Unbelievable

Also by John Shelby Spong

Honest Prayer

Dialogue in Search of Jewish-Christian Understanding
(with Rabbi Jack Daniel Spiro)

Christpower (compiled and edited by Lucy Newton Boswell)

*Life Approaches Death: A Dialogue on Medical
Ethics* (with Dr. Daniel Gregory)

The Living Commandments

The Easter Moment

Into the Whirlwind: The Future of the Church

Beyond Moralism (with the Venerable Denise Haines)

*Survival and Consciousness: An Interdisciplinary Inquiry into
the Possibility of Life Beyond Biological Death* (editor)

Living in Sin? A Bishop Rethinks Human Sexuality

*Rescuing the Bible from Fundamentalism: A Bishop
Rethinks the Meaning of Scripture*

*Born of a Woman: A Bishop Rethinks the Virgin Birth and
the Role of Women in a Male-Dominated Church*

This Hebrew Lord: A Bishop's Search for the Authentic Jesus

Resurrection: Myth or Reality? A Bishop Rethinks the Meaning of Easter

Liberating the Gospels: Reading the Bible with Jewish Eyes

Why Christianity Must Change or Die: A Bishop Speaks to Believers in Exile

The Bishop's Voice: Selected Essays (1979–1999)
(compiled and edited by Christine Mary Spong)

Here I Stand: My Struggle for a Christianity of Integrity, Love and Equality

*A New Christianity for a New World: Why Traditional
Faith Is Dying and How a New Faith Is Being Born*

*The Sins of Scripture: Exposing the Bible's Texts
of Hate to Reveal the God of Love*

Jesus for the Non-Religious: Recovering the Divine at the Heart of the Human

*Eternal Life: A New Vision—Beyond Religion,
Beyond Theism, Beyond Heaven and Hell*

Reclaiming the Bible for a Non-Religious World

The Fourth Gospel: Tales of a Jewish Mystic

*Biblical Literalism: A Gentile Heresy—A Journey into a New
Christianity Through the Doorway of Matthew's Gospel*

Unbelievable

Why Neither Ancient Creeds Nor the Reformation Can Produce a Living Faith Today

John Shelby Spong

HarperOne
An Imprint of HarperCollinsPublishers

HarperOne

While I have relied heavily on the Revised Standard Version, the New Revised Standard Version and the King James Version in quoting scripture, I have in every case used whatever wording seemed to my ear to be most faithful to the original text.

FIRST EDITION

Library of Congress Cataloging-in-Publication Data.

Names: Spong, John Shelby, author.
Title: Unbelievable : why neither ancient creeds nor the reformation can produce a living faith today / John Shelby Spong.
Description: FIRST EDITION. | San Francisco : HarperOne, 2018.
Identifiers: LCCN 2017023227 | ISBN 9780062641298 (hardcover)
Subjects: LCSH: Christianity—21st century.
Classification: LCC BR121.3 .S75 2018 | DDC 230—dc23 LC record available at https://lccn.loc.gov/2017023227

18 19 20 21 22   LSC   10 9 8 7 6 5 4 3 2 1

To My Special Wife
Christine Mary Spong

AND

My Wonderful Daughters
Ellen Elizabeth Spong
Mary Katharine Spong
Jaquelin Ketner Spong

AND

In Memoriam
Joan Lydia Ketner Spong
(1929–1988)

Contents

Preface

I look back with some amusement on the fact that I have introduced all of my recent books as "probably my last book." In all honesty I must confess that this has been accurate. At the time I was engaged with each "last book" I had no idea that another lay hidden under the doormat, but that happened to be so. A new book was always born in the process of going over the present book. I did not mean to be dishonest. The fact remains that I have thus far written five "last books." I think I can guarantee that this current volume, however, will be my last.

I am now in my eighty-seventh year of life and when this book comes out in 2018 I will be (if I am still living) in my eighty-eighth year. It continues to be a rich and full life. So far in the study for this book no subjects have presented themselves, but if they had I would have to say no. The reasons for that statement will be clear as this preface unfolds.

I have no regrets. Some of my best books have been written in these twilight years of my life. I look at *Eternal Life: A New Vision—Beyond Theism, Beyond Religion, Beyond Heaven and Hell, The Fourth Gospel: Tales of a Jewish Mystic,* and *Biblical Literalism: A Gentile Heresy,* for example, my three "last books," and feel a great sense of accomplishment. Like those predecessors, this new book, *Unbelievable: Why Neither Ancient Creeds Nor the Reformation Can Produce a Living Faith Today,* is based on the experience of finding that the traditional words of religion have lost their believability; for me, it became a necessary piece of work to clear away things that had not been dealt with in previous books. It is a fitting culmination to a writing career that has extended for almost fifty years.

Let me tell you a story, a true story. My wife and I had planned on finishing my lecturing career at the end of June 2017. We had actually planned on doing it earlier, but the invitations continued to come. It seemed as though they would never cease. With all of the travel and sleeping in a wide variety of circumstances, it became harder and harder to prepare and to make the lectures. Yet I continued to love to do it. Still, Christine and I decided that June would be it. We agreed that perhaps if an invitation came that was just irresistible we might consider it, but by and large June 30, 2017, would be the end. Consequently we planned these last few months carefully, with the goal of returning to some of our favorite places.

We began by returning to the Chautauqua Institution in western New York. I think I have been there on eight different occasions. It is a rich diet. In recent years I was there with Roger Rosenblatt, who brought with him each week a series of stars from the world of Hollywood, television, Broadway and the arts. We met Tom Brokaw, Jim Lehrer, Jane Pauley, Garry Trudeau, Julie Andrews and her daughter Emma Walton Hamilton, Alan Alda and many others. Roger introduced them all and called forth the inner self of each. Earlier I had also spent a memorable week with Buckminster Fuller. During each weekday morning these lectures followed a worship service with a noted preacher.

The 2:00 P.M. slot each afternoon was the theological hour and the time when I spoke. I introduced a book about every two years, and for the last three times I was there the recorded attendance was more than two thousand people a day. About twenty-five percent of my audience was Jewish. I love that place deeply. So in 2016 we went back to Chautauqua to introduce *Biblical Literalism: A Gentile Heresy*. It was a highlight in our lives.

This was followed by a period of time in the mountains of western North Carolina near Highlands and Cashiers. Christine and I have gone there annually for years, climbing a mountain a day. We always saved the hardest mountain, Chimney Top, for the last day. We had failed to make it to the crest in 2015, having halted about a hundred yards from the top because we did not feel up to scrambling/climbing the last bit. It was for us both a crushing defeat. We charged it off to age. That summer of 2016 we went up again, not expecting to reach the top, but just to see how near we could come. We made it all the way, and filled with the celebratory sense of achievement, we came back home in a rainstorm that was quite refreshing. We looked like drowned rats!

On Sunday and Monday nights I lectured to about two hundred people at the Church of the Incarnation in Highlands. I had been a lecturer there for a number of years and knew the audience well. Most of them were summer tourists, who were the intellectual leaders in their communities all over the South, but they listened with their ears attuned to a new dimension of understanding.

We then enjoyed some family time at the wedding of my brother's only daughter, Ashley, and her husband, Mark, in New Orleans. It was a joy to be with my deceased brother's family. Next we visited with our children and grandchildren in Vermont.

After that we set off for Marquette, Michigan, to begin the fall lecture schedule. Following our visit to Marquette we planned to take our last European tour. First, there would be a relaxing trip down the Rhine River. When that was ended we were to take a train to Paris and do lectures at the American Cathedral in that city, where the dean, Lucinda Laird, is a former priest of our Diocese of Newark, New Jersey. Then we would stay in Paris for an additional two days to do lectures and media events for our

French publisher, Karthala Editions, which was bringing out two more of my books in translation in 2016.

We were then scheduled to go to the United Kingdom, starting first in Glasgow, followed by an appearance at a conference at the Gladstone Library in Wales. We were to be there for seven days in all, and I would actually be doing a lectureship named for my mentor John A. T. Robinson and myself, the Robinson-Spong Lecture on Contemporary Theology. One does not get a chance to fulfill a lectureship in one's own honor very often! Following that we would go to Birmingham and London, including visiting St. James' Church, Piccadilly, a wonderful church in London. We were to return to the United States about the first of November. It was, however, not to be.

We got to Marquette on Friday night, September 9. Nothing was scheduled that evening except for a lovely dinner party at one of Marquette's top restaurants. It was a delightful time seeing old friends and renewing relationships. We laughed and enjoyed ourselves greatly. My first assignment was at the University of Northern Michigan at 11:00 A.M. on Saturday. I got up early, went to the fitness center and got in my regular four miles on the running track. Returning, I took Christine to breakfast, came back and showered, shaved and dressed to get ready for the day. That was when it happened. Suddenly I was on the floor and unconscious. I say *unconscious* for that is what it seemed like, but I was high above my body, surveying the whole scene. I was wonderfully at peace. I did not feel a thing. Suddenly those attending me felt a need to cut off my clerical shirt. I watched them do it and then I truly did enter into unconsciousness. I later asked Christine what had happened and she told me that they had cut off my shirt, just as I had seen them do, in order to place sensors on my body. They even gave the shirt back to Christine. I have it now. It was quite surreal, but in fact it was a stroke hitting the right side of my body, which I could no longer move. That was September 10, 2016. I stayed in the Marquette Hospital for about a week before being transported in a medically equipped plane to Morristown, New Jersey, where I spent an additional two weeks in the hospital, learning slowly and patiently to walk again. As I write this, I seem fully recovered. I now walk on my treadmill every day, I am able to go to church every Sunday and recently took great delight in watching my wife run a half-marathon in Richmond. I still have trouble writing. Oh, I can do it all right, but as yet no one can read it! I expect that to improve with time.

That little stroke means that this will be my last book. Fortunately for me it was already largely written. All it needed was the usual copyediting and correcting for delivery to Harper. We even met the deadline, although Harper had waived the limit and agreed to receive it whenever it arrived. I was delighted to send it in prior to the due date.

That is my story. I have received over thirty thousand pieces of communication, by mail, through my column and by Facebook, since my stroke. I appreciated every one of them, but the inability to write, and the sheer volume of the messages, has made it impossible to respond to them in person, no matter how grateful I am. Perhaps this brief acknowledgment will serve to show my gratitude.

My wife Christine deserves more credit for this book than anyone else. She had heard it, piecemeal, in lectures, and while I was the sickest she amused herself by typing parts of it. She was also familiar with it because it had appeared in my column, which she had edited. I had even written columns ahead to cover that time I would be away in Europe. So my column wound up on a positive note. I will not resume the column, but I hope the folks at my website, A New Christianity for a New World (johnshelbyspong.com), will soon find a replacement to carry out its vital ministry. I wrote the column for fourteen years, and it was always a pleasure.

My thanks go to Drew University and especially to Jesse Mann, the theology librarian. He assisted with the bibliography and was most gracious. Drew has been a serendipity in my life.

Perhaps the greatest experience I discovered in this sickness is how deeply my family cares for me. Children and grandchildren came to see me and I loved it. We have had tremendous conversations, which have made the ordeal a beautiful thing. I am particularly and eternally grateful for the love and attention that have been given to Christine and me.

I wish to thank Rosemary Halstead, secretary at St. Paul's Church in Morris Plains, for serving as my secretary and working on my column for all fourteen years, as well as for typing much of this current book. I could not have done it without her.

My thanks to my HarperCollins team for a lifetime of support: Mark Tauber, my publisher; Mickey Maudlin, my editor; and the best manuscript manager and copyeditor, Lisa Zuniga and Kathy Reigstad, that I have ever known. They are incredible.

My thanks also go to Kelly Hughes of DeChant Hughes in Chicago, who Harper hired to handle the launch of most of my books. Kelly is a lively and competent young woman.

Above all I wish to thank my host of readers who encouraged me to keep writing. That support has meant a lot to me. I must give up the column now, but while I wrote it I was carried by their support. I thank each of them personally.

Finally, this book reflects my dedication to that group of people who sustained me for a lifetime; chief among those are my wife and daughters. I dedicate this book to them.

Shalom!

John Shelby Spong
Morris Plains, New Jersey

PART I

Setting the Stage

Why Modern Men and Women Can No Longer Be Believers

It was my daughter Jaquelin Ketner Spong, the recipient of a Ph.D. degree in physics from Stanford University, who once said to me: "Dad, the questions the church keeps trying to answer, we don't even ask anymore." I was quite startled, for it painted a picture of the irrelevance of religion that was profound. Could the enterprise to whose institutional expressions I had dedicated my entire professional life really be this out of touch? Could it ever again be a force possessing the ability to shape the life of the world? Could the system of thought that had for centuries dominated Western understanding and the Western world finally be at the end of its life? These were troubling questions.

Theology was once called the "queen of the sciences," and it garnered enormous respect in the great academies of learning, but now it appears no longer to be able to attract the brightest and best into its ranks. Indeed, one must almost apologize for spending one's time in this academic arena. This is not a new phenomenon. When I was an undergraduate at the University of

North Carolina in the early 1950s, my faculty advisor, Dr. Louis Katsoff, who was also head of the Department of Philosophy, asked on our initial interview why I wanted to major in philosophy. "Because I want to be a priest in my church," I replied. I had come out of a culture in the South where such a vocation still carried a great amount of cachet. Dr. Katsoff punctured that assumption quite quickly. "Why do you want to spend your life dealing with a medieval superstition?" he asked. For my entire career in that department I constantly had to defend and to justify my choice. There was, however, still enough of a religious veneer in our society that I could proceed with my chosen profession.

When finally armed with my undergraduate degree in philosophy, with substantial work in the life sciences, which particularly attracted me, and with my master's degree in divinity from the Protestant Episcopal Theological Seminary in Virginia, I began my career as the rector of St. Joseph's Episcopal Church, located right off the campus of Duke University in Durham, North Carolina. My 11:00 A.M. congregation was made up primarily of married graduate students from Duke in various fields, but medicine and chemistry stand out in my memory as dominant, supplemented by undergraduates, who were mostly female students. This imbalance was caused by the fact that the church was next door to East Campus, where female students were housed, and not because of a sexist bias.

Sunday after Sunday in that church I had to deal with how traditional Christianity, which I represented, interacted or failed to interact with brilliant, educated graduate and undergraduate university students. One learns quickly in such an environment that claims for the "authority of the Bible"—filled, as that book is, with stories of an invasive, supernatural deity performing miracles—are ignored, and all attempts to define "the true faith," or to pronounce anything that deviates from a traditional understanding to be "heresy," is more a conversation-stopper than it is a way to dialogue. I also learned in that church and from that congregation that there was, and I suspect continues to be, a yearning for a meaningful religious experience or, at least, a way to have one's life enhanced by something beyond itself. The desire to believe in this something or to feel oneself to be embraced by a sense of transcendent wonder appears to be well-nigh universal. On this frontier that seems to exist between contemporary knowledge and religious yearning, I was destined to spend most of my ordained life. I kept recalling the words of the seventeenth-century French philosopher and theologian Blaise Pascal, who wrote: "The heart has its reasons that reason knows not of."*

Even now, looking back on my career, there is no doubt that I had times of success working on this frontier. Surprisingly enough, I lived out my life as a priest not in what might be thought of as liberal parts of either my nation or my church, but in the most traditionally conservative parts. My first congregation, just off the campus of Duke, grew while I was there with a significant surge of new members. I called them the "converts." They came primarily from small-town, fundamentalist religious backgrounds, both Roman Catholic and Protestant. When their religious training collided with the thought that bombarded them from this great university, they abandoned fundamentalism in droves. I appeared to offer them a way to continue to be believers that they had not known before. That pattern continued in my other priestly assignments, all of which were in traditional parts of the United States. I served a church in the agricultural belt of eastern North Carolina, in Tarboro. Then I moved to the small city of Lynchburg, which was thought of as the northern edge of "conservative Southside Virginia." Next I became rector of a

---

* *Pensées.* See bibliography for details.

church in the heart of Richmond, Virginia, that called itself "the Cathedral of the Confederacy." During the American Civil War both Robert E. Lee and Jefferson Davis were regular worshippers. In all of these congregations my appeal was to those who had either abandoned the religion of their childhood as no longer relevant to the life they were living, or, at the very least, packed their religious upbringing into a compartment of their lives, where knowledge or new insight would never be allowed to challenge it. The success I enjoyed in each of those places led me into the delusion that I had discovered the doorway into a new Christian future.

That all changed in 1976 when I was elected the bishop of the Diocese of Newark, an area that encompasses the New Jersey suburbs of New York City, with its incredible diversity. A brand-new perspective on ministry was forced into my awareness.

I learned, first, that a bishop exercises little leadership over local congregations. His or her influence is guided mostly by example over a long period of time. Most local congregations dance to the tune of their established membership, and in most cases the personal security of that membership is bound up with what they might call the "faith of our fathers."* (I am sure they also meant "mothers," but that was not always either obvious or emotionally accurate.) I also learned that most clergy are either unable or unwilling to engage the great theological issues of the day because of their perception that to do so will "disturb the faith and beliefs" of their people. Indeed, that was the reaction that my initial theological reflections as bishop prompted.

The first hint I had of this reaction came very shortly after my election, before the glow of pride had been allowed to be enjoyed for more than a day. Election as a bishop is followed, in the

---

* From an English Catholic hymn by Frederick William Faber 1849.

Episcopal Church, by a confirmation process. During this time what I believed was to be examined deeply. I had already written three books. My thoughts were out there, in the public arena. The first book, entitled *Honest Prayer,** challenged the presuppositions behind the traditional activity we call prayer. The second was *This Hebrew Lord,*† which challenged some of the traditional theological assumptions that have been built up through the centuries in regard to the central symbol of the Christian story, Jesus of Nazareth. Doctrines such as the Incarnation and the Holy Trinity that once had made contact with the thought forms of their day were, I suggested, no longer registering with this generation. There was nothing in either book that had not been discussed openly in my theological training. This was my first awareness of the gap between the academy and the pew, to say nothing of the gap in honesty between what clergy both knew and believed and what they were willing to say. There is a game being played in contemporary church life where truth is suppressed in the name of unity.

The third book was entitled *Dialogue in Search of Jewish-Christian Understanding.*‡ It was co-authored with a brilliant rabbi named Jack Daniel Spiro. He had read my book *This Hebrew Lord* and had challenged me to a series of dialogues in which the members of my congregation would be forced to engage their stereotypical prejudices about Jews and the members of his congregation would be forced to engage their stereotypical prejudices about Christians. When one steps outside the circle of one's own religious history to engage another's religious history, the pious religious clichés of the past simply do not work. How can we present the typical Christian claim that Jesus is "God's

---

*   See bibliography for details.
†   See bibliography for details.
‡   See bibliography for details.

only son" to a congregation of Jews who believe that God is so awesomely one and holy that to suggest that God had a son seems like blasphemy?

This dialogue lifted me into a new level of notoriety; it was covered by local radio, television and the print media, but it then became a national story, at least in religious circles, coming into the awareness of the increasingly non-religious population and even the thoroughly secular population through the *Washington Post.* My attempts to speak to a non-traditionally religious body of people was seized upon or attacked by church representatives who were not sure they wanted someone who violated traditional boundaries to serve as one of their bishops. Apparently my positions, all of which were widely taught and understood by the theological seminaries—including the one that had trained me for ordination—had challenged, frightened and threatened the religious world.

I also noticed in this struggle that while the attacks on my faith from my religious critics gained a good bit of public notice, in secular society the matter was regarded as little more than a dispute within the sphere of the religious world. It certainly did not create a desire for anyone to look again at the faith system from which they had significantly moved away. My critics could not see that the faith they wanted to define in the most traditional forms appealed not at all to those who had left organized religion and who had no desire to return to its antiquated forms of worship. So out of touch with reality were these traditionalists that they really did believe that if they kept Christianity inside its recognizable framework of creedal beliefs, someday "the lost sheep" would find their way back into the fold. To confirm a bishop who did not guard that tradition meant that the fox of secularity had entered the hen house of the church! Only disaster could result. So in their minds I was the heretic who could not be allowed entrance to a position of authority.

My opposition was led by ultra-conservative church publications whose titles betrayed their position. *The Living Church* and *The Certain Trumpet* were two of them.* I was shocked by this experience and for the first time disillusioned at what seemed to me to be a bleak Christian future.

Controversy in the Christian church is seldom just about biblical exegesis and theological formulations. By and large people do not want to engage these issues publicly, perhaps because they know deep down that their religious convictions cannot stand much public scrutiny. So most church fights and even divisions are on social issues such as racial prejudice, equality for women or members of the lesbian, gay, bisexual and transgender community, or issues of human sexuality like birth control, abortion and the ordination of women to be priests and bishops. Those issues, in which the church has little expertise, have split the "body of Christ" into competing splinter groups, rival hierarchies and mutually exclusive claims to be "the true church."

So while my confirmation seemed to be based on "heretical claims" found in those first three books of my writing career, the meaning that gave it passion was my participation in the civil rights movement, the women's liberation and ordination movement and the gay rights movement. These were surely in the background, but the fact that I was not a "true believer" in the formulas of the past became visible for the first time. Had I not been elected bishop, my theology would have remained hidden.

Far more than these critics in the church recognized, however, these theological issues had been bubbling beneath the surface, waiting for an opportunity to erupt publicly. My election as a bishop provided just such an opportunity. The issues, though, were not new; they had simply been repressed. Friedrich Nietzsche had

---

* *The Living Church* is still published and is the "voice" of tradition. *The Certain Trumpet* is no longer published.

declared in the nineteenth century that God is dead. Few people
paid much attention to Nietzsche, however, who was widely regarded as a madman. In 1960 a group of theologians emerged
in the United States who called themselves the "God is dead
theologians."* They achieved a certain amount of notoriety, being
featured in the cover story in *TIME* magazine on April 8, 1966. In
the larger Anglican family that housed my Episcopal Church there
were two sitting bishops who stirred these waters. In England John
A. T. Robinson broke out of the pack with a book published in
1963 entitled *Honest to God,*† which touched a nerve in the English population, becoming hotly debated first in the English papers,
then in the world press and finally entering into conversations in
the pubs and among the cabbies of the nation. Generally the world
devoured Bishop Robinson's thought, while the established church
resisted it. In the United States it was a bishop named James Albert
Pike whose books *A Time for Christian Candor* and *If This Be
Heresy*‡ also broke out of the boundaries of the church to be read
by a critical-thinking world, while generally being criticized and
reviled by the church hierarchy.

By and large, what the world relished, the church abhorred.
John Robinson, in that exquisitely understated English manner,
was marginalized by the Church of England. He was left to wal-
low in the rather secondary role of an area bishop and was never
allowed to head up a major diocese. He finally resigned from the
bishop's office and went back to his career as an academic. In
the United States traditional voices, led by the bishop of South
Florida, Henry I. Louttit, Sr., constantly threatened Bishop Pike
with a heresy trial, which was averted ultimately by Bishop Pike's

---

* Among them were William Hamilton, Thomas J. J. Altizer, Paul van Buren and many
  others. See bibliography for their books.
† See bibliography for details.
‡ See bibliography for details.

resignation and his move into a think tank. Robinson and Pike were not the only ones who were battling on this frontier, but they were the major ones in the struggle for relevance.

In Roman Catholicism that church's most brilliant ordained scholars, who dared to move beyond the defined boundaries of "orthodoxy," were harassed, silenced, removed and marginalized. One thinks of Edward Schillebeeckx, Hans Küng, Matthew Fox, Leonardo Boff and Charles Curran. Lay Roman Catholic scholars, especially female Roman Catholic scholars, could get away with a great deal more—and they did. They were simply ignored or were denied the privilege of speaking at or teaching in Roman Catholic schools. Joseph Ratzinger, first as the cardinal inquisitor and later as Pope Benedict XVI, led this attempt at suppression.

Observing these events in church life was a little like watching Humpty Dumpty being lived out in history. The theological consensus of the past was being broken into thousands of pieces, and "all the church's horses and all the church's men" could not put it back together again!

Important

At first the response of institutional Christianity was to seek a renaissance in security-offering churches, where the old-time religion was offered, together with modern music and charismatic, show-boating evangelicals who had more volume than conviction and were content to say to people: "You do not have to think about these things; you only have to trust and obey." The just-under-the-surface crisis in faith would soon go away, they assured their increasingly large audiences. That movement has, however, proved not to be the wave of the future. The great expansion of evangelical religion, with its rise of mega-churches, has now crested and has actually begun its inevitable retreat. The second generation of evangelical leaders has not been as compelling as the first. Some of those churches have morphed into feel-good places that avoid controversy and critical thought to concentrate on easing their people's way through life. The biggest sign of the demise of organized religion in our generation, however, has been the statistical downward spiral of mainline churches, most of which know too much to play the security games of their past, but which have not yet figured out what to do as they move into the future. Signs of death in organized religious circles are, therefore, rampant. Churches are closing, merging and fading. Budgets are shrinking. Programs and staff are all declining.

In Europe Christian churches increasingly look and act like museums. Church attendance is down in many cases to less than ten percent of each country's population. That decline is not denomination- or tradition-specific. It is true in the Roman Catholic countries of Spain, Italy and France. It is also true in the Protestant countries of England, Scotland and Scandinavia.

A recent poll conducted by the Pew Research Foundation suggests that in the American electorate the religious affiliation category called "none" now equals in numbers those who call themselves evangelicals, as well as those who call themselves Roman Catholics. Among those who are defined today as "millennials"—that is, those who were born from 1979 on, who have reached maturity in the twenty-first century—the religious category called "none" is now the majority category.*

There clearly have been changes of dramatic proportions in people's attitudes toward religion. This is not just a phase or a passing phenomenon. It is a rising tide that gives every evidence of being tomorrow's norm. If nothing is done to address this crisis, the ultimate result seems to be clear. Christianity appears to be destined to take its place along with other religions and deities of human history that have died. The God of Christianity will be in a long line that has included Baal, Chemosh, Marduk, the gods

---

* See Pew Research—Millennials—Church Preferences. Internet research.

of Olympus and the deities of the mystery cults. Each is now a lost chapter in the human pursuit of a spiritual dimension. At the same time, if Christianity is to survive it must undergo so radical a transformation that people may well see no continuity between the Christianity of yesterday and the Christianity of tomorrow. Death could well come in either direction. Is there, however, still a choice to be made? Are Christians to be immobilized by the fear of failure? I am not willing to adopt that path. I vote for a radical rethinking of our religious symbols. I vote for a reformation that will be so total that many people will think that Christianity has already died. To stand by idly and do nothing is for me not an option. This book will push in this new direction.

So I vote for a risky future that includes a radical rethinking in which every symbol of our religious past must be examined, replaced or reconfigured. I recognize that calling this process a "reformation" is to use an historically loaded term. I will address that in the next chapter, but I know of no other word that can bear the weight of what I believe is necessary. I have decided to keep the word, while both recapping and stating that what we need today is far, far more than what that word has previously meant.

Would contemporary men and woman be interested in dealing with a group of theses in Lutherlike fashion? It is worth a test. If we opened the gates to a real debate, would modern people be prepared to contemplate and discuss theological ideas? We would have to get beyond their caustic reply: "He has abandoned every aspect of traditional Christianity." Perhaps we need to say that every aspect of medieval Christianity *needs* to be abandoned. A thesis, in this reformation scenario, would be short, succinct and to the point. I have decided on twelve theses, which cover everything from God to Christ to prayer to life after death. In my weekly column, over a period of about two years, I engaged my audience with the possibility of just such a debate, a reformation.

I was encouraged. Finally, I decided that the time had come to put all those theses together in a primer—this book—and to invite a vigorous debate. Hence the title of this book, *Unbelievable*.

I am not ready to surrender Christianity to a secular future. I am not willing to abandon the Christ experience, which I still find real, simply because the words traditionally used to describe that experience no longer translate meaningfully into the language of our day. I *am* willing to sacrifice all claims to possessing a literal Bible, literal creeds or historical liturgies in the Christianity that I seek to create, but I am not willing to sacrifice my conviction that there is something real that draws me beyond myself, which I call "God." I am not willing to cease being a member of a church that has the courage to seek after the truth of God. I search in the motto of the seminary I attended for the truth of God, "come whence it may, cost what it will."* I claim today and will in the foreseeable future claim for myself the title "Christian," but I reserve the right to define what that title means. I am not willing to allow the word "Christian" to be claimed and defined exclusively by the voices of the past. I invite you, my readers, to journey with me into this new arena. I am convinced that when the ultimate history of the Christian church is written, my efforts will not be thought of as radical at all, but as not nearly radical enough. I am content, however, to leave that verdict up to the future. Let the reformation begin!

---

* Attributed to Dr. William Sparrow, a nineteenth-century theologian.

PART II

Stating the Problem

2

How the First Reformation Began

On October 31, 1517, so the story goes, a solitary monk named Martin Luther approached the great doors of All Saints' Church in Wittenberg, Germany, on which he planned to post a document entitled "The Dispute over the Power and Efficiency of Indulgences." History has renamed that document "The Ninety-Five Theses." It was designed to call the entire Christian church into debate.

What Luther was supposedly doing on that day was not particularly unusual. In academic circles throughout Europe, it was normal to post topics for public debate in public places. This was the way theological exploration was conducted. What flowed from that posting, however, was a surprise to Luther. He had touched a match to a massive amount of incendiary material, creating an explosion and lighting a fire that Luther himself could never have controlled, much less extinguished.

Wittenberg's All Saints' Church, known then as the "Castle Church," was uniquely qualified to be the place where this blaze was ignited. It was also called the "Church of Relics," claiming among its treasures vials of milk supposedly drawn from the breasts of the Virgin, straw allegedly taken from the manger of

Jesus and even the body of one of the "Holy Innocents," those male babies said to have been murdered by Herod in his attempt to destroy in his infancy God's promised deliverer!

In Luther's mind it was clear that institutional Christianity had ceased to be the "body of Christ" serving the world. It had instead become a profitable business, designed in such a way as to increase and even to enhance the church's worldly power. In order to finance its institutional needs, which included the building of a new basilica at St. Peter's in Rome, the Vatican had endorsed the practice of selling "indulgences." A "sinner" could purchase one such indulgence and thereby forgo the need to repent. By challenging this practice, Martin Luther was striking a blow to the economic well-being of the Christian church of his time. Beneath that debate, however, was a deeper challenge to all of the authority claims being made by the church on its journey through history.

By the sixteenth century the power of the Christian church was so deeply entrenched in the life of Europe's culture that for anyone to challenge its claimed authority to define truth was regarded as an act of heresy. That which was named "Mother Church" was the vehicle through which the "Father God" spoke to the world of men and women. An all-male ordained hierarchy, which stretched from the local priest all the way to the papal office, was acknowledged as the only proper channel through which that and the will of God could be discerned by human beings. That claim is what Luther was challenging.

Over the centuries the hierarchy had in fact defined the content of Christianity. The Nicene Creed had been adopted by Christian leaders at the Council of Nicaea in 325 CE, and it was believed to have summarized the "essence of the Christian faith" *for all time*. The church claimed for itself the sole right to interpret the sacred scriptures. That was not a difficult claim for the church to maintain in that day, for few people, other than the clergy, could either read or write. Most of the great universities of Europe existed primarily to train the clergy. The average layperson learned the stories of the Bible, not by reading the biblical text, but by looking at pictures painted by the world's great artists, whose actual knowledge of the Bible was minimal. Almost every church had something called "the Stations of the Cross" on its walls. This was a pictorial display of the final scenes in the life of Jesus. How closely those stations followed the biblical narrative was of little concern. No one bothered to check. The images, along with those in the stained-glass windows, were simply absorbed.

The sixteenth century was also an age of almost unchallenged belief in a literal final judgment. God was regularly portrayed as a supernatural, all-seeing figure who lived above the clouds, watching human behavior. God wrote down, it was said, the deeds and misdeeds of all the people in the "Book of Life," which would determine the eternal destiny of each individual soul. The difference between heaven and hell was enormous, so the bliss of heaven and the peril of hell were regularly made quite vivid, both in the sermons of the clergy, to which the people listened week after week, and in paintings depicting "Judgment Day" that they regularly saw. The fires of hell quite literally terrified the masses. Guilt was the coin of the church's realm, and it permeated the emotions of every "sinner" with whom the church had to deal. Being able to buy an indulgence provided security, for the indulgence assured them of the forgiveness that was, they were quite certain, the only doorway into heaven. Time in purgatory could also be shortened for loved ones by the purchase of an indulgence. A strict behavior-controlling system was held in place by these practices. Unbeknownst to Luther, he was about to pull the linchpin on this entire way of life, causing it to come crashing down in ruins.

For at least two hundred years after Luther, Europe was roiled by this Reformation conflict. Traditional circles tried valiantly to re-establish the religious authority of the past and to impose it anew on the entire social order. At the same time, those who had been the repressed victims of this religious control system reveled in their new-found freedom and rejoiced in the future opportunities that were opening to them. They, therefore, resisted any attempt to harness or to stop the winds of change. Conflict between yesterday and tomorrow engulfed the Western world. A thirty-year war raged across Europe as traditionalists and reformers fought to impose their understanding of God on their opponents. The sinking of the ships of the Catholic Spanish Armada sailing toward Protestant England was even said to have proved that God was on the side of the reformers.

The traditionalists had the power of history and authority on their side. They could quote the doctrines and dogmas of the church, which they believed reflected God's will. The reformers needed a counterclaim, and they found it in the authority of the Bible, almost always literally understood and called the "Word of God." So "the church teaches" became the claim of one side and "the Bible says" became the claim of the other. When both sides in any conflict believe that they speak for God, the result is that each side demonizes the other. That was the backdrop through which each side, in that moment of history, endured the bitter and destructive struggle that we call the Reformation.

Martin Luther, the almost-accidental originator of this sixteenth-century reform movement, opened the doors for changes that he had never even imagined. Those doors would never close again in the same way. Feelings were destined to reach an emotional intensity not seen before in human history. Was Luther talking about the pope or the devil when he wrote: "The prince of darkness grim, we tremble not for him. His rage we can endure, for lo his doom is sure. One little word shall fell him.''* That one little word was "alone." It was by faith "alone," not by works or deeds, that salvation was accomplished. Indulgences were works! The result of this struggle was, therefore, always inevitable. In time, Martin Luther was condemned by the church, excommunicated as a heretic and driven into hiding. His life in danger, he was protected by certain political princes of Germany, who saw in Luther's upheaval a way to break the power and control of the Vatican and thus to allow both the nation states of Europe and their wealth to develop independent of religious control. It was a tumultuous time in European history.

For so much anger, hostility, war and bloodshed to be displayed and for so many people to be persecuted, incarcerated and killed seems strange today when we seek to identify the substance of the debate that broke Catholic hegemony apart. Just as today's church controversies tend not to be rooted in doctrinal issues, the battles of the Reformation were not about real issues of faith or belief. The Reformation ultimately was not fought over what a Christian must believe to be a Christian, but over issues of institutional authority and power.

Both sides in this moment of conflict still read the same Bible, still recited the same creeds and still sang the same hymns. Liturgical patterns did change, but for the most part the ancient liturgies of the church were all not only still recognizable, but they were also conducted in the same churches. Protestant polity became more democratic and less hierarchical. The people in Protestantism had more decision-making involvement, while Catholicism continued to operate under the slogan: "Father knows best." For the most part, despite the intensity of the struggle, the essence of the Christian faith continued to be talked about in

---

* "A Mighty Fortress Is Our God," Martin Luther 1529.

traditional and recognizable ways. The primary change was that
doctrinal debate was no longer controlled by the church hierarchy; in other words, the church was no longer acknowledged as
the final arbiter of truth.

In reality this single change opened up other vast arenas for
transformation. From the leaders of science, freed now from ecclesiastical control, came a new understanding of how the world
operated, which challenged the Christian formulas of antiquity.
Changes began to come in unceasing waves, each building on
the last. The result of these and so many other cascading insights
was that traditional Christian concepts became less and less intel-
ligible to more and more people. Those are the facts that are still
today building pressure for a radically new kind of reformation.
This one will not be about issues of authority; it must focus on the
substance of Christianity itself. The questions which Christians
are forced to ask today are qualitatively different from those that
the Christians of the sixteenth century were asking. We want to
know whether the idea of God still has meaning. We ask whether
the historical creeds commit us to things that we cannot possibly
still believe. We wonder how or if we can still use those creedal
words with integrity. Can those fourth-century documents still
be authoritative? Can there still be a definition of ultimate truth?
Are not the claims of an infallible pope or an inerrant Bible both
ridiculous in today's world?

That is the place where we must begin the process of finding
new words for our faith. The old words have lost their ability to
serve in this way. This journey will go beyond the clichés of yesterday and will call us to a new faith for tomorrow. It will be an
exciting adventure. This may be the theological ride of a lifetime.

3

Differentiating the Experience from the Explanation

"Time makes ancient good uncouth."* James Russell Lowell, the poet who wrote these words, understood the difference between an experience and the way that experience is explained. So important is this distinction for our later theological work that I want to impress it onto the memories of my readers with two rather commonplace illustrations.

First, consider the motion of the sun. It rises in absolutely the same manner each day in the east and sets each day in the west. Look, however, at the variety of ways that this experience has been explained in human history. The Egyptians explained this natural phenomenon by suggesting that their god, Ra, rode his chariot across the sky each morning surveying the earth. The sun was the visible wheel of the chariot. Other ancient people explained the sun's rotation as a heavenly body circling the earth, making the earth appear to be the center of the universe. Later,

---

* From Lowell's 1845 poem "The Present Crisis," adapted to become the hymn "Once to Every Man and Nation."

others believed it was caused by the planet earth turning on its axis as it made its annual elliptical orbit around the sun. The experience being described was identical, but each explanation reflected the time in which the explainer lived and the level of knowledge that the explainer possessed.

Now look at the experience of the physical disorder called epilepsy, a phenomenon that affects only a small minority of people, but is common enough to be universally recognized. A first-century epileptic seizure was identical with one that occurs in the twenty-first century. The way epilepsy was explained in the first century, however, differs so widely from the way it is explained in the twenty-first century that one would hardly recognize that the same thing was being described. It is hard to relate "demon possession" to the "electrical chemistry of a brain cell." These illustrations point to the distinction between an experience, which can be real and even eternal, and the explanation of that experience, which is always time-bound and time-warped.

Jesus, whatever else he was, was a first-century person in whose life people believed that they experienced what they called "the divine" coming together with what they identified as "the human." The explanations of that experience are what we find in the pages of the New Testament. Those biblical explanations inevitably reflect the worldview of the first century, the time in which the experience lived. No one can escape their own frame of reference. So first-century experiences will always be explained in terms of first-century thought forms, first-century presuppositions and first-century vocabulary. If we also literalize the explanations that were framed in the first century, we literalize the frame of reference in which those explanations were cast. One cannot, therefore, literalize the biblical narrative without literalizing a mentality that is both dated and doomed. Biblical literalism thus quickly becomes biblical nonsense.

The creeds of the church represent a fourth-century attempt to codify that Jesus experience, whatever it was. The creeds thus reflect the dualistic worldview of the Greek mind that dominated fourth-century thought. If we literalize the creeds or claims for their eternal infallible truth, we are inevitably literalizing the frame of reference of this long-passed era. No explanation can ever be identified with the experience or even the truth that it seeks to explain.

Therein lies the problem: Christianity, having recorded its first-century explanations of the Jesus experience in scripture, and its fourth-century explanations in creedal statements, then proceeded to make excessive claims for authority of those explanations, essentially freezing them into their first- and fourth-century frames of reference. Literalized words are always doomed words since our perception of truth is constantly expanding and changing.

The explosion of knowledge over the last five hundred years in the West has rendered most of the biblical and creedal presuppositions unbelievable. They rise out of a world that no longer exists. Yet churches continue to operate as if eternal truth could be placed into these earthen vessels, proclaiming that in both the Bible and the creeds ultimate truth has been captured forever. The result is that Christianity seems less and less believable to more and more people.

Can the Christ experience be separated from the dying explanations of the past? That is the current theological imperative. If we cannot achieve this separation, then surely Christianity will continue its relentless journey into a declining irrelevance. If we can, however, the result will necessitate a reformulation of Christianity that is so radical that Christianity as we know it may well die in the process.

Death, however, appears to be the only realistic alternative. I cast my vote for the latter. I would rather die in controversy than die in boredom. I post in this book a call for a new reformation, framing that call in the form of twelve theses. I will state them as sharply and as provocatively as I can. People need to feel the dead weight of traditional theological claims before they can open themselves and their ancient words to new possibilities. I will use the traditional words to lay bare the claim. Then I will seek to point out a new direction. It will not be easy, for we must use human words to define non-human truths. My readers will hear the familiar words. They will learn that external, non-human truths cannot be captured in these traditional concepts. It will be an interesting experience, perhaps even transformative.

Lowell said it so clearly: "Time makes ancient good uncouth."

THE TWELVE THESES

1. God

Understanding God in theistic terms as "a being," supernatural in power, dwelling somewhere external to the world and capable of intervening in the world with miraculous power, is no longer believable. Most God talk in liturgy and conversation has thus become meaningless. What we must do is find the meaning to which the word "God" points.

2. Jesus the Christ

If God can no longer be thought of in theistic terms, then conceiving of Jesus as the incarnation of the theistic deity has also become a bankrupt concept. Can we place the experience of "the Christ" into words that have meaning?

3. Original Sin

The biblical story of the perfect and finished creation from which we human beings have fallen into "original sin" is pre-Darwinian mythology and post-Darwinian nonsense. We have to find a new way to tell the old story.

4. The Virgin Birth

The virgin birth understood as literal biology is totally unbelievable. Far from being a bulwark in defense of the divinity of Christ, the virgin birth actually destroys that divinity.

5. Miracles

In a post-Newtonian world, supernatural invasions of the natural order, performed by God or an "incarnate Jesus," are simply not viable explanations of what actually happened. Miracles do not ever imply magic.

6. Atonement Theology

Atonement theology, especially in its most bizarre "substitutionary" form, presents us with a God who is barbaric, a Jesus who is a victim and it turns human beings into little more than guilt-filled creatures. The phrase "Jesus died for my sins" is not just dangerous, it is absurd. Atonement theology is a concept that we must escape.

7. Easter

The Easter event gave birth to the Christian movement and continues to transform it, but that does not mean that Easter

was the physical resuscitation of Jesus' deceased body back into
human history. The earliest biblical records state that "God raised
him." Into what? we need to ask. The reality of the experience
of resurrection must be separated from its later mythological explanations.

8. THE ASCENSION ?

The biblical story of Jesus' ascension assumes a three-tiered universe, a concept that was dismissed some five hundred years ago.
If Jesus' ascension was a literal event of history, it is beyond the
capacity of our twenty-first-century minds to accept it or to believe it. Does the ascension have any other meaning, or must we
defend first-century astrophysics?

9. ETHICS

The ability to define and to separate good from evil can no longer
be achieved with appeals to ancient codes such as the Ten Commandments or even the Sermon on the Mount. Contemporary
moral standards must be hammered out in the juxtaposition between life-affirming moral principles and external situations. No
modern person has any choice but to be a situationist.

10. PRAYER

Prayer, understood as a request made to an external, theistic
deity to act in human history, is little more than an hysterical
attempt to turn the Holy into the service of the human. Most of
our prayer definitions arise out of the past and are thus dependent
on an understanding of God that no longer exists. Let us instead
think of prayer as the practice of the presence of God, the act of

embracing transcendence and the discipline of sharing with another the gifts of living, loving and being.

11. LIFE AFTER DEATH

If we are to talk about eternal life with any degree of intellectual integrity, we must explore it as a dimension of transcendent reality and infinite love—a reality and love that, when experienced, let us share in the eternal.

letting us share in the eternal

12. UNIVERSALISM?

We are called by this new faith into radical connectedness. Judgment is not a human responsibility. Discrimination against any human being on the basis of that which is a "given" is always evil and does not serve the Christian goal of offering "abundant life" to all. Any structure in either the secular world or the institutional church that diminishes the humanity of any child of God on any external basis of race, gender or sexual orientation must be exposed publicly and vigorously. There can be no reason in the church of tomorrow for excusing or even forgiving discriminatory practices. "Sacred tradition" must never again provide a cover to justify discriminatory evil. The call to universalism must be the message of Christianity.

Can a new Christianity be forged on the basis of these twelve theses? Can a living, vital and real faith that is true to the experience of the past, while dismissing the explanations of the past, be born anew in this generation? I believe it can, and so to engage in this task I issue this call to the Christian world to transform its holy words of yesterday into believable words of today. If we fail in this task there is little reason to think that Christianity, as presently understood and constituted, will survive this century. It is my conviction that we must move beyond theology, beyond creeds, beyond human perceptions to catch a new vision of the Christ. This book will be my attempt to do just that.

PART III

Thesis 1: God

Understanding God in theistic terms as "a being," supernatural in power, dwelling somewhere external to the world and capable of intervening in the world with miraculous power, is no longer believable. Most God talk in liturgy and conversation has thus become meaningless. What we must do is find the meaning to which the word "God" points.

4

The Challenge of the Copernican Revolution

The laws by which the world operates have not changed since the dawn of time, but the way human beings explain and understand those laws has changed dramatically over the centuries of human history. As a direct result of these changes, the primary way that Western human beings of recent millennia have conceptualized God has gradually lost its meaning and has become discredited. In the past, God—whether the Christian God or some other deity—was the answer to almost everything that human beings could not otherwise explain. "Theism" was the name of the operative definition of God that people used, both consciously and unconsciously. That definition saw God as "a being" that dwelled outside the boundaries of this world, endowed with supernatural power and periodically intervening in history to answer prayers or to impose the divine will on life in this world. It is this definition that has been rendered nonsensical by the advance of knowledge. Today in the hearts and minds of most educated people in our Western world a huge question mark lives in the place that theism once occupied. A crisis of faith is now afflicting modern men and women. Because most people are unable to separate this human definition of God from the reality of God, there is a feeling abroad that God is dying, or perhaps has died. As I noted earlier, this is not a new idea. The death of God was officially announced to the Western world in the nineteenth century, and we have not been able to get our heads around that debate since. If theism is the only way in which God can be understood, then the death of theism seems to leave us with *a-theism* as our only alternative.

As this realization dawns, the Christian world divides into two mutually exclusive camps. The first is made up of those who cannot step out of the security system that theism created for them. The second is made up of those who, unable any longer to affirm the symbols of their religious past, have become members of what I call the Church Alumni Association. These people want not just freedom *of* religion; increasingly they fight for freedom *from* religion. There is little room left over for anything else.

This division marks the "culture wars" of modern politics, driving each side toward fiercely held and mutually exclusive positions, between which there is and can be little room for compromise. Polarization, created in large measure by the death of theism, has become the political reality into which our modern world is living.

As each new generation grows into maturity, however, the direction in which this world is moving becomes clearer. The religious institution, along with traditional religious thinking, is declining at breathtaking speed, while non-religious secularity appears to be the ascending majority. Enormous fear accompanies this transition. As yesterday's theistic security system reveals its rapid decline, the voices of its adherents become more strident, more aggressive and even more warlike. It is not surprising to see terrorism, which almost always has a religious component, become the plague of our time, as zealots seek to impose the discarded religious values of the past on a post-religious generation, seemingly willing, sometimes even eager, to destroy themselves and much of the world with them in the process. This activity reflects, I believe, the depth of the human anxiety that emerges within us when one of the major bulwarks in the human security apparatus, namely the theistic God, begins to die and that death penetrates human awareness.

The secularists are winning, *not* because they are "anti-God," but because the forces which have brought about the diminution and the subsequent abandonment of traditional religious thinking cannot and will not be reversed. New insights rise with regularity as human knowledge expands, is tested by reality and is adopted in the form of revised operating principles in our world. There will be no turning back from these insights to embrace anew the definitions of yesterday.

Once one dismisses the theistic understanding of God as a literal being, who lives in a distant place to which no one has ever been—who sees all our deeds and misdeeds, records them and then rewards or punishes us according to our deserving—then one has to face the fact that God, as God has been traditionally understood, looks very much like an adult version of the child's dream of Santa Claus. The mythical North Pole elf is "making a list and checking it twice" to determine who is "naughty or nice," so that a proper abundance of Christmas joy may be left at the house of that person. Just as children outgrow their Christmas fantasies, so adult Christians must outgrow their religious fantasies. We cannot help but wonder if the theistic God is anything more than a relic of the childhood of our humanity. Once that possibility is opened, it can never really be dismissed again. The world does not move backward or retreat from truth once that truth has been articulated and then entered. What were the explosions of knowledge that spelled the death of our theistically understood God? They came in waves as the world evolved into modernity.

In the sixteenth century, the revolution began in the mind of a Polish monk named Nicolaus Copernicus, who from his monastic cell studied the movement of heavenly bodies. His calculations led him to a startling conclusion. The earth is not the center of a three-tiered universe! This insight, an incredible breakthrough in knowledge, also had significant religious consequences. The Bible was written from that earlier perspective of a three-tiered universe—heaven above the earth, hell below—and claims had been regularly made by the church that the Bible was "the inerrant word of God." With the discovery of Copernicus, however, the inevitable conclusion was that if the three-tiered universe was wrong, the Bible was also wrong! Copernicus did not publish his thinking widely, so the hierarchy of the church just ignored his work, hoping that no one else would notice. Johannes Kepler, however, not only noticed it, but he accepted it and even improved on it by explaining that the earth's orbit around the sun was not circular, but elliptical. Kepler's mother was put on trial for being a witch, but Kepler himself generally escaped the wrath of the controllers of orthodoxy.

The third major person in this first incredible breakthrough was Galileo Galilei, a well-known public figure of the seventeenth century, who was a mathematician, an astronomer, a recognized man of letters, a writer, the builder of a telescope, the father of a nun and a personal friend of the pope. He was, in effect, a person who could not be ignored. Building on the work of Copernicus, he published a paper demonstrating that the sun could not possibly revolve around the earth. The religious leaders struck back, asserting that the "truth" of the Bible must be protected from this onslaught. Galileo was put on trial for heresy, a capital crime in that day, which was normally punished by burning the heretic at the stake. The literal Bible and Galileo could not both be right. At that time in history, the Bible was the stronger of the two. So Galileo's accusers quoted from the Bible—from the tenth chapter of Joshua, to be specific, where the sacred text announced that in answer to Joshua's prayers, God stopped the rotation of the sun around the earth in order to provide Joshua with an extended period of daylight in which to kill his enemies. Since the Word of God itself spoke of the sun rotating around the earth, they quickly concluded that Galileo had to be wrong. He was found guilty and ordered to the stake. Before the fires were lit, however, a plea bargain was entered and accepted. For his part Galileo renounced his own findings, and he promised never to write about these things again. He also accepted "house arrest" for the balance of his life. In exchange for these concessions his life was spared.

Truth, however, cannot be suppressed simply because it is not convenient for those who are threatened by it. So, undaunted by Galileo's fate, successive scientists—first the few, then the many—began to study and to validate Galileo's insights. Our knowledge of the size and shape of the universe expanded exponentially. In the second half of the twentieth century, space travel ensued. Soon the Hubble telescope was launched and the heavens became increasingly available to our study. How then could one still portray God as dwelling above the sky? Would that mean that God is somewhere between the earth and the sun around which the earth rotates? Or was God rather to be relocated *beyond* the sun? That would place God somewhere in the galaxy we call the Milky Way, a galaxy of which our sun is nowhere near the center. Next, much to our surprise, we discovered that there were several hundred billion stars in our galaxy and perhaps as many as one trillion galaxies in the universe. Was God outside the whole universe? So where *is* God, we wondered? The supernatural theistic being we called God, who supposedly lived just above the sky, became less and less believable. A deity who cannot be located somewhere soon tends to be located nowhere. What does it then mean in such a world to say: "Our Father, who art in heaven?" Jesus, the supposed author of this prayer, clearly did not know anything about either the location of heaven or the size and shape of the universe. The authority of the Bible and even of Jesus began its slow, but steady retreat.

In 1991, the Vatican, seeking to accommodate itself to this new reality, finally issued an official statement in which the obvious was acknowledged: "We now believe," the Vatican said in effect, "that Galileo was right." It was not an apology to Galileo, but it was probably as close as that institution, which claims for itself infallibility in "faith and morals," could come to offering one. There has been, however, nothing from church leaders to address the impact of this knowledge on the traditional religious understandings of God. Despite that silence, theology and reality continue to drift away from each other.

If the Bible was wrong on this issue, about what else might it also be wrong? In the centuries since Copernicus, Kepler and Galileo, people would have to answer that question again and again. By the end of the twentieth century, with the theistic God dislodged from the assumed divine dwelling place and much more known about our vast universe, a contemporary theologian could write a book entitled *Taking Leave of God.*[*] Another could write: *Christianity Without God.*[†] As with Galileo, these authors would not be seen by the church as leading us to a new God definition, but rather as heretics, perhaps even as atheists, who must be marginalized by a threatened church. Is the denial of theism the same

---

[*] Don Cupitt. See bibliography for details.
[†] Lloyd Geering. See bibliography for details.

as atheism? Is there no other alternative? If not, then God was obviously beginning to die. That, however, was just the beginning of the problems that traditional religious formulas faced. We have just begun this chronicle of the human thought journey in which the meaning of the theistic God has faded.

5

The Impact on Theism
from Isaac Newton
and Charles Darwin

I n the growth in knowledge about the shape and size of the universe, God was dislodged from the realm we call heaven, and in that process God was for the first time in human history left with no dwelling place. As the growth of knowledge continued, all the things that we once attributed to this theistic definition of God began to be explained with no reference to God's supernatural power at all. We discovered, for example, that sickness was caused by germs, viruses, cholesterol, blood clots and cell malfunctions called cancer. It was not divine punishment inflicted on sinners by the record-keeping deity who looked down from above the sky. So sickness, in our most recent century, began to be treated not with prayers and sacrifices, but with antibiotics, chemotherapy, radiation, surgery, blood thinners and many other treatments. Sickness became secularized and God was largely removed from the medical arena.

Next, the God who once was believed to control the weather patterns, the God who punished a sinful world at the time of Noah with excessive rains that created the great flood and who

later stopped the rains from falling in the days of Elijah to produce a punishing drought, began to disappear as a causal agent in
the weather. Human beings increasingly spoke of weather fronts,
high and low pressure systems, El Niño winds and the collision
of tectonic plates underneath the sea that resulted in earthquakes
and tsunamis. We learned to track tropical depressions as they
crossed the oceans from Africa and formed the hurricanes that
pounded the Western hemisphere with devastating power. Prayer
addressed to that deity who lived above the sky proved to be ineffective in turning a hurricane away from human communities.
When a popular evangelical preacher in the United States suggested that New Orleans was struck by hurricane Katrina as punishment because that city had been the birthplace of a well-known
lesbian comedian or that the earthquake that devastated Haiti
was God's punishment of the Haitians for expelling the French
in the early years of the nineteenth century, his comments were
nothing more than fodder for late-night comedians.* God had
clearly been removed from any role in the weather patterns. The
theistic God had been forced into a full-scale retreat.

A major influence in creating this new way of looking at the
physical world was the English mathematician and physicist Isaac
Newton. Born in the middle years of the seventeenth century,
Newton studied the apparently fixed patterns of the vast universe
to which Galileo had opened us, only to discover that this world
operated in a mathematically precise way. The laws of the universe
were fixed, unchanging, immutable and predictable. There was no
place in Newton's worldview for supernatural power to operate, for
magic to occur or for God's miraculous abilities to be displayed.†

---

* Both of these comments were widely attributed to Pat Robertson, America's best-
   known television preacher and the son of a former United States senator from Virginia, A. Willis Robertson.
† *The Principia*. See bibliography for details.

Once again, it was a newly understood reality, one that called into question the term "act of God," a phrase that is still used by insurance companies with which the biblical story appears to provide ample illustrations. Could God turn the waters of the Nile River into blood to facilitate the escape of the Hebrew people from slavery in the land of Egypt? This was but the first of many divinely inspired plagues, the Bible tells us, which culminated in the divine plan to inflict death (shall we say "murder"?) on the first-born male in every Egyptian household. The final plague formed the background for the liturgy of the Passover, which was in turn the background for the Christian Eucharist. That is why Jesus is referred to as the new "Paschal" or "Passover" Lamb.

Once the credibility of God's invasive, miraculous power was called into question, the entire theistic framework of religion began a rapidly accelerating decline. The deity, defined theistically, whose dwelling place in the sky had been destroyed by Galileo, was now in the position, thanks to Newton, of not doing the traditional works of God. We began to wonder if this dislocated, apparently impotent deity really existed and why we needed this deity. In the words of the English biblical scholar Michael Goulder: "God did not have any work to do."[*] The Bible, now seen as a dated and fallible book, began to collapse. This constant retreat of the theistic concept of God from the life of our world and from our consciousness did not stop there, however.

In 1831, a man named Charles Robert Darwin, who earlier in his life had sought ordination as an Anglican priest, was offered a job as a naturalist on a ship called the *Beagle,* captained by a man named Robert FitzRoy. Darwin accepted this position and thus began a five-year journey around the world, during which time he studied life, the environment, the adaptation of living things to

---

[*] Michael Goulder and John Hick. *Why Believe in God?* See bibliography for details.

that environment, and fossil records. The latter in particular gave him the opportunity to examine the slow, incremental changes in various species of plant and animal life. A careful scholar, Darwin processed his data for almost thirty years before he published his findings in 1859 in a book entitled *On the Origin of Species by Means of Natural Selection.** The result of that book's publication was stunning and long-lasting in human thought. *On the Origin of Species* also presented a radical new challenge to our understanding of God.

Darwin documented meticulously his key theory in regard to the origins of life, which set him immediately in radical opposition to the traditional religious understandings. He saw life, including human life, as one interconnected whole. From that perspective, the idea of a special creation of human beings in "the image of God," as proclaimed in the Bible (Gen. 1:26–27), was called into question. Darwin dramatically changed the cultural definition of human beings. Before Darwin we thought of ourselves as "just a little lower than the angels," but after Darwin we began to think of ourselves as "just a little higher than the apes." In the process, and now from a new direction, Darwin called into question the accuracy of the Bible on many levels, including the way the Bible was thought to tell the story of how Jesus brought salvation. Darwin's challenge could not be ignored. *Unbelievable* was the only word to describe it.

Traditionalists struck back immediately, first ridiculing Darwin: "On which side of the family is your ape ancestor?" That was, in effect, the question the Anglican bishop of Oxford, Samuel Wilberforce, asked Thomas Huxley in their famous debate on Darwin in 1860 in the Oxford University Museum of Natural History. When ridicule no longer appeared to be a winning strategy, a group of

---

* See bibliography for details.

Presbyterian clerics associated with the Theological Seminary in Princeton, New Jersey, struck back with concerted attacks in the name of what they called "the fundamentals" of the Christian faith. Aided by the financial support of the Union Oil Company of California (UNOCAL), this group, in the first quarter of the twentieth century, sent out a series of newly composed pamphlets addressing those fundamentals to hundreds of thousands of religious leaders around the world.

Next, a man named John Scopes, a science teacher in Dayton, Tennessee, with the encouragement of the American Civil Liberties Union, agreed to test a state law forbidding the teaching of anything in the public schools of Tennessee that directly contradicted the "clear teaching of Holy Scripture." In 1925, for the crime of teaching Darwin's theory of evolution, he was convicted and fined in a trial that brought wide exposure to the conflict between science and religion.* Then came a concerted political attempt to force into the science departments of the tax-supported schools of the United States a pseudo-scientific theory called "creation science," to temper what supporters called the "faith-destroying" impact of Darwin's thought. Later, "creation science" was repackaged for a second assault on the public schools, but this time under the name "intelligent design." Both were finally declared unconstitutional by the courts under the provisions of the Constitution that called for the separation of church and state.† Yet truth, no matter how challenging, can never finally be determined by either majority vote or a court case.

Darwin's theory was an enormous breakthrough in understanding the truth of our biological origins, and it is now fully established in every citadel of higher learning in the developed

---

* See the Scopes Trial.

† Creation Science went to the Supreme Court. Intelligent Design was stopped in a lower court.

world. There is no Western medical school in the world today that has not organized its curriculum around Darwinian thought. The political debate over what can be taught as science in the public schools is now conducted only in rural and small-town districts, primarily in what is called "the Bible Belt" of the South, sometimes still reaching to the level of the governor's office in such states as Arkansas, Louisiana or South Carolina. Even the governor of Wisconsin, the son of a Protestant clergyman, seeking the presidential nomination of the still southern-based Republican Party in 2016, refused to answer a question about whether or not he "believed in evolution."* It was easier not to respond than it was to line up with Darwin.

When the smoke of this battle cleared, however, the accuracy of a "literal" Bible, the "infallible" pronouncements of a pope, together with the theistic understanding of God had all become unbelievable. They had been battered into submission. Suddenly, the Genesis creation story began to be reinterpreted in fascinating ways, but the transformative process in religious thinking continued in its apparently relentless retreat from Western consciousness. Slowly, but surely, as the insights of Darwin penetrated the minds of Western people, what once had been thought of as the "revealed truth" of the Bible was on the verge of collapse.

After Darwin there appeared to be no such thing as a perfect creation on which the God who lived above the sky could look with approval and pronounce it not only good but finished, as the Genesis creation account had suggested (Gen. 1:1–2:4a). For Darwin, creation was an ongoing, never-to-be finished, evolutionary process. Human beings were thus forced to draw some radically new conclusions. Without an "original perfection" in

---

* This was Scott Walker, who was among the first candidates to exit the race for the Republican nomination that year; February 15, 2015; http://time.com/3710087/scott-walker-evolution/.

creation itself, there could not have been a fall from perfection into something that was called "original sin." If we did not fall into "original sin" by an act of willful disobedience, there was no need to be baptized "for the remission of sin." The idea that unbaptized babies were bound for hell became ludicrous. There was also no need for us to be "saved, rescued, or redeemed" from a fall that never happened. This meant that the story of God sending Jesus or incarnating the divine person in the human Jesus to overcome "the fall," or to "die for our sins," was reduced to little more than pious nonsense. Everywhere we looked the traditional religious patterns began to fall into disuse.

If the story of human life is one of "unfinishedness," incompleteness, rather than a fall into sin, then the work of God is not to save us from our sins, but to bring about human completeness or wholeness. God cannot logically rescue us from a fall that never happened, nor can God restore us to a status we never possessed. So what does it mean to say that "God was in Christ reconciling" (II Cor. 5:19) or to insist on the centrality of a doctrine called "the Incarnation." As theologian Paul Tillich noted, it was at the recognition of these realities that there was "the shaking of the foundations" of religious thought.* Those religious systems based on traditional assumptions began to collapse. Thinking people began to recognize just why it was that Christianity must change or die! The need for reformation was becoming imperative. Before the process would reach crisis proportions, however, the screws would be given more turns, so our story continues.

---

* For Tillich's book of that title, *The Shaking of the Foundations,* see bibliography for details.

6

Dealing with the
Insights of Freud

First there was the revolution in astrophysics led by Copernicus, Kepler and Galileo. In that revolution, the comfortable assumption that God lived just above the sky, watching over us, recording our deeds and misdeeds in the Book of Life and ready to intervene on our behalf when needed, was challenged. Then came the revolution led by Isaac Newton, in which human beings were forced to see that they lived in a universe that operated according to predictable, consistent natural laws. The next onslaught against theistic thinking came in the nineteenth century from a naturalist named Charles Robert Darwin.

The early part of the twentieth century brought a further onslaught against traditional religious thinking. It did not take the form of an active campaign against religion, though to many it felt that way. It was rather a journey into a new understanding of truth and of reality in which the theistic definition of God simply did not fit. This twentieth-century attack was led by an Austrian doctor of Jewish parentage. His name was Sigmund Freud. Born in 1856 in a small city in what was then the Austro-Hungarian Empire, Freud did most of his work in Vienna before being forced

—— to flee to England to escape the murderous rage against the Jews led by Adolf Hitler. Freud's frontier was not the size of the universe, as it had been for Copernicus, Kepler and Galileo, the laws that govern the universe, as it had been for Isaac Newton, or the origins of life, as it had been for Charles Darwin. Freud, rather, was to make his mark by exploring the unconscious dimensions of life, something that few people in Freud's day were aware even existed, much less exercised any control over our lives and activities. So great was Freud's impact on human thinking that by the time of his death in 1939, even people who had never read a word that Freud had written were talking about such things as "Freudian slips," the device of rationalization, and even the symbols present in our dreams.

It was Freud's stated conviction that the force behind the creation of all religious systems was the need present in human beings to bank the fires of anxiety born in what he called "the shock of existence." By this he meant the moment that self-conscious awareness appeared in the evolutionary process. Freud believed that religion was simply the human projection into the sky of a protective parental figure of our own creation. This deity used supernatural power to deal with all the anxieties of self-consciousness, such as meaninglessness and the certainty of our mortality.

—— To guarantee that this theistically defined, divine parent figure could and would come to our aid in times of need, human beings developed, Freud stated, the two major aspects of almost every religious system.* First, we fashioned ritual acts designed to please God; second, we sought to order our lives on the basis of God's "rules" so that, as obedient children, we would succeed in winning God's protective favor. Liturgy was largely designed, he argued, to flatter God. Religious people called it "praise," but

---

* *The Future of an Illusion*; see bibliography for details.

Freud argued that it was nothing other than flattery. In these acts of liturgical flattery, believers called God by every honorific title we could imagine: "Almighty," "All-Loving," "Most Merciful," and hundreds more. We wrote and sang flattering hymns to God like: "How Great Thou Art," "The Heavens Declare the Glory of God" and "Praise Him, Praise Him, All Ye Little Children."* In every way imaginable, we told God how wonderful and praiseworthy God was.

Since flattery in human discourse, Freud noted, is always manipulative, he assumed that this was also its purpose in liturgy. Human praise for the theistic deity was designed, he said, to cause God to look favorably on us and our needs.

The same controlling motivation was also present, Freud argued, in the religious pressure used to make people obey God's will and to abide by God's rules. How did we know what God's will was? Our religious mythologies developed legends about how God's laws were dictated by God to a faithful servant, usually on a mountaintop where the God from above the sky came down to meet the designated leader at a midpoint between heaven and earth.

Knowing that obedience to God's rules was not always possible (the Torah, for example, contained 613 laws—one could not remember them all, much less obey them), religious liturgies focused on confessions of our failures, on pleas for God to have mercy and on the need for the fallen to be saved or rescued. The image of the theistic God began to look more and more like the face of a punishing parent or perhaps that of an ultimate judge.

One only has to look at our God language to validate these Freudian insights. The theistic God was a being like us human beings in all details, except with human limitations removed. We

---

* "How Great Thou Art," based on a poem by Carl Gustav Boberg 1885; "The Heavens Declare . . . ," based on Psalm 19; "Praise Him . . . ," author unknown.

called God infinite and immortal because we knew ourselves to be finite and mortal. We called God omnipotent and omnipresent because we knew human life to be powerless and ultimately bound by space. We called God omniscient because we knew ourselves to be limited in knowledge. Only a deity not bound by our weaknesses could address the anxieties of our limits and provide us with the security we sought. Then we named this deity "Father" or "Almighty Father," which served to make Freud's insight all but irresistible. Next, we offloaded onto this projected supernatural parent figure all of the anxieties of our birth into self-consciousness. The religious institutions then sought to control these anxieties by keeping their adherents in a state of dependency in which, like children, they did not worry about what they did not or felt they could not understand. People were then exhorted to be "born again," never to grow up, never to take responsibility. It was no wonder that the parental word "Father" became the name for the church-appointed representative of this theistic deity.

Under the power of Freud's insights, our theistic understanding of God seemed less and less real. Relentlessly, our theistic view of God was stripped from our minds. With this major bulwark against the chronic anxiety of self-consciousness now mortally wounded, we should not be surprised to note that this anxiety the theistic God was created to hold in check came roaring back. The twentieth century saw the world experiment first with the security found in a controlled society called fascism and, second, with the security found in a classless society called communism. When both of these systems failed, we opted for an increasingly secular society in which God was mentioned only on the fringes of life, while we put our search for meaning and security into the pursuit of wealth, material possessions and various forms of physical gratification. No matter how hard we tried, however, the emptiness at the center of human life could not be overcome. We then tried other coping devices, drugs, alcohol and even suicide. As the poet and playwright Edna St. Vincent Millay wrote: "God is dead and modern men (and women) gather nightly around the divine grave to weep."*

Then to our horror, we watched rising from the ashes of our dying religious systems a harsh militancy. Its adherents might be "Christians" who killed at a Planned Parenthood center, or "Muslims" who, in suicidal missions, sought to destroy those who had taken religious security away from them. Could human life make it without a viable theistic deity? We were about to find out.

When these, and many other breakthroughs in our understanding of truth that are too numerous to mention, are added together, the picture becomes astonishingly clear: God understood theistically has been mortally wounded. Will all religious yearnings die with this theistic deity? Can human beings live without self-destruction, if the security blanket of religion is removed, leaving us alone to cope? That remains to be seen. When we can go no further down this one-way street of no return, finally we begin to raise a different question: Can the reality of God be experienced in a non-theistic way? Reconstruction is always more difficult than deconstruction, but it is far more important, and that is the task that now lies before us.

---

* *Conversation at Midnight.* See bibliography for details.

7

A Place to Begin—
Being Not a Being

In the light of our expanded knowledge, the God that we had understood theistically turned out to be our own creation, one in which we human beings tried to fit God into the kind of words that met our needs. While seeking to describe our experience of "the Ultimate," we discovered that we had only human words and human concepts with which to do it. Those definitions served us for a while, but they have now visibly run their course and are disintegrating. All human definitions, we are learning, ultimately turn out to be both time-bound and time-warped. No one should be surprised when a human definition dies, even the definition of that which we call God. Nonetheless, we are forced to put words onto our experiences. We have no other option. So our task must inevitably be to try to find a non-theistic way in which we can talk about "the Holy." It is not an easy assignment, but it is a necessary one.

A mid-twentieth-century theologian named J. B. Phillips tried to capture the essence of what I am trying to do when he entitled his book *Your God Is Too Small.** The meaning of God, he and

---

* See bibliography for details.

I contend, cannot be limited to the scope of the human mind. It is hard, however, for humans to admit that reality. The task of a new reformation is not to redefine God, changing one set of limited human images for another, but to find a way to point ourselves beyond every human boundary, most specifically beyond the boundary of words. This means that here I must begin with negatives. If ultimate truth can be engaged at all, it will always be, to quote the apostle Paul, "in a mirror dimly" (I Cor. 13:12). So we work first with negatives, asserting at the very least what we believe God is not!

1. God is not "a being," not even "the supreme being." A being is something that exists in time and space, but we are trying to describe that which is ultimate, unbound, meaning that such terminology—the category of existence—cannot be used. Our first step then requires that we move beyond the idea of God as a being and contemplate the possibility that God is "Being itself." This step inevitably shifts the vocabulary of theology and makes us newly aware of the paucity of language. We are beings; we exist in time and space. How can we describe "Being itself"? "Being itself" does not exist in time and space. What does it do to understanding and to language to suggest that maybe time and space exist inside "Being itself"? Are we just playing word games? Some will surely make that accusation, but the search for truth means that we must absorb that charge. I think we can make the case that human beings are able to experience that which words cannot describe and that the experience itself can still be valid and real. To support this possibility, I turn first to the spiritual genius of the Jewish people. Among the Jews, God's name could never be spoken because God's "being" could never be grasped by the human mind. So the Jewish name for God became an unpronounceable set of consonants: YHWH. When Jews came to this unpronounceable set of Hebrew letters in their scriptures, they

made no attempt to speak this name, but rather, were trained to say the word *Adonai,* which means "the Lord." Jews were taught that they could not speak the name of God because that name was part of God's being.

Through the centuries, people have tried to ferret out the meaning of God's unpronounceable name. In the Jewish sacred story this name was revealed to Moses at the burning bush (Exod. 3:14). Jewish scholars, trying to translate that name, became convinced that these consonants reflected the source of God as "Being itself," not *a* being, though they would not have used those words. So the suggestion was made that YHWH meant "I am who I am." In our day theologian Paul Tillich would translate this name for God as "the Ground of Being." Others sought to clarify this idea, suggesting that this name meant "I will be what I will be" or "I am that which causes all things to be." So this set of four unpronounceable letters became a symbol, a Jewish symbol if you will, for that which is ultimate, holy and real. In this way of approaching the "Holy" the Jews were suggesting that God could be experienced, but never defined. Likewise "transcendence" and "being" could be experienced, but never defined. The spiritual genius of the Jews thus gave us a doorway through which to walk beyond theism without walking beyond God. God is not *a being;* God is the *Ground of Being.* It is a start, but it is still just a first step.

There are other hints in that biblical and thus still Jewish treasure trove of the divine-human encounter we call the Bible that might also carry us beyond the traditional idea of God found in the theistic language of men and women. Let me refer briefly to three of these biblical insights.

In the thirty-fifth chapter of Isaiah, the prophet seeks to respond to the question of how people will know when the kingdom of God is dawning in human history. In his answer Isaiah does not refer to such theistic images as the messiah descending to the earth from the realm of heaven. He speaks rather of a world transformed, a world alive and whole in the oneness of God.

"Water will flow in the desert," he answered, causing the crocuses to grow in this unlikely environment. It was a striking first image of transformation. Then he went on to say that the kingdom of God would become visible in the outbreak of human wholeness. Paraphrased thus, Isaiah says: "The eyes of the blind will be opened, the ears of the deaf will be unstopped, the limbs of human beings will no longer be lame, crippled, withered or limited and the voices of the mute will once again be heard" (Isa. 35:5–6). The presence of God, Isaiah was seeking to communicate, will be seen not in *a being*, but in the image of human beings *achieving wholeness*. It was a different insight, perhaps a new breakthrough in human consciousness. The realm of the human and the realm of the divine driven to their depths were not separate, he was suggesting. Isaiah the prophet was using the vehicle of words to speak of a reality beyond words. The divine can be seen only in and through the human. One must look inward not outward to experience the meaning and reality of God.

A similar note is struck in a parable that Matthew alone records, known as the parable of the judgment (Matt. 25:31–46). A parable by its nature is filled with symbols and pointers. No parable can be literalized. In this parable, a character called "the Son of Man" is cast in the role of the judge who comes at the end of time to inaugurate the ultimate reign of God. This judge begins the final process by separating the nations and the people of the world into two mutually exclusive camps. One he calls *the sheep* and the other he calls *the goats*. Listen to the details of this parable.

The sheep are invited into *the presence of God*, while the goats are assigned to what is called *outer darkness*. The standard by which the judgment was rendered, however, was identical. The sheep were those who were destined to become one with God. How was this to be accomplished? The sheep were those who, when God appeared before them as one who was hungry, they fed God. When God appeared before them as one who was thirsty, they gave God drink. When God appeared before them as one who was homeless, they took God in. When God appeared before them as one who was sick, they ministered to God. When God appeared before them as one who was imprisoned, they visited God. At the same time, those who were condemned to be apart from the meaning of God were those who did not do any of these things for God. Both groups were shocked and both began to question: "When did we see you hungry, thirsty, homeless, sick or imprisoned?" They had no memory, no recollection of responding either positively or negatively to this God presence. Then came the clarifying answer of this parable. God is not a being separate from the human. If you do not and cannot see God in the face of the hungry, the thirsty, the homeless, the sick and the imprisoned, then you cannot see God at all. God is not an external being; God is present in the faces of the least of these—our brothers and our sisters.

— Please note that none of the requirements that religious systems appear to think are important received the slightest bit of attention in this parable of the judgment. The Son of Man never asked either the sheep or the goats whether they had "accepted Jesus as their personal savior," whether they believed the words of the creeds and were therefore "orthodox" or even whether they were regular attenders at worship. No one asked either group if they had contributed generously to the church or to a religious institution. The only question raised was whether or not God had been experienced as part of the human!

A third, but still not dissimilar, idea found in the Bible appears

in the first epistle of John (4:16). Once again, apparently in answer to the human question about the definition of God, the letter writer—presumably a wise elder statesman of the Christian
movement—replied: "God is love. If one abides in love, one abides
in God."

It was such a short and simple thing to say. There was no need
to write a long theological tome to clarify the issue. In this statement, also, there was no separation between God and love or
between the divine and the human. Indeed, the divine and the
human appeared to penetrate each other. Note that while the
assertion was made that God is love, this simple definition was
never reversed. Nowhere in the text was it said that "love is God."
God cannot be defined. While God may be present in the experience, the experience can never be identified with God.

The common theme in each of these biblical vignettes is that
God is not a being separate from the beings who are human. God
is not a being to whom beings can relate; God is rather "Being
itself." God is not a noun that needs to be defined. God is a verb
that needs to be lived. It was and is an ancient idea, but perhaps
because it is not always a satisfying idea, it never grasped the core
of our humanity. "Being itself" does not offer us a lifeline to security. It does not promise us aid in time of need. It does not put
the supernatural at the service of the human. It does not teach us
how to manipulate the divine for the benefit of the human. What
these minority voices out of the Bible call us to do, however, is
to step beyond a theistic understanding of God and to open ourselves to a new way to approach the Holy. It suggests that we are
part of the Holy. Theology turns into anthropology. This is where
reformation begins; it must not, however, be where it ends. So we
press on.

8

The Quest for God:
A New Form

It was a sixth-century-BCE Greek philosopher named Xenophanes who wrote: "If horses had gods, they would look like horses." Xenophanes was pointing to the reality that all of us face when we try to speak of or to conceptualize that which we acknowledge as the ultimate reality, or what theologian Paul Tillich referred to as "our ultimate concern."* Yet our inadequacy in moving beyond our limits cannot be an excuse for not venturing into this realm at all. We human beings will never be able to speak of the Holy, of that which we call God, except in the language of the human, but speak we must; life and our humanity require it. Because we can conceptualize the ultimate "other," we cannot help but speak of it. So we are inevitably driven beyond the patterns of deconstruction into the task of reconstruction. It is not easy, it sometimes requires backing and filling and approaching the subject from several different perspectives to cover all the possibilities, but it is nonetheless an essential aspect of our humanity.

Who then is God?—or perhaps we should rephrase the ques-

---

* In *Systematic Theology*, vol. 1. See bibliography for details.

tion and ask: What then is God? Is the very idea of God a delusion of human creation? I do not think so. Can we then assert that God is real even if not part of the reality we can process? I do believe God is. These answers reveal simultaneously both my deepest conviction and the ultimate difficulty of trying to place this conviction into the vocabulary of human language. It is easy to understand why we fall again and again back into the limitations of theism, which leads us into one dead end after another.

So walk with me now slowly as I seek to find my way through this human thicket. Earlier in this book I stated that there is a difference between an experience and an explanation. That distinction is critical for theological thinking. An experience can be real, even timeless, but in order for that experience to be shared with another, it must be explained. Every explanation of an experience, however, is inevitably bound up in the limitations of human experience. Explanations are couched in the language of, the level of knowledge possessed by and the presuppositions embraced by the explainer. They are thus reflective of the subjectivity in which the explainer lives.

God, I believe, is an experience that is real. Creeds are, however, nothing more than attempted explanations of that God experience. Theology thus represents little more than human attempts to organize the explanations. Doctrine then becomes only the attempt to enforce the theology arrived at in those creeds. Finally, dogma develops, which is doctrine literalized and turned into idolatry! All theological systems are, therefore, finally nothing but coercive human creations. Religion is not and never has been based on a divine revelation. No religious system escapes this inevitable pathway that it must walk. The idolatrous nature of all religion, however, should not be used to hide from us the fact that the experience behind the idolatrous religious system can still be real. That forms a new place to begin. The reason such religious systems are constructed is to protect the original experience, because that experience was so transformative that it was imperative that it be shared and then passed on. So I begin this search for a way to enter the reality of the God experience with this complex, even circular analysis. I begin with what I know, which must be what I can demonstrate. We must, after all, start somewhere.

I am a subject; that is my and every other human being's uniquely human perspective. As a subject, I can experience and interpret things outside myself. This is one gift that ultimately sets self-conscious human beings apart by degree if not by kind from every other living thing. All living creatures can and do experience happenings, but only self-conscious human beings can interpret those experiences in words, and our interpretations will always reflect the limits of our humanity.

My doorway into God is to take my God experience seriously and then to live into it as deeply as I can. Whether or not I am delusional will be addressed later. For now I will assume my own rationality. How do I experience God? First, I experience God as life. Life, at least as we understand it, is a reality that emerged on this planet out of lifeless matter some 3.8 billion years ago. Life began as a single cell, which had the capacity to create a second cell. Then life began to express itself in a remarkable number of forms. Plants are living, insects are living, animals are living, but only self-conscious creatures can interpret the life that flows through all living things and which all living things can experience.

"I am alive" are words that only self-conscious creatures can utter. Meditate on the fact that human beings alone can say the words "I," "me" and "myself." We alone can use the verb "to be," which is the basis of every language. We alone know that we are alive, and that we have the ability to experience something beyond ourselves to which we feel somehow related. Life is thus for human beings something that places us into a mystical moment of transcendence. I can share in something that I know is not limited by my humanity. So I assert that we are related to a transcendent dimension of existence called life. Life flows through me, even as I am aware that I am part of it. It is the regular pattern of our humanity to name that transcendent dimension of life "God." Now look at what follows from the experience of transcendence. If God is the source of life, then the worship of this God forces me into the task of living—living fully. Then that which we call God becomes visible in others in the fullness of the depths of our ability to live.

The transcendent dimension of life that we call God is not separate from me. God is revealed in me and through me. The word "God" becomes not the name of God, but rather my name for the transcendent dimension of my own life. God is the name for the power and the source of life. Perhaps that is what the author of the book of Genesis meant when that writer wrote a myth of creation in which it was said that God breathed the life (or the *nephesh*) of God into the first human being. God originally was not perceived by this writer as external from us; God was rather met in the life we lived. This means that no matter how many times we pretend that God is a being like us, we are always driven by our experience to see that God remains the power of life within us. God is the life force made visible when we live fully. That is where I start this quest, but that cannot be the terminal point. So we move on to probe our experience of transcendence even more deeply.

Love is another reality that we human beings can both experience and name. Perhaps it is true that every living thing experiences that which human beings call love, but lesser forms of life cannot interpret it as we do. If love is the power that enhances life, then is not love the meaning found in the process of photosynthesis that draws plants into the life-enhancing rays of the sun? Is not love in the instinctive behavior of the mother cat licking the fur of its kittens or the mother cow giving the warmth of its body to the newborn calf? Is not love that force in the worker bees and drones of the hive that drives them to protect the nest and also to feed the queen? Is not love in the milk that fills a mother's breasts so the child can nurse, and in the process of nursing simultaneously feel the security of the mother's body? Is not love present in the parents of every species that seems programmed to fight off enemies to protect the life of the young? Love is the meaning of the life we give to another. None of us can create love. None of us can give love until we have received it. So love is also a reality that relates us to something beyond ourselves. That is the meaning of transcendence. Love gives life. The unloved offspring of every species will die. Love thus relates us to something beyond ourselves.

Love, however, is never disembodied, never found or experienced apart from life. Love passes through us. It neither originates nor terminates in us. We receive it, and only having received it are we able to pass it on. Love does not keep to be consumed later as "leftovers"; it cannot be preserved. It must be shared or it will die. So love opens each of us to a dimension of the human experience that is transcendent. Love relates us to something that is real, but something that we can neither create nor destroy. God is the name by which we call this experience of love. If God is love, the only way we can worship God is by loving others. The more we give love away, the more we make the experience of God visible. God is not a being, external to us; God is experienced in the presence of love. God is the dimension of transcendence flowing through us.

Whatever God is or might be, the fact remains that only self-conscious human life can interpret the experience of this power that is obviously present in the universe. It is the experience of love that allows the boundaries between one human being and another to fade, enabling us to enter the life of another so deeply that he or she becomes part of who we are and we become part of who he or she is. Suddenly individualism, that human development which we have for so long extolled, begins to look like a mirage, something perceived at the edges of life, not at its depths. Human oneness appears to be the deeper truth. We are bound to each other and are a part of something greater than any of us can be. God is our name for this reality. It is a place to begin. God!

These ideas flow readily into the suggestion that God is not a being, but "Being itself." God is the Ground of Being in which our being is rooted. God is the timeless eternity to which we are attached. So if God is Being, then the only way we can worship God properly is by having the courage to be all that each of us can be. The more deeply and fully we can be ourselves, the more God, who is Being, becomes visible. The missionary thrust of this understanding can never then be "to convert the heathen"; it can only be to enhance the being of others, to give life to others and to enhance love in others. These are the marks found in our experience of transcendence. They now become the footprints of the Holy, the experience of the dimensions of transcendence, the experience of God's reality. It is a place to begin.

When we insist that God is personal not impersonal, what we are saying is that the God experience drives us into a deeper humanity. When the Christian church asserts, in words attributed to the apostle Paul, that God is that in which we "live and move and have our being" (Acts 17:28), we are saying that God is the life we live, the love we share, the Being in which we are united. If we do not get this first point correct, all else will collapse into a theistic formula that dooms God to die. God is. Because God is, I live, I love, I am. Does that mean that God exists? I do not know what that question means. I experience God; I cannot explain God. I trust my experience. I will return to this formula again and again before I close this book.

9

Our Definition of God: Evolving, Never Fixed

I conclude in this chapter the discussion of the first of my twelve theses in my hope to initiate a new reformation. I began with the crucial task of reimagining God, which is foundational in all religious thinking. I have struggled to be careful with the way I use words. I have sought to be thorough and clear, so as not to ask of words what they cannot deliver. To accomplish the intended reimagining is to force human language to expand to the point that language itself becomes symbolic, pointing to truth while no longer pretending to be a vessel that is able to contain truth. This process is not an easy one and it raises anxiety in the minds of those who hear it for the first time, especially those rooted in the unbelievable religious symbols of yesterday, who search for the security of certainty. Their security, when found, always turns out to be just another bit of idolatry. Religious honesty requires the admission that certainty in religion is always an illusion, never a real possibility. Religion, which was born in the need to provide security for self-conscious creatures wrestling with issues of mortality, finitude and meaning, now finds itself forced to admit that it has no security to offer. Radical insecurity must now come to be seen as a virtue, which we must learn to embrace as central to our religion.

I began this discussion by once again positing a distinction between experience and explanation. An insect can experience the presence of a bird, but no insect has the frame of reference out of which it could ever describe to another insect what it means to be a bird. Similarly a horse has the ability to experience the presence of a human life. No horse, however, has the frame of reference that would enable it to describe to another horse what it means to be human. We understand each of these illustrations well enough, but when we drive these conclusions into the realm of the human, we begin to assume a capacity for human life that we would never attribute to a lesser creature. A human being, I am quite convinced, has the ability to experience God, but no human being has the frame of reference that would enable that person to describe to another human being what it is like to be God. This means that all of our creeds, our doctrines and our dogmas are human-bound definitions that are, in the last analysis, nothing but human creations; none is the product of what we have called "divine revelation."

The obvious conclusion to which I am driven is that while I am quite confident that human beings can experience the presence of God, I am now utterly convinced that it is completely beyond the realm of human competence to explain what it means to be God. One would not understand that, however, by listening to the God talk bandied about in most religious assemblies. Religious people generally do not recognize how unbelievable that God talk is. That is why doing serious theological thinking in a public place or through a public medium is so difficult and so fraught with peril. Most people cannot bring themselves to embrace the levels of ambiguity that theology requires. They will not be drawn to the enterprise of probing the symbols of our faith story for meaning. They will not want to do the painstaking, slow and laborious work of clearing their minds of normal human presuppositions.

This debate will, therefore, never be a popular one with the majority of religious people. It is something that we struggling searchers will have to do for them, whether they want it done or not. They are, in any event, not the audience I seek to reach. I want to speak to those who know that the religious assumptions of their childhood can no longer form the answers for them. I speak for those whose god is so small that they have dismissed this god from the realm of their reality. I speak to that which someone once called the "God-shaped hole" that seems to permeate the human consciousness—a hole that we try to fill, but into which nothing ever really fits. The difficulty in filling the hole in no way, however, diminishes the importance of this task. So I continue to walk this path and I invite others to walk with me. The journey is always, I believe, worth the effort.

Let me confess that I undertake this journey as a Christian. Because my call for church reform is radical, and for many alarming, I think it is important to state, both up front and clearly, that I am a Christian both by choice and by conviction. I do not understand Christianity as a religious system with fixed points of revealed truth, however. I see it rather as an evolving home in which I dwell happily. The forces that created and that continue to create this evolving faith are a rising human consciousness, an ever-expanding body of human knowledge and a growing capacity to achieve human insight. I do not think that Christianity is now or ever has been an unchanging tradition. This faith system did not drop from heaven in some newly revealed dimension. We rather evolved out of Judaism, breaking its boundaries in the process. We then incarnated ourselves in a variety of forms throughout history, riding each one until it broke open, unable to contain the meaning we struggled to communicate.

During each of our historic phases we Christians made excessive claims for every one of these forms. We had delusions of infallibility for our leader and inerrancy for our sacred story. We made dogmatic claims that sought to transform what were partial truths at best into ultimate truths that we pretended constituted the "one true faith" practiced by the "one true church." Each of these delusions would, in time, be abandoned as too small to be what we claimed it to be, but that abandonment was achieved only after fierce rejection of each new possibility and accompanied by the intense persecution of those people or ideas that propelled the change. It was also marked by institutional attempts to dig defensive trenches around the "true faith." Christianity has no ultimate stated certainty; it is an ever-evolving faith system, into which we are privileged to walk if we are to live into the future. I believe that we as a church will endure only so long as we are willing to live in flux. Human beings will inevitably create and recreate the religion they need to survive. Christianity is a human vehicle designed to allow that creative process to go on and on and on. This is what I mean when I identify myself as a Christian.

As consciousness grows and expands, the conclusions of yesterday become inoperative. We recognize that they have become unbelievable and can no longer inform the faith of tomorrow. If one has literalized yesterday's conclusions in order to form a set "orthodoxy," which resists change arising from any source, then the religious system of that era will be sick unto death. When our defined gods are so obviously human creations, they will inevitably participate in human mortality. Theism is only the latest of the God casualties. The experience lives on, while the explanation dies.

Allow me to illustrate this with a central Christian symbol, the idea of God as a Trinity. Is this truth a truth about God or is it a description of human experience? Is knowledge of God's being

ever a human possibility? Are not definitions of God always definitions of human experience? Theology thus is always about my
understanding of God; it is not about God. The doctrine of the
Trinity, therefore, describes a stage in the evolution of human experience. It was certainly not a revealed truth, nor was it the way
the earliest Christians understood God. Paul, for example, was
clearly not a Trinitarian. For the Jewish Paul, God was "one" and
nothing approached or modified that "oneness." Paul says in Romans that God "designated" Jesus as "Son of God with power according to the spirit of holiness by his resurrection from the dead"
(Rom. 1:4). God is the designator, Jesus is the one designated;
that is not co-equality or Trinitarianism. Paul said that the life
Jesus lived, he lived to God (Gal. 2:19). We become alive to God
through Jesus, he asserted. For Paul, Jesus was a doorway into the
ultimate; Jesus was not himself the ultimate. God, as "Father,"
reflected ideas from the childhood of our humanity. God was the
protective power that human beings sought desperately to access.
To make the power of God work for them was the essence of
worship and of religion. This distant, powerful, parent deity was
believed to have the ability to place a protective shield around the
faithful human life. Natural disasters such as the flood at the time
of Noah resulted, people believed and stated, from the human
failure to keep God's law. Our hymns still express that hope. We
sing, "Eternal Father, strong to save, whose arm hath bound the
restless wave."* Floods, tidal waves and tsunamis, however, reveal
that the restless waves cannot be and are not bound by the divine
hand.

Christianity at its infancy, like all religions, was childlike,
based on a protective deity. In many ways, early Christianity was
a religion of fear and control. Because we had failed to be pleas-

---

* William Whiting 1860.

ing to God, Christianity thus became almost totally a religion of penitence, guilt and pleas to God for mercy. It was a system that did not allow us to grow up. We were children seeking to please the powerful "Father" or parent God. It is hard to grow up until we leave the "Father's house."

Developing Christology was one of the things that allowed us to begin to grow out of this childlike religious form. Christology arose in the late third and early fourth centuries with the suggestion that God had entered human life, which served to give human life a dignity it had not had before. As Christianity came to understand itself in this new way, we began to tell the story of the Father God who, by drawing near to us, suffered the consequences of being in the human arena of pain and death and who called us into a new level of humanity. Of course, in the telling of it, the Jesus story got corrupted. The idea that God could take on human form, however, meant that we had come to an awareness that humanity might have a potential we had never realized before. This represented a major shift in consciousness. Next we began to entertain the story of the Holy Spirit, which served to universalize the Christ story. Now all people, not just Jesus, could be God-filled. There was no longer anything unique about a God-filled humanity. Maturity had begun to set in. This set the stage for our next step. Discovering a humanity that was the medium through which "the Holy" could be seen and experienced as present became a new possibility.

Another turn in consciousness was about to be discovered and entertained. That is the door on which we are knocking today. Maybe the human and the divine are the same. We file that now with the promise to return to it after we have looked at the Christ story. An evolving Christianity is not our fear, but our hope.

We move now to the Christ story.

PART IV

Thesis 2:
Jesus the Christ

If God can no longer be thought of in theistic terms, then conceiving of Jesus as the incarnation of the theistic deity has also become a bankrupt concept. Can we place the experience of "the Christ" into words that have meaning?

10

Escaping the Idolatry
of the Incarnation

S ome years ago, when I was in conversation with the
dean of a theological seminary, he made what he surely
thought was a safe assertion: "I base my faith on the Incarnation." The Incarnation was for this dean a kind of
Maginot Line. He had already implied in both word and action
that I was no longer a "true believer." To his dismay I responded:
"I do not." Surprised at my claim, though I suspect he saw it as
confirmation of my heresy, he was silent. Once a Maginot Line is
challenged, silence always follows. I turn in this chapter to what
has become for traditional Christians a code word: "incarnation."
What does "incarnation" mean? It is clearly not a biblical concept. It reflects rather the fourth-century dualistic Greek mindset
in which it was born. It asserts that the external, theistic, supernatural God has taken on the form and flesh of a human life. In
that process, Christian theologians asserted for centuries, against
all evidence to the contrary, that neither the divinity of God nor
the humanity of Jesus' biological life had been compromised in this
affirmation they called "the incarnation." These ideas made no
rational sense, but they were repeated again and again. The clear
implication has been that they do not have to make sense. One does

not question a theological mantra; one only repeats it. So fourth-century Christians placed these words into the Christian creed: "For us and for our salvation, he came down from heaven and was incarnate by the Holy Spirit of the substance of the Virgin Mary and was made human."

The clear implication of this creedal assertion was that in Jesus a form of God had entered into human life. Jesus was thus a divine being in a human disguise. After all, "incarnation" literally means "enfleshment." Charles Wesley assumed this when he wrote "Hark! the Herald Angels Sing," one of his best-known Christmas carols, which includes these words: "Veiled in flesh, the Godhead see; hail the incarnate deity."* Because of this strange and alien note in the biblical theology found in this hymn, it is my *least* favorite Christmas carol.

If Jesus was God in human form, then all of the miracles claimed for him in the New Testament made sense. Jesus could give sight to the blind, hearing to the deaf, wholeness to the crippled and lame and voice to the mute because he was "God incarnate." Jesus could even raise the dead, for he shared in the eternal life of God. Jesus could expand the food supply so that the hungry could be fed, and lead to victory the forces of goodness over the armies of our enemies, because Jesus was God in human disguise.

As this tradition developed, it broadened its Jesus narrative to address problems as they arose. For example, if the external God, who lived above the sky, was to take on human form, a landing field on which this deity could arrive on the stage of human life had to be prepared. God could not be forever bound by the limitations of human life, however, so there also needed to be a launching pad from which the incarnate God could be propelled

---

* Wesley wrote this hymn in about 1739.

back into God's natural domain in the heavens. In time both of these mythological elements, and many others, were added to the Jesus story. Like all other explanatory narratives in the faith experience, they were all too soon literalized and became part of what traditional-thinking Christians called "orthodoxy."

When the theistic concept of God was battered by the expansion of knowledge, however, the idea of incarnation became more and more nonsensical. Nonetheless, it would take hundreds of years before this aspect of our dated theological language would become apparent and begin to fall apart. That day has finally come.

The skies are filled with planets, suns, stardust, dark matter and black holes and the universe appears to be infinite. There is no supernatural being living beyond the clouds, watching over life on planet earth. The laws that govern the twists and turns of life are the fixed laws of nature. They are not amenable to the intervention of a supernatural deity, who can change the course of history to bring about the military victory of a favored nation or to create different outcomes in the exigencies of human life for those who pray properly. Human life is not a special creation made in the image of God. All life emerged from matter and then evolved into the complexity that marks our world today. The theistic definitions of God have been splintered on the hard rocks of reality, which inevitably means that so has the idea that this theistic deity would somehow, "in the fullness of time," incarnate the divine being into a human form. Incarnation in any literal sense is revealed to be little more than a pious hope, an unfulfilled dream. What then does it mean—or indeed what could it mean—to assert, as Paul does, that "God was in Christ" (II Cor. 5:19) or that God had emptied the "being" of God into the life of a servant, "being born in the form" of the human (Phil. 2:5–8)?

Paul was a Jew. For a Jew God could not be defined or discussed as if God were an object that we could observe or control. God could be experienced only as a presence that transformed human life and drew it beyond its boundaries. So we need to ask: What was Paul's experience, which caused him to use language that could ultimately be interpreted as "incarnation" by those who needed to define the experience? Can that experience be recovered? Is it something into which *we* could walk? Literalized inside human language, this concept makes no sense to modern ears. Must we Christians then still confront the world with this claim as if we were people endowed with the inarticulate sounds of unknown tongues? Can we deny every aspect of our literal creedal affirmations about Jesus and still call ourselves Christians? Can we still be Jesus' disciples? I believe we can, but not until we extricate ourselves from the creedal language of the fourth century, including the language of "incarnation."

Can the divine be seen in the human? That is where we must begin. Can the human be pulled beyond its limits until it becomes the vehicle through which the divine is able to be experienced? What was there about this Jesus that lent itself to what is now thought of in the strange language of "incarnation"? What was it that caused the words "my Lord and my God" to be placed by the author of the Fourth Gospel into the mouth of the one once called "doubting Thomas" (John 20:28)?

We come to these questions in the only way we can. We must begin with negative statements because we, as human beings, are not capable of saying what God is, so we limit ourselves to saying what God is not or what God cannot be. People did not see miraculous power in Jesus and then move from that experience to the conclusion of his divinity. The power of Jesus was experienced long before people attributed miracles to his presence. No one prior to the writing of Mark in the eighth decade ever seems to have associated miracles with Jesus. This fact surprises many. Paul, who wrote between 51 and 64 CE, never spoke of Jesus as a worker of miracles. The Q document, if its existence can be definitively established (I am quite skeptical), and if once established it can be dated as earlier than or even contemporaneous with Mark, contains no miracle narratives.* The Jesus of supernatural acts seems to be a late-developing portrait that people painted of him. The power of Jesus, as one through whom a God presence was seen, had been experienced long before miracles were attributed to him. The claim that God was revealed in Jesus in a special and unique way also had nothing to do with narratives that asserted his miraculous birth. No miraculous or virgin birth story emerged in the Christian tradition until the ninth decade, and it had disappeared from the tradition by the end of the tenth decade. It was neither essential nor beneficial to the claim of divinity for Jesus. That fact also surprises people.

No, there was something far earlier and perhaps more profound about this Jesus that caused his followers to make the God claim for him. It was, I believe, the breaking down of all the boundaries and barriers by which we human beings separate ourselves from one another. The power of God seen in Jesus was the overcoming of all our fears and divisions. In his presence and through the experience of his life, the barrier between Jew and Gentile, Jew and Samaritan, male and female, Israel and Judah, bound and free, rich and poor, and life and death all faded away. In Jesus there was a humanity that included all and that dismissed none. In this Jesus a human community without boundaries could be seen. God was the power of life, the passion of love, the Ground of Being that draws all lives into a new humanity. That

---

* The healing of the centurion's servant is a possible exception to this rule. I dealt with that exception in my book *Biblical Literalism: A Gentile Heresy.* See bibliography for details.

was the experience that drove first Paul and later many others to say of this Jesus: "God was in Christ" (II Cor. 5:19).

God is not a being who can invade and take over human life. Jesus is not God in disguise. Jesus is the fully human one in whom a separated world finds a new unity. Incarnation language today will never give us that. That kind of language needs to be abandoned, not because the experience it seeks to articulate is wrong, but because the words used to communicate its meaning no longer communicate the depth of that experience. God did not invade the world; rather, the human became the vehicle through which the divine could be and was met and engaged.

Why do we seek to make it so difficult? Why do human beings insist that theological ideas must be literalized in order for them to be true? Do we not understand that theological idolatry can kill faith just as easily and just as quickly as biblical literalism can kill faith? The journey into Christ must carry us beyond both.

This is now the established principle through which we will begin to look at the traditional way the Jesus story has been told. Before we have completed this task we will have looked at that story from many different angles and examined it from many different perspectives. It will never look the same once this process is engaged.

The Collapse of the
Salvation Story

As the insights of Charles Darwin began to percolate throughout the educated world, it became clear that it was not just the integrity of the Bible that was at stake; a far deeper threat from Darwin came to be perceived by believers. On that deeper level no saving compromise could ever become possible. Both contemporary knowledge and the primary way in which the Christian story was told could not ultimately co-exist; one or the other had to be wrong and would finally be forced to die. The battle was on and the primary Christian myth that involved a good creation, followed by a fall into sin, which then required the rescue operation, which God mounted in Jesus with its climax on the cross of Calvary, producing the pious claim that Jesus "died for my sins," all of that was destined to come crashing down. It would take a couple hundred years for this challenge to the traditional way in which the Christian faith was articulated for the victory of the new knowledge to be complete. Today, we live in the aftermath of that total triumph.

The first challenge that traditional Christianity had to face was that there never was an original perfection from which we human beings had fallen. Life studies confronted us with an evolving process that was not only real, but was significantly unfinished. It was a view of our origins that was both ongoing and incomplete. At this very moment, for example, galaxies are still being formed and various species of plant and animal life are still being born while some are becoming extinct. A perfect and completed creation was seen as an oxymoron. It is only at this moment that we begin to understand that human life sits at the top of the food chain with no natural enemies. We are the current winners of the battle for survival, but uneasy should be the head that wears that crown. Human beings have *not* had "dominion over the beasts of the field" since the dawn of time (Ps. 8:6–7). The Bible is clearly not factual.

Some sixty-five million years ago the dinosaurs occupied the top rung in the world's food chain. They too had no natural enemies. Those dinosaurs, like *Homo sapiens* today, had no reason to believe that their ascendancy would ever be challenged. That is, however, not the way that evolution works. In the ever-churning evolutionary process, when one door is closed on one form of life, it opens to another form of life. In that ancient moment of dinosaur supremacy in the history of this planet, something radical, unexpected and dramatic happened. Today's major scientific conjecture is that there was a collision between our planet and a giant meteor, perhaps one as large as Mars. This collision may have been so powerful that it knocked earth out of its primary orbital path around the sun, changing our planet's climate measurably for a significant period of time. Perhaps it raised a level of dust that would not settle for generations, scrambling all of the forms of life in a chaotic way. Whatever it was that happened, we know that the dinosaurs became extinct and that with that extinction, the age of the dominant reptiles came to an end. The door was thus opened for the mammals to rise in ascendancy.

Our first mammalian ancestor appears to have been a mouse-like creature that inhabited the grasslands of eastern Africa. From that single ancestor, the mammals proliferated in a number of directions. There were many widely differing types of mammals, and each species joined in the struggle for supremacy. Some, like the mouse, beaver and opossum, were rodents. The cat family included creatures as small as tiny kittens, as well as midsize wildcats and mountain lions, and larger panthers, tigers and lions, the latter of which was given the title "king of the jungle." Then there was the mammoth family of mammals, which included the now-extinct mammoth, the elephant, and possibly both the hippopotamus and the great whale, which seem to have been distantly related. There was also the hominid family, which included small monkeys, larger orangutans, gorillas, the great apes and ultimately *Homo sapiens.* For millions of years, representatives from each of these mammalian subsets struggled among themselves and with each other for supremacy until finally the superior brain found in the hominid line led to their domination of the animal world. This victory was achieved relatively recently, perhaps within the last four to six million years.

Nothing, however, in this long evolutionary process pointed to the original perfection claimed by the dominant Christian myth. No form of life is today what it was originally, nor is it what it will always be. Life is never set. It is always in flux. No part of life reflects a state of unchanging perfection, as the Bible's creation story suggested. The corollary of this insight is that no form of life ever "fell" from perfection into what we came to call "sin." Physical reality knows only an evolving world of trial and error.

The theological ramifications from that insight proved to be stunning for Christianity. The building blocks in the creation myth were scattered precipitously. If there was no original perfection, there could have been no fall from perfection into original sin. If there was no fall into sin, there was no need for a "savior" to rescue us. One cannot be rescued from a fall that never happened, nor can one ever be "restored" to a status that one has never possessed. The idea that Jesus on the cross paid the price of our fall in order to save us from sin thus becomes an idea that no longer makes any sense to anyone. This ancient form of telling the Christ story has collapsed before our eyes. It has become unbelievable. Yet we continue to build liturgies and say the ancient words about Jesus that constitute something like a foreign language to modern ears. What does it mean today to say: "O Lamb of God, who takes away the sins of the world, have mercy on us"? Is there any reason for us to continue to think that these non-sensical words will ever be able to translate themselves into meaningful worship for modern *Homo sapiens*?

We human beings were not made in a special act of creation, nor were we created in the image of God. Like every other form of life, we have journeyed over billions of years from a single cell into our various levels of complexity, consciousness and self-consciousness. As recently as the middle of the twentieth century we learned of our DNA relatedness to all living things. We now know not only that we share a 99.9 percent identical DNA with the great apes, but also that we share a DNA connection with the clams, the cabbages and even the plankton of the sea. Life is all one expression of an evolving whole. There was no original perfection followed by a fall into original sin. There was only the slow and gradual unfolding of life in an evolutionary process. There were howls of protest in religious circles as these realities began to be processed and established as true. No credible challenges to this explanation of our origins, however, have yet been found. The world has changed. The primary way we have been telling the Christ story is wrong.

So how do we today account for the reality of evil? Is it simply a part of life? Are we nothing more than the survivors of a tooth-and-claw struggle? If human beings are connected with every other life-form, then how do we tell the story of Jesus? Is there anything from that story that we can maintain? While the theological forms of yesterday no longer hold water, must we give up the experience just because the human explanation of that experience has become bankrupt? Is the reality of "transcendence," "otherness" and "God" dependent on the truth of ancient mythology? I do not think so, but I do know that our explanations today cannot begin at the same place where they began in our religious past.

Human beings share the gift of life with every living thing, both plant and animal. Is there something common to all forms of life? Is there a common reality in which all living things share? I think there is. Studies reveal that every living thing, including human beings, is survival-oriented. Illustrations that support this premise are not difficult to find. Survival drives the evolutionary process. It is found in plant life and in all animals. The illustration of this comes from my own travels and observations.

Mangrove trees, freshwater plants, but now found living in a tidal river flowing into the Coral Sea in North Queensland, Australia, have developed, in the service of survival, an elaborate root system that filters out much of the salt contained in the river water before it can kill the tree. When excessive salt still threatened the life of these trees, they somehow devised a means to guide the salt to particular leaves, which then turned orange and fell off the branches. These came to be called the "sacrificial leaves." They died that the tree might live. Mangrove trees do not appear to be capable of *planning* this means of adaptation. They are thus driven by a natural process that is survival-oriented.

Parakeets living in the Amazon jungle receive life-sustaining nutrients from the seeds of the fruits that grow in the jungle. The problem is that these seeds are toxic, so the food required for their survival can also kill them. These parakeets, however, have learned to go daily to certain places in the forest, called "clay licks," where the soil is filled with anti-toxins. Here they ingest the dirt, getting their fill of anti-toxins in the process, a step that then enables them to eat their toxic food and still survive.

Also in the jungles of the Amazon, wasps and ants live in a relationship that makes their mutual survival possible. Ants build their nests in the lower branches of the trees, while wasps build their nests above the ants. These positions make survival possible for both. The primary enemy of the wasps is another kind of ant, known as army ants, who want to climb up the tree to the wasp nests in order to devour the larvae, thus killing the nest. The wasps are helpless against these army ants because they have only stingers with which to defend themselves. The laws of nature, however, are that the army ants will not go past the regular ants' nest in the tree, so if the wasps build above the regular ants, they are safe.

As suggested above, the regular ants also benefit from this arrangement. The primary enemy of these ants is the anteater, a small animal which climbs the trees with ease and will eat a whole ant nest. The anteater, however, is driven off by the stinging wasps. The ants make the wasps' survival assured, and wasps do the same for the ants. Nature is survival-specific. By that I mean that the laws of nature protect the various species. Wasps and ants do not talk to each other; they simply do as instinct dictates.

There are no native mammals on the Galapagos Islands, because there is no freshwater to sustain their lives. Pirates, however, who used these islands as hideouts, once imported some goats so that they would have a fresh meat supply whenever they landed there. Over time the stomachs and kidneys of these wild goats adapted to the briny water, the only water available in those islands, in order to survive.

Our biology itself has dictated to self-conscious human beings a survival mentality that is our highest value. That desire for
survival inevitably means that we are self-centered. We do not
respond well to people who are different—those who look different, speak a different language or worship a different God—
because we have judged them as a threat to our survival. So to be
human is to be prejudiced, tribal and sectarian. Self-centeredness
is rooted, not in our morality, as we once thought, but in our biology. It is a given, not a consequence! That is the universal human
experience that our ancestors once called "original sin." The experience was real; the interpretation was false. We are not "fallen
sinners"; rather, we are incomplete human beings. Our old theology is dead. The door begins to open on a new way to tell the old,
old story.

PART V

Thesis 3: Original Sin

The biblical story of the perfect and finished creation from which we human beings have fallen into "original sin" is pre-Darwinian mythology and post-Darwinian nonsense. We have to find a new way to tell the old story.

12

The Garden of Eden

The perfection of God's world is described again and again in the text of the Genesis story of the Garden of Eden (Gen. 1–3). We read that God saw all that God had made and pronounced it good. We learn that this world was a fertile garden, but it lay fallow without a person to till it. To overcome this problem, Adam was created. We are told that "every tree that [was] pleasant to the sight and good for food" began to grow in the garden, but we are then advised that all of these regular trees grew in the company of two special and unique trees. One was called "the tree of life"; the other, "the tree of the knowledge of good and evil." Four rivers provided water for this garden, known as the Garden of Eden. Two of them were named the Tigris and the Euphrates, which would tend to locate them in what came to be known as Mesopotamia. This garden was also said to possess gold, bdellium and onyx. Why the garden's first human inhabitants needed these valuable treasures is, however, never stated. The man, Adam, was given the power to rule over all things. In his world there was no such thing as evil.

When the woman was created in the second creation account out of the man's rib, Adam's ability to rule over all things was compromised just a little.* The woman, we are led to understand, was human like Adam, but she was designed to be dependent, the male "helpmeet." So his authority over her was not as complete as it was over the members of the animal kingdom. For example, though Adam had "named" her, as he did all the other creatures, her status as a human being gave her a freedom and a power that no other creature possessed. The stage was thus set for evil to enter Eden through this presumably "weak link" in creation. It was still a very patriarchal world!

This was a story full of fantasy and wondrous elements. Snakes that could walk on two feet and speak understandable human words to a human being were in the cast of this garden's characters. Human deception and the ability to cast blame, to say nothing of the human capacity to engage in both rationalization and projection, were portrayed. Fascinating explanations were offered for things that ancient people obviously observed, but could not otherwise explain. Why did snakes slither on the ground, eating dirt in the process? Why did women endure pain in childbirth? Why did the man struggle to eke his living out of the apparently hostile ground?

The contest and tension in the third chapter of Genesis is between the wily serpent and the woman. The "tree of the knowledge of good and evil" was forbidden to the two human beings. "Forbidden fruit," we all recognize, exercises a particular attraction. Why was it forbidden? How would it taste? Its fruit was apparently so appealing that the woman allowed it to enter her fantasies. She circled this tree daily, looking at it from every angle. A fixation was clearly developing.

The serpent, we are told, was at this time "more subtle than

---

* Genesis 1–3 contains two different accounts. The older one (Gen. 2:46 through 3) is the Adam and Eve story and the later one (Gen. 1:1 through 2:4a) is the Seven Day Creation story. They have been merged in the text.

any other wild creature that God had made," so the serpent noticed the attraction between the woman and the fruit of this tree and began to move in on Eve, the snake's target. Was this serpent a phallic symbol, depicting sexual desire and fear simultaneously? A case could certainly be built for that supposition.

The conversation began with the serpent reminding the woman of the prohibition. The text says "Did God say that you should not eat from any tree in the garden?" Eve responded: "We may eat of the fruit of the trees in the garden, but God says 'You shall not eat of the fruit of the tree that is in the midst of the garden, neither shall you touch it lest you die." (Gen. 2, 3). Death was the punishment for that act.

Such a harsh punishment for so minor a misdeed must have seemed to Eve to be both severe and unwarranted, perhaps even wrong and unjust. From then on the snake began to toy with Eve, as a cat might do with its prey. "You will not die," the snake said. There must be some other divine reason for this prohibition. Then the serpent offered this possibility: "God knows that if you eat of this tree, you will become like God, knowing good and evil." God wants no such competition, the snake assured Eve. It was a subtle and an appealing stab into the weakness of the snake's victim, and it landed squarely on its target.

The woman, the text tells us, saw that this fruit was good for food, that it was a delight to the eyes and that now she believed it might make her wise. The temptation was too great to resist and so she picked it and ate it. Disobedience at that moment was said to have entered God's perfect world! Not willing to be alone in her act of disobedience, she then gave some of the fruit to her husband, Adam, and he also ate.

The result? The narrative tells us that their eyes were opened and that they felt shame; they knew that they were naked. A sexual theme is always close to the surface in this account. They then proceeded to cover their shame with fig leaf aprons. Then, we are told, they heard the rustling of leaves in the garden. God had come down in "the cool of the evening" to take God's daily walk with God's friends, Adam and Eve. Before this moment, God had always been a welcome presence. Now, however, things had changed. God was now perceived as a punishing judge. So Adam and Eve hid themselves in the bushes of Eden from this judgmental deity. In this primitive myth, the all-seeing God's supernatural power was obviously deficient, because God was unable to find Adam and Eve. So God called out to them: "Adam, where are you?" In the game Hide and Seek one hides so as not to be found. This, however, was the first time that Hide and Seek had been played in human history, and Adam apparently did not yet understand the purpose or the rules; so he called back to God, saying: "Here I am, Lord, hiding in the bushes." God responded: "What are you doing in the bushes?" Adam explained: "I was ashamed of my nakedness. I did not want you to see me, so I ran away and hid."

This was a new level of human understanding. God picked up on it immediately. "Who told you that you were naked?" Presumably Adam and Eve had been naked from the moment of their creation, but they had never noticed. From where does this self-awareness, this shame, this sense of inadequacy come? Then it dawned on God just what this behavior meant: "Have you eaten of the tree of which I commanded you not to eat?" The man was trapped. The deeply human quest for survival set in. Finger pointing, guilt, excuses and rationalization appeared for the first time. "It was *that* woman," Adam said, "You know, God, the one *that you made*. She gave me the fruit and yes, I ate it." God turned to the woman, but she also had a scapegoat: "It was the serpent that beguiled me and I ate."

At that moment, presumably for the first time, self-conscious creatures had to take responsibility for their deeds, so divine punishment was handed out. The serpent was cursed to be hated above all creatures and was condemned to crawl forever on its belly. Enmity would always exist between the serpent's offspring and the woman's offspring. Once again the sexual overtones are overt. The woman's punishment was that she must forever bear pain in childbirth. The man would have to eke out a living from the ground, which, God predicted, would bring forth more briars and thistles than good food to eat. The ultimate punishment, however, was that all living things would have to die. "Dust you are and to dust you shall return." Since death was universal, the sin that caused death had also to be universal.

God then banished them from the garden. Now that they knew good from evil, it was deemed imperative that they not be allowed to eat from the tree of life and escape mortality. Adam and Eve could never again live in Eden, within God's presence. Our destiny as human beings was to live somewhere "east of Eden,"* forever separated from oneness with God. An angel with a drawn sword was placed at Eden's gate, eternally guarding it from human "re-entry." Fallen human life was destined to die.

That is the story, as told in the ancient Jewish myth of creation. Early Jewish readers of this story never saw it in moralistic terms. For them, this was the story of human beings growing into self-awareness, learning to discern between good and evil, ceasing to be children dependent upon the heavenly parent for all things and finally having to enter their maturity and to assume self-responsibility.

Augustine and subsequent Christianity, however, read the creation story as a literal narrative, accounting for the way in which

---

* This biblical phrase was used as the title of a 1952 novel by John Steinbeck. See bibliography for details.

sin and evil had entered the world. The perfection of God's perfect world had been destroyed; the source of evil had been identified; human life had fallen into sin. The account of this myth in Genesis, now validated as the "Word of God," set the pattern for the omnipotence of God. God was not so much the source of life and love, as God was the focus of judgment. Human beings were now to be defined as fallen, corrupted and evil. No one, it was said, could escape this indelible reality. Human beings were doomed to be punished with death. Our only hope was to throw ourselves onto the mercy of God. The ramifications of this definition abounded.

Baptism was then developed to wash symbolically from the newborn human life the stain of Adam's original sin. If an unbaptized child died "in the sin of Adam," that child was said to be bound for hell. The Eucharist then became the foretaste of the heavenly banquet, the sign of our salvation. The deepest human yearning was now couched in terms of rescue from this inescapable original sin, avoidance of the punishment due us. So it was that Jesus came to be understood as the savior, the rescuer, and the redeemer. This theology trod roughshod over the idea of Jesus "who came that they might have life and have it abundantly" (John 10:10). Human potential was trumped by guilt and behavior control. So we created hymns such as "Throw Out the Lifeline," "I Was Sinking Deep in Sin When Love Lifted Me" and "O Savior, Precious Savior"; we also sang of that "Old Rugged Cross" on which Jesus "for a world of lost sinners was slain."*

This was the new template against which Christians would tell the Jesus story. It was also the backdrop against which all Christian liturgies would be developed. This kind of Christianity

---

* "Throw Out the Lifeline," Edwin S. Ufford 1888; "I Was Sinking . . . ," James Row 1912; "O Savior . . . ," Frances R. Havergal 1870; "Old Rugged Cross," George Bennard 1913.

reigned unchallenged for centuries. It is, however, dying today. The question I have to ask is: Was this really the essential message of Christianity? The institutional church certainly claimed that it was so. I believe, however, that original sin obscures rather than illuminates that essential message. We have only just begun to scratch the surface of Christianity in these pages. As we move forward, perhaps we can decipher that message more clearly.

PART VI

Thesis 4:
The Virgin Birth

The virgin birth understood as literal biology is totally unbelievable. Far from being a bulwark in defense of the divinity of Christ, the virgin birth actually destroys that divinity.

13

The Story of the Virgin Birth

It was the idea of a fall into "original sin" that formed the background of the way Christians told the Christ story that is now embedded in our traditions and creeds. Once that central linchpin is pulled, everything else falls of its own irrationality. It was to save a fallen world that Christianity proclaimed Jesus had come from God in a rescue operation. But how can those, however, who have not fallen be rescued in any meaningful way? The traditional way of telling the Jesus story turned Jesus into the agent of the God who lived above the sky and so came to our rescue. It reflected the dualism of the Greek world into which Christianity got translated from the second century on. It was this dualism that ultimately shaped the creeds, the most enduring version of which was adopted at the Council of Nicea in 325 CE.

Nicene Christianity has come to be understood as "original" and "orthodox" Christianity. Few people embrace or understand just how foreign Nicene Christianity was to the original Jesus experience. What people tend to call "traditional Christianity" is, in fact, a fourth-century creation imposed on the original Jesus story. It would have been quite foreign to Jesus, and it has become

quite foreign to the world we inhabit today. The worldview in
which traditional Christianity was formed has in fact died, and
with that death has come the demise of the Jesus story as previously told. The bad news is that, because of new information,
people are now struggling to make sense of the Jesus story, which
they can no longer translate into believable categories today. The
good news is that there is little or nothing about that traditional
view of Jesus that is original to the Jesus experience.

   We turn now to aspects of the Jesus story that need to be scraped
clean of the fourth-century creed and placed into a very different—
some would say revolutionary, even heretical—frame of reference.
When, however, one is seeking to chart a new reformation, one
must deconstruct first. There is no other place to begin. So I now
examine anew the psychological framework in which Jesus has
been proclaimed in order to create faith in this Jesus in our time.
We begin with the creedal assertion that Jesus was "conceived by
the Holy Spirit and born of the Virgin Mary." There is no possibility that this story could ever be reconciled with our knowledge
of biology, so there is no possibility that the virgin birth was ever
meant to be literally believed.

   Almost all of us at one time or another have participated in a
Christmas pageant. We have been angels or shepherds, wise men
or Joseph, the Virgin Mary or even one of the animals located
around the stable—a camel, a sheep, a lamb or a cow. Early in my
ministry, I served the congregation of Calvary Parish in Tarboro,
North Carolina, the county seat of Edgecombe County. Around
that county, at almost every crossroads where a service station
and a country store were located, this church had created mission
congregations. I was thus responsible also for churches in such
rural North Carolina villages as Old Sparta, Speed and Lawrence.
There were two additional mission churches in Tarboro itself, one
rooted in racial segregation and the other in the social divide be-

tween owners and workers. Since every church had a Christmas pageant, I had to attend numerous pageants each year! That was, to put it frankly, "cruel and unusual punishment" for a priest. I knew the color, size and shape of every bathrobe in Edgecombe County, for that is what all the characters wore as costumes—except for the Virgin Mary, of course, who was always dressed in pastel blue. It is because of our adult familiarity with Christmas pageants that the birth narratives found in the gospels of Matthew and Luke are to this day writ large in our memories. The way we remember them, however, is as a single blended narrative, which is not the way they appear in the Bible. So first we look at some "biblical facts"!

Paul, who was the first Jewish author of any material that would later constitute the New Testament, appears never to have heard about Jesus having had a miraculous birth. Paul wrote between 51 and 64 CE, and all he says about the origins of Jesus is found in two places. In Galatians, probably the second epistle to be written, dated about 52 CE, he says of Jesus that he "was born of a woman" (Gal. 4:4). I submit that this is not particularly newsworthy! The word Paul uses that is translated "woman" is *gunaikos,* which is the word from which we get our word "gynecology," and it has absolutely no sense of "virginity" in it. The second and last Pauline reference to Jesus' birth was in Romans, written in the middle years of the sixth decade of the Christian era. Here Paul writes, making a messianic claim, that Jesus "was descended from David, according to the flesh" (Rom. 1:3). Since royal descent was always through the male line, there is no way Paul could have written this line if he had ever heard of or entertained any idea of a virgin birth.

The second author of a work that got included in the New Testament was Mark, the first gospel to be written. Mark is dated in the early seventies of the Common Era. Once more we find no story of Jesus' birth. God enters Jesus in Mark's gospel only at his baptism, which occurs in Jesus' adult life.

Later in Mark's gospel, this author portrays Jesus' mother as coming with his brothers to seize Jesus, because people were saying, "He is beside himself" (Mark 3:21)—that is, he is "out of his mind." That is not the way a woman would act toward her adult child if an angel had literally said to her at his conception that he "will be called the son of the Most High, and . . . he will reign over the house of Jacob forever" (Luke 1:32–33). Mark clearly also had never heard of the virgin birth.

It is not until the ninth decade, in the writing of Matthew, that the story of the virgin birth makes its entry into the Christian tradition. Matthew also introduces in his story of the virgin birth such unique features of our Christmas observances as the star in the east, the magi, the gifts of gold, frankincense and myrrh, the slaughter of the "Holy Innocents" by King Herod and the flight of the holy family—Joseph, Mary and the Christ child—into Egypt to escape Herod's wrath. These details are uniquely Matthean, appearing in no other book of the Bible. *Is Luke jewish?*

The third gospel to be written, Luke, which appeared in the late ninth or early tenth decade of the Common Era (circa 89–93), gave us a second birth story. It is the details of this version with which we are most familiar, since Luke provides the story line that has been followed by most of our Christmas pageants. This is where we find such familiar details as the annunciation to Mary in Nazareth by the archangel Gabriel, informing her that she is to be the virgin mother of the messiah (Luke 1:26–38); the journey by Joseph and Mary when she is "great with child" from Nazareth to Bethlehem to be "enrolled" (Luke 2:1–5); the story of "no room at the inn" (Luke 2:7); the birth, presumably in a stable although the only hint of a stable in the text is that an animal's feeding trough becomes the manger in which the infant is laid

(Luke 2:7); the angels appearing to hillside shepherds to announce that "unto you is born this day in the city of David a savior who is Christ the Lord," and their subsequent urging of the shepherds to go seek the baby in Bethlehem (Luke 2:8–20). The angels give the shepherds only two clues: "You shall find the child wrapped in swaddling cloths [not *clothes,* as it is so often misread] and lying in a manger" (Luke 2:12). The shepherds go, find the babe and return to their fields, while "Mary kept all these things in her heart and pondered them" (Luke 2:19). These uniquely Lucan additions to the story of Jesus' birth also appear nowhere else in the Bible. They are the products of Luke's mind only.

What does this brief analysis of the biblical details of Jesus' birth mean? It means that contradictions in the birth narrative abound. It means that we cannot assume that any of these details were originally regarded as "literal" history. In Matthew the holy family appears to live in Bethlehem, in a house over which a star can stop. Immediately after Jesus' birth, they are forced to abandon their home and flee to Egypt to avoid the wrath of Herod. In Luke, however, we read that Mary and Joseph live in a house in Nazareth and are required to journey to Bethlehem only by the decree of Caesar Augustus to be "enrolled." Furthermore, Luke makes no mention, following the birth in Bethlehem, of Jesus fleeing to Egypt for safety; rather, he is incorporated into the tradition of the Jews by being circumcised on the eighth day and presented in the Jerusalem Temple on the fortieth day; then with his parents, Mary and Joseph, he makes his way leisurely back to their home in Nazareth. Matthew gives us the narrative of the wise men, while Luke, who seems to know nothing of this, gives us the narrative of shepherds. Is either of these two authors writing a firsthand memory? Certainly the two stories cannot be harmonized.

In the final gospel to be written, John (circa 95–100 CE), the story of the miraculous birth of Jesus has disappeared altogether, a fact that most people are surprised to discover; that element simply is not there. More than that, on two occasions in this gospel, Jesus is referred to simply as "the son of Joseph" (John 1:45, 6:42).

No reference to the birth of Jesus occurs anywhere else in the entire Bible. This is all there is. Two deeply contradictory narratives, related in two separate books of the New Testament, form the totality of the Bible's story of Jesus' birth. The birth tradition that most of us meet at Christmas has been built by blending these two irreconcilable narratives into a single story in which all the contradictory details have been quietly blunted.

The first step in our understanding of the meaning of the virgin birth tradition is, therefore, to take the time to note exactly what the Bible says about the origins of Jesus. It is not what most of us have been taught. When that truth registers for the first time, people begin to ask questions that are almost frantic. Are there *any* facts here that we can trust? Were these fanciful stories written by their original authors as history? Let me state at once that there is not a chance that any of the birth details in either Matthew's or Luke's version of the virgin birth are either accurate or literally true! The data supporting this conclusion are overwhelming. Stars are masses of burning gas; they do not announce earthly events. Wise men do not follow a star that travels through the sky so slowly that they can keep up with it. No star is equipped with a GPS system that allows it to guide Oriental magi to the proper destination. A convenient supply of gold, frankincense and myrrh is not kept available, or camels at the ready, just in case a star does appear. Angels do not break through the midnight sky to sing to hillside shepherds. Shepherds do not go in search of the divine child armed only with the two previously mentioned clues. Especially is this so when the town of Bethlehem is said to be crowded with visitors drawn by a decree issued by the Roman emperor! Virgins also do not conceive. Every one of these scriptural details is mythological. None of them is or can be literally true.

Matthew seeks to ground each detail of his birth story in the predictive powers of the Hebrew scriptures. He accomplishes this task only by the wildest stretch of the text imaginable. Just for starters, the word "virgin" does not occur in the Hebrew text of Isaiah 7:14, a passage that Matthew uses in creating his virgin birth story. Nonetheless, Matthew tries to build his "virgin" story on this text. If that is not strange enough, Matthew reads this text to say that this non-existent virgin "will conceive." In Hebrew the text in Isaiah 7:14 does not read, "Behold, a virgin *will conceive*," but rather, "Behold, a woman *is with child*." The two are not the same! One can also search these birth narratives and discover that many familiar details simply are not biblical. No stable is mentioned anywhere in Luke's story, nor is an innkeeper ever referred to. There are no camels on which the wise men ride in the text of Matthew's story, and there is no reference anywhere to the magi being three in number. We have sung "We Three Kings"* so long that we have inserted the number itself into the gospel.

These facts shock people when they first hear them, but by and large these details continue to remain a part of our Christmas seasonal fantasies. They are also constantly being reinforced in our minds by the artifacts of the season. We send Christmas cards that depict angels singing to hillside shepherds or with a turbaned man sitting on a camel looking up at a star. We portray Joseph as a strong, silent male standing behind a kneeling mother watching an infant lying in an animal's feeding trough. Crèche scenes are built on our lawns, in churches, in our homes and in our consciousness. We sing reinforcing hymns such as "While Shepherds

---

* "We Three Kings," John Henry Hopkins 1857.

Watch Their Flocks by Night." We extol the "Silent Night" in which Jesus was born in the "Little Town of Bethlehem."* All of these references serve to burn these literal images into our minds. Then we discover what the Bible actually says. Truth is sometimes disturbing.

---

* "While Shepherds . . . ," Nahum Tate 1700; "Silent Night," Joseph Mohr 1818; "O Little Town of Bethlehem," Phillips Brooks 1868.

14

The Actual Details
Behind Jesus' Birth

In all probability Jesus was born in Nazareth. That is surely
the assumption made in Mark, the first gospel to be written. The names of both of his parents do not appear to be
historically known. The name Mary, as the mother of Jesus,
is first mentioned only in the eighth decade in Mark. All of the
biographical details of her life that purport to come before that
time are clearly mythological.

There are, however, a series of biblical facts about which most
people seem to be unaware. How many people, for example, realize that the name Mary, the presumed name of Jesus' mother,
appears only one time in Mark, the first gospel to be written; and
on that occasion it is placed on the lips of an anonymous member
of a crowd, who shouts out about Jesus: "Is not this the carpen-
ter, the son of Mary?" (Mark 6:3). Note also that in this initial
biblical reference to Jesus' family, Jesus is the one who is the car-
penter. There is no Joseph. Joseph would not enter the story until
Matthew, about a decade later (see Matt. 1–2). Even there the
biographical details that Matthew ascribes to Joseph are drawn
from the story of the patriarch named Joseph, found in the book
of Genesis (37–50). It is also not until Matthew that we get our

second reference to the suggestion that the name of Jesus' mother is Mary. Luke uses the names Mary and Joseph in his later birth narrative, presumably having taken them from Matthew.* It is worth noting, just to complete the record, that nowhere in the Fourth Gospel is the mother of Jesus called Mary. In that gospel she is referred to only, and repeatedly, as "the mother of the Lord."

One other little-known fact is that when the gospels were written, the followers of Jesus were defending him against the charge of the critics of the Jesus movement that their founder was "base born"—that is, illegitimate. How do we know that? We find hints of it in the texts of the gospels themselves. In the reference just mentioned from Mark's gospel the anonymous voice in the crowd calls Jesus "the son of Mary." Every Jew would know that to refer to a grown man in Jewish society as "the son of a woman" was to suggest that his paternity was unknown.

Matthew deals with this same theme overtly in his birth narrative, where he has Joseph debate what he must do with his pregnant, betrothed wife who, he believes, is expecting someone else's child (Matt. 1:19). When Luke has the mother of Jesus say in the song of Mary, called the Magnificat, that God has "looked upon the low estate of his handmaid" (Luke 1:48), we might infer a covert reference to her being pregnant outside of marriage, for there was no estate more lowly in first-century Judaism than that of an expectant mother with no male protector. Finally, in the Fourth Gospel another voice in the crowd during a discussion of Jesus' origins shouts out to Jesus: "We were not born of fornication" (John 8:41). The clear implication of this remark is that Jesus was.

---

*   I make the assumption that Luke had Matthew available to him as well as Mark. He rewrites Matthew's story to remove from it elements which he disliked like magi and hints of kings and their wealth, substituting humble shepherds in their places. My authority for doing this is Michael D. Goulder's book *Luke: A New Paradigm*. See bibliography for details.

That is the background against which the story of the virgin birth is introduced into the Christian narrative. Matthew is the originator of that story, and to this day the way he handles it is vivid, strange and overtly controversial.

Matthew introduces his supernatural virgin birth story with seventeen of the most boring verses in the Bible. We call them "the genealogy." Here Matthew seeks to ground Jesus in the literal DNA of Jewish life. He is first the descendent of Abraham, the father of the Hebrew people. Then he traces the Jesus line to King David. Jesus is also the son of David, fulfilling one of the major ingredients in Jewish messianic expectations. Some future messiah must re-establish the throne of King David. Next he traces the line that produced Jesus, stretching from King David to the Babylonian exile. Jesus' ancestors had lived in and through that exile, the most desperate moment in Jewish history—at least until the Holocaust in the twentieth century. Then Matthew continues the ancestral line until he reaches Jesus himself.* Most readers skip over these "who begat whom" verses quickly as being of no great value. No one would think of reading these verses today as a lesson in corporate worship.

Hidden in this boring genealogy, however, is, I believe, the hint that unlocks the meaning of the story of the virgin birth, so we turn to these verses in search of that vital clue. Matthew includes in the line that produced Jesus four ancestral "mothers." It was quite unusual in that day to place women into any genealogical line, for women were thought of more as incubators than as co-creators of the life of the unborn child. In addition to that, each of the women named was well known to Jewish readers, for their stories were told in the ancient scriptures with which Matthew's Jewish readers would have been quite familiar.

---

* He does this through Joseph.

The first of these women was named Tamar. Her story is found in Genesis 38. She is the daughter-in-law of Judah, one of the twelve sons of Jacob. Tamar becomes pregnant by Judah, which would have been called incest in Jewish society. That pregnancy results in twins named Perez and Zerah. The line that produced Jesus, Matthew suggests, flowed through Perez, one who was a product of incest. It is a strange connection that Matthew is making.

The second ancestral mother in his list is Rahab. Her story is told in the book of Joshua (chapters 2 and 6). In that narrative Rahab is a prostitute who runs a brothel located inside the walls of the city of Jericho. She entertains and protects Joshua's spies and presumably later marries one of them. It is through the prostitution of Rahab that the line that produced Jesus flowed. Tamar was guilty of incest, Rahab of prostitution. Is a pattern developing?

The third ancestral mother in Matthew's genealogy is Ruth, the daughter-in-law of Naomi. Her story is told in the little book that bears her name, but the interpretive secret is found only in chapter 3. After Naomi's husband Elimelech and her two sons Mahlon and Chilion have died, she returns with Ruth, her widowed daughter-in-law, to Israel, where Ruth gleans for grain in the fields of a man named Boaz, who happens to be a distant kinsman of Naomi's husband. During the harvest, Ruth comes up with a fully worked out plan to seduce Boaz. After much wine has been consumed following a day on the threshing floor Boaz becomes very drowsy, finally lying down on the floor in sleep. Ruth puts a pillow under his head and a blanket over his sleeping body. Then she climbs under the blanket with him.

When Boaz awakens the next morning, he finds a strange woman with him under his blanket. "Who are you?" he asks. "Marry me," she responds (in effect), "for you are the nearest of kin." It is a fascinating story. Eventually, after trying unsuccessfully to pass her off to someone he thought was even more closely related, he does!

The final ancestral mother in Matthew's genealogy is identified only as the wife of Uriah the Hittite. We know from other sources, however, that her name is Bathsheba. Her story is told in chapter 11 of II Samuel. She is the woman whose adulterous affair with King David led not only to her pregnancy, but also to the calculated murder of her husband, Uriah, while he served in King David's army. The line that produced Jesus, Matthew was saying, flowed through the adultery of Bathsheba.

Does it not strike you as strange that Matthew, who was the first to relate the narrative of the virgin birth, chose to introduce that narrative by suggesting that incest, prostitution, seduction and adultery are all in the line that produced Jesus? Is this not an unusual way to defend one's founder against the charge of illegitimacy? Was Matthew saying that just as a convicted felon, executed in a public place, could be the life in which God is best seen in human history, so too could a child called "illegitimate" be the life in whom God was met in a new way? I think this possibility needs to be taken seriously. In the virgin birth story Matthew claims a holy origin for Jesus, but then he seems to add that God can raise up a holy life even through incest, prostitution, seduction and adultery. I submit that this is a powerful witness!*

In the introduction to this section on the virgin birth, I stated that if the Christian church insists on interpreting the virgin birth as literal biology, it will make Christ's divinity, as traditionally understood, impossible. That is for many traditional-thinking Christians a rather startling claim, so let me be more specific.

We understand reproduction today in a way that the first-

* For a much fuller treatment of these four ancestral mothers of Jesus, I refer readers to my book *Biblical Literalism: A Gentile Heresy.* See bibliography for details.

century authors of the gospels could not and did not. No one in that day knew that women produced egg cells. Nor did they understand that a woman is genetically a co-creator of every life that has ever been born. The assumption of the first century was that pregnancy occurred after the analogy of a farmer planting his seed in the soil of Mother Earth. Mother Earth added nothing to the genetic makeup of the planted seed, which grew out of the soil. The only purpose of the soil was to nurture the seed in order to bring it to life. The existence of egg cells containing genes from the woman would not be confirmed by Western science until many centuries later. When that insight was confirmed, all virgin birth stories ceased to be biological possibilities; indeed all virgin birth stories died.

Virgin birth stories were originally created to explain extraordinary human power. Each virgin birth story of antiquity (and there were many) paired a divine agent with a virgin female. Since in the minds of the ancient world the virgin mother added nothing except incubation to the divine offspring, there was no need to remove her from the reproductive act. Only the male agent had to be replaced by the divine spirit or the God figure to produce a deity masquerading in human form. All of these assumptions disappeared, however, when the egg cell of the woman was discovered. Now we know that every child born receives half of his or her genetic code from each parent. The product of a union between a deity and a human virgin could now never be either fully human or fully divine, which was the claim that Christians made for Jesus. Indeed such an offspring would inevitably and biologically be half human and half divine. The meaning of the virgin birth in Christianity was thus lost, and a literal understanding of it made Jesus begin to seem something like a mermaid or a centaur, that creature in Greek mythology that had a human head attached to an animal's body, a blend that was neither human nor divine. Although a modern understanding of genetics has rendered all virgin birth stories inadequate to account for what they were designed to explain, the virgin birth is a symbol that has been literalized by the masses.

There was one other, related church tradition or doctrine that collapsed under the weight of these developing facts. If the mother of Jesus had passed on to her son half of her own human genetic makeup, she too, as a child of Adam, would inevitably have passed on to him the stain of the fall into "original sin," which we considered in chapter 3. Jesus would, like every other person, have been corrupted by original sin, since only his father was divine, not his mother. When the Roman Catholic Church declared in the nineteenth century that the mother of Jesus had herself been born without sin, or "immaculately conceived," they sought to address this glaring new problem. Theology does adjust to reality whenever reality comes too close to threaten ancient formulations.

There was in Jesus something that his followers believed could not have been produced by human beings alone. In the fullness of his humanity, they stated, the fullness of God had been met and experienced. That was the original Christ claim before it was literalized in stories of the virgin birth. The virgin birth tradition was designed to proclaim exactly that: that Jesus had in him something of the divine. The virgin birth was never universally believed even in the earliest developing Christian tradition. Of the five major writers of the New Testament, two, Paul and Mark, appear never to have heard of it. Two others, Matthew and Luke, offer quite different versions of it. The last, John, appears to have dismissed it. Our task is not to believe it, but to understand it.

PART VII

Thesis 5: Miracles

In a post-Newtonian world, supernatural invasions of the natural order, performed by God or an "incarnate Jesus," are simply not viable explanations of what actually happened. <u>Miracles do not ever imply magic.</u>

15

When Miracles
Entered the Bible

In almost every religious tradition there are tales about the supernatural power that God somehow makes available to human beings. The forces of the world are said to have been changed or manipulated by an invasive divine power for human benefit. The Bible is no different, but strange as it may seem to some, miracles are not a dominant or even an early theme in Hebrew scriptures. Few people seem to be aware, for example, that in the older portions of the Bible, miracles understood as supernatural events are generally limited to the narratives that have gathered around two pairs of gigantic Hebrew heroes. These two pairs are made up of the "twin towers" of the history of the people of Israel: Moses, the father of the law, and Elijah, the father of the prophets. So powerful was each of these two figures in the biblical narrative that their immediate successors, Joshua in the case of Moses, and Elisha in the case of Elijah, were also caught up in these developed tales of supernatural power.

If we take away the cycle of stories that have gathered first around Moses and Joshua, and second around Elijah and Elisha, the Hebrew scriptures are almost devoid of miraculous stories. That fact surprises people. Oh, one might stretch the content of what we call "miracles," at least in that older portion of the Bible, by including such things as the forty days of rain before the flood that starred Noah, or the astonishing pregnancy of Sarah, the ninety-year-old wife of Abraham, but most such accounts are regarded as heightened natural stories more than divine intervention stories, so they do not qualify technically as supernatural events.

It is fair, therefore, to say that for all practical purposes miracles enter the Hebrew tradition with Moses, then they carry over to Joshua before disappearing in the Bible for almost four hundred years. Miracles then reappear in the Elijah story and carry on to Elisha, before disappearing again for about eight hundred years. Finally, they reappear in the New Testament in the stories that gather around Jesus of Nazareth. The pattern set in the Hebrew scriptures is followed, for these miraculous acts are then said to carry over to Jesus' disciples in a manner that appears to replicate first the Moses/Joshua stories and then the Elijah/Elisha stories.

So my first observation is that miracles are not scattered throughout the biblical story as so many people seem to think; they are gathered around heroic figures. Great segments of the Hebrew Bible are devoid of miraculous happenings, including most of the Torah, most of the writings of the prophets and all of what we call the "wisdom literature," including such works as the Psalms and Proverbs.

The next stop in this analysis is to look at the content of the miracle stories that do appear in the biblical narrative. We start, therefore, with Moses. He was, says the book of Exodus, called into leadership by a strange natural phenomenon that occurred in the wilderness (Exod. 3). We call it the burning bush. Moses was herding the sheep that belonged to his father-in-law in the land of Midian, because he had been forced to flee Egypt after murdering an Egyptian overseer who was beating a Hebrew slave. When Moses discovered that this murderous deed had been seen by others, he fled for his life into the wilderness within the borders of Midian.

The regular place of meeting in the Hebrew scriptures between a single man and his potential wife was at the well. In the division of labor in Hebrew society, women went to the well each day to draw water. On this particular day the seven daughters of Jethro, the priest of Midian, went for water. Shepherds from another tribe rose to drive the women away. Moses came to the rescue and banished these shepherds. In gratitude Moses was taken into Jethro's home and ultimately married one of the seven daughters, a woman named Zipporah (Exod. 2).

These biographical details regarding the life of Moses were clearly part of the folklore of the Hebrew people, including the story of his birth and his being saved from the order of the pharaoh that Jewish boy babies must be put to death. In an effort to save Moses from this fate, his mother placed him in a basket lined with pitch, which allowed him to float on the Nile until he was rescued by the daughter of the pharaoh and raised as her son in the royal court (Exod. 1). This story reflects a similar, but much earlier, narrative regarding another Middle Eastern leader named Sargon, one of the first kings to rise out of Mesopotamia. He too was drawn out of a river and saved.

In all of the stories about Moses we need to remember that while the actual man appears to have lived in the thirteenth century BCE, the stories about him found in the Bible were not recorded until at least the tenth century BCE. This means that all of these Moses stories floated in oral transmission for about three hundred years before being written down in the Bible. History is thus quite difficult to separate from fantasy or mythology. The Moses cycle of stories can hardly be viewed as history. They are more like folk tales that have been magnified in the telling and retelling than they are history. They seem to serve the purpose of validating the hero, Moses, and the role he was destined to play in the tribal history of the Hebrew people.

Supernatural events, which we have regularly called miracles throughout our religious history, make their first appearances in the Bible in Moses' early leadership recounted in the tribal history of the people of Israel. The only thing we need to question is whether these miracles are real, observed and happened as a part of history, for that is the claim that religious people make for them. No matter how one approaches the subject of miracles, one has to admit that the biblical narrative regularly presents their origins as quite bizarre, and appears to argue against miracles ever being thought of as literal events that actually occurred in history.

God was said to have equipped the reluctant Moses with miraculous powers (Exod. 4:1–9) for his first leadership position, which was to guide the people to freedom out of Egypt. Moses carried a rod in his hand. God told him to cast the rod to the ground, and when he did, it became a snake. Next Moses picked up the tail of this snake and it once again changed into a lifeless rod. It was a rather impressive trick. This was to be a God-given sign to the pharaoh and his admirers that Yahweh, Israel's deity, was powerful and was with Moses. The second supernatural trick with which Moses was endowed by God on this occasion was initiated by his placing his hand inside his tunic. When he drew it out it had turned leprous, which presumably would cause people to fall back in fear. Then Moses, at God's instruction, returned his leprous hand to his tunic, and when he pulled it out it had become clean. Strange as it seems, this is the place where supernatural, miraculous power enters the biblical story. It is not an impressive beginning. When Moses and his brother Aaron did in fact use both of these miraculous tricks in negotiating with the pharaoh, the Egyptian ruler's own court magicians, were able to replicate each one! The first miracles to appear in the Bible were thus not unique, special or even determinative. The superiority of Moses' God was, however, demonstrated when Moses' snake devoured the snakes of the Egyptians (Exod. 7:10–12).

God thus had to up the miraculous power that Moses possessed over the natural world, validating him as God's special deliverer. To do this the series of what are called the plagues of Egypt began (Exod. 7:14–11:10). Moses and God first turned the Nile River into blood. It was a dramatic story. To Moses' dismay, however, the magicians of Egypt could do the same thing, so the pharaoh was not impressed with Moses' supposedly God-given power.

The second plague was a plague of frogs that overran the land, filling the Egyptians' houses, bedchambers and even kneading bowls. Once again, however, the Egyptian magicians did the same thing, so the pharaoh was not moved.

The third plague was a plague of gnats. Finally the Egyptians failed to reproduce this miracle, so power began to tilt toward Moses. In rapid succession came other plagues, miraculously produced by Moses and Aaron. There was the plague of flies, the plague that killed Egyptian cattle, the plague of boils, the plague of hail, the plague of locusts and the plague of darkness. The biblical narrative portrays the pharaoh after each plague as relenting and agreeing to allow the Hebrews to depart, only to change his mind when the plague was lifted. Sometimes the text says that the pharaoh hardened his heart (Exod. 8:15, 9:34), which presumably would render him culpable, while on other occasions the text says that God hardened the pharaoh's heart, presumably so that God could hit him with another plague (Exod. 10:20, 27, 11:10). The God-originated miracles appeared to be rather vindictive.

It is a strange story on many levels. If God had infinite power, why, we have to wonder, was not one plague sent of such severity as to accomplish the Hebrews' escape? Why are these nature miracles so ineffective as to have to be repeated and changed? If God was the one who hardened the pharaoh's heart, why was God working against the divine purpose? If the plagues represented the supernatural power of God, why could the Egyptian magicians replicate them, at least at the beginning? Is this a convincing way to introduce miracles to the biblical story? This is, however, the way that the miraculous enters our Judeo-Christian religion!

The final plague, which was supposed to have resulted in the initiation of the liturgy of the Passover (Exod. 12), combined supernatural power with deadly tribal prejudice, but according to the biblical text this last plague finally succeeded in bringing freedom to the enslaved Hebrew people. On this occasion, Moses' request of God was that he send the "Angel of Death" throughout the land of Egypt to slay the first-born male in every household. Jewish families were to be protected from this murderous plague by placing the blood of the slaughtered paschal lamb on the doorposts of Jewish homes. The Angel of Death, seeing the "magical blood," would "pass over" that home and bring death only to Egyptians. That is the source of the observance of Passover in Hebrew history.

So in our attempt to understand miracles in religion, we note the fact that they entered the biblical story in the service of tribal needs, to validate the quest for Hebrew freedom and to inflict pain and suffering, or to deliver people from the perils of life. Miracles were found in the ability to manipulate the forces of nature in order to create suffering for the enemies of the chosen people. It was not a particularly noble way for miracles to be born.

Were miracles real? Did those who related them believe that they actually happened? Or were they simply part of tribal folk tales designed to reveal God to the Hebrew nation? Could the religion that was destined to grow into Judaism have developed without the element of the miraculous? Can religion today survive if the miraculous is omitted?

We draw no conclusions at this point; we seek only to establish the facts.

We search out the biblical case, which is so often known only vaguely. Conclusions will come, but not before the facts are clear. At the beginning, however, it appears that miracles may not be moral or even desirable. Perhaps Christianity would be better off without them, or perhaps we should learn to view them in a radically different way.

16

The Miracles in the Moses/Joshua Story

O nce miracles are established as part of the life story of the founder of the Hebrew nation, they proceed to grow in power and intensity. Again we trace them briefly.

The exodus from Egypt was successfully achieved for the slave people of Israel on the night of the Passover, as we saw in the previous chapter. While the Egyptian people were mourning the death of the first-born male in each family, the Hebrew people, having eaten their meal, which did not, as would have been usual, include leavened bread for they had no time to wait for the bread to rise, made their way into the wilderness (Exod. 12:34). Once again, as soon as the plague was over the pharaoh changed his mind. Not wanting to lose his source of cheap labor, he organized his military to begin a pursuit of the escaping slaves, to return them to their bondage. The Hebrew people appear to have gotten a three-day head start before Egyptian pursuit was initiated. That lead resulted in the most significant miracle to be recounted in Hebrew history. We know it as the parting of the Red Sea (Exod. 14). It has been dramatically portrayed in motion pictures such as *The Ten Commandments*, directed by Cecil B. DeMille and released in 1956. This movie is still reshown on television annually, usually during Holy Week, so it is indelibly in the minds of many people. As a supernatural event, however, there are some serious problems connected with this biblical story.

First, if the text is referring to what we today call the Red Sea, and if the escaping slave people's plan was to return to what they called their Promised Land, then they went far out of their way. Second, the Red Sea is approximately two hundred miles wide, which would make the miracle quite stupendous. Third, the words in the Hebrew text that are translated "Red Sea" are *Yam Suph,* which literally means not "Red Sea," but "Sea of Reeds." That body of water *would* be located on a direct route; it was an area of swampy land where the Suez Canal would later be built. So the dominating miracle that we refer to as the parting of the Red Sea may be considerably less dramatic than we once believed. Once again, we need to remember that the stories about Moses were written down some three hundred years after the fact. In other words, these stories went through the oral transmissions of perhaps as many as fifteen generations before being written down. This was ample time for heightening the story to include elements of the miraculous.

If the Hebrew people headed toward the Sea of Reeds before they learned of the pursuit of the military power of Egypt, then the drama was no less real; the circumstances were still daunting. In front of them was swampy marshland. Behind them, but visible in the distance, were the Egyptian soldiers clad in heavy armor and mounted on iron chariots drawn by horses, the predecessors of the modern tank. It was a fearful sight. Navigating the swampy land would be slow and enormously difficult for the Hebrew people, but not to continue their journey to freedom was to fall into the hands of their heavily armored enemies. Death appeared to await them no matter what they chose. Death in the swamp was, however, less certain and less inevitable, so they chose, I suggest, to keep moving. Traveling with little more than the clothes on their backs, they began to navigate the swampland. They were well into it before the Egyptian battalions finally arrived at the swamp's edge.

Undaunted by what lay ahead, the Egyptian forces pressed on into the swamp, but their soldiers, with the weight of their armor, could not navigate, and so they began to sink, stuck in the mud. The iron chariots were even less mobile; they began to sink deeper into the marshland with each turn of the wheel. The Hebrew people continued their slow plod through the swamp. They were slowed to a bare crawl, but the Egyptians had been stopped cold. In time the Hebrew people reached dry land and could continue their journey. The Egyptian army, however, was incapable of navigating the swamp. Their only choice ultimately was to extricate themselves and return to the land of Egypt. The Hebrew people had been delivered from their peril and were now able to reclaim their nomadic heritage and continue their journey across the wilderness. God had delivered them from Egyptian bondage.

As the story was passed on through the generations, it clearly grew. The Hebrews did not navigate the swampland, the evolving account said; the waters parted instead, and they walked through on dry land. The Egyptians did not get stuck in the mud; the parted waters closed and drowned the Hebrews' enemies. Moses was then said to have sung a song to the Lord for the divine deliverance provided to the escaping slave people at the Sea of Reeds (Exod. 15:1–18). There is some indication (Exod. 15:21) that Miriam, Moses' sister, actually composed their song of triumph, but it was too great in memory to have been attributed to anyone other than Moses, so it became known as the Song of Moses.

Whatever its original circumstances, that event now became a sign of God's power over water, and it was destined to be repeated frequently in Hebrew history. Once safely in the wilderness the Hebrews began to face other problems, and their miraculous deliverance by God through the parting of the waters would become a familiar theme in Hebrew history. It was regarded as a miracle of the first order.

The second well-known miracle associated with Moses in the wilderness years had to do with the shortage of food. Two months after departing from Egypt, the Hebrews began to find the realities of nomadic wilderness living oppressive. Food was scarce and they began to express resentment. At least as slaves in Egypt there had been food to eat, they said. You have brought us into this wilderness to die of hunger. In the Numbers version of this story they are quite specific: They missed the cucumbers, melons, leeks, onions and garlic that they had had in Egypt (Num. 11:5)! Moses takes this complaint to God, who is said to have responded with the promise to rain bread down from heaven (Exod. 16:4). Whatever the germ of history that was originally in this story (some point to the white, flaky substance that falls to the ground from the tamarisk tree), by the time it was written in the Torah it had been skillfully edited. Here we read that God sends manna from heaven on six days of the week. God does not send it on the seventh day, so that neither God, by sending it, nor the people who gather it will have to violate the Sabbath (Exod. 16:13–30). The manna is always sufficient even then, for they gather it on the sixth day to have provisions for the Sabbath.

This is the first biblical episode in which the theme of expanding the food supply appears. It will, however, occur again and again in the biblical story. There were other apparently miraculous events that marked the life of Moses, but all of them seemed to include power over nature. Splitting bodies of water and expanding limited food sources were the major ones.

When Moses died in the land of Moab without entering the

Promised Land (Deut. 34), another crisis appeared for the chosen people. Was God with the whole Hebrew nation or only with God's chosen leader Moses? Was the death of Moses also the end of their God's special focus? That anxiety was met by wrapping a Moses miracle story around his immediate successor, Joshua. We read that story in the third chapter of the book of Joshua. God says to Joshua: "This day I will begin to exalt you in the sight of all Israel, that they may know that as I was with Moses, so I will be with you" (Josh. 3:7). The symbol was clear. Another body of water impeded the Hebrew people from crossing into the Promised Land. This time it was not the Red Sea, but the Jordan River. It was in the flood season. When those bearing the Ark of the Covenant stepped into the swollen river, the waters parted and the children of Israel crossed over the Jordan River on dry land. Moses' power over nature was now with Joshua.

A second illustration of this miraculous power was described in Joshua 10. On this occasion Joshua stopped the sun's orbit around the earth to allow his army more daylight to destroy the fleeing Amorites. Joshua ordered the sun to stand still in the sky. It was probably the first instance of daylight saving time! The principle was established: The miraculous power over nature revealed in the life of Moses was now present in the life of Joshua.

Miracles had now entered the biblical tradition in the first pair of heroic figures, Moses and his successor, Joshua. They were nature miracles only, but the concept of miracles would grow, as we shall see as the biblical story continues to unfold.

Elijah and Elisha—
Miracles Expanded

Miracles expressing the reality of invasive, supernatural power designed to meet human needs disappear for all practical purposes in Hebrew scriptures after the death of Joshua. There will be a hiatus of some four hundred miracle-free years. Oh yes, biblical writers will still speak of God's great power in defeating Israel's enemies, but this was done through strength of arms for which God was simply given credit. It was not the result of binding the forces of nature in the service of Israel's needs, as it had been in the Moses/Joshua cycle of stories. Then, in the latter years of the ninth century BCE, another portrayal of the miraculous suddenly reappeared. It corresponded with the rise of another Hebrew hero. His name was Elijah, and he was destined to become known as the father of the prophetic movement.

This second series of miraculous accounts would parallel the Moses/Joshua cycle in a number of ways. First, miracles in the life of Elijah were then stretched to include the life of Elijah's successor, who was named Elisha. Other familiar themes develop when we look closely at the Elijah/Elisha narratives. Elijah emerges in the Hebrew scriptures in I Kings 17. He will be the featured life in that story, but for only eight chapters. Elisha will join him midway in Elijah's career. Elijah's departure from this world is told in II Kings 2. Packed into these few chapters, however, are a wide variety of heroic stories, many of them revealing Elijah's power over nature. Echoes of Moses and Joshua are clearly present in this narrative.

Elijah is introduced as a Tishbite from Gilead (I Kings 17:1). He breaks on the scene as the "trouble-maker of Israel" and its King Ahab (I Kings 18:17). To him is attributed the power to stop the rain, creating drought. He was also thought to have the ability to call down fire from heaven. King Ahab saw him as a powerful and personal enemy, and was always seeking Elijah's life.

Elijah was driven into hiding by both the drought and King Ahab's assumption that Elijah was responsible for it. The text tells us that he hid in a cave near a brook called Cherith. There he had water to drink and, at God's command, was fed by ravens each morning and each evening with both bread and meat (I Kings 17:1–6). When the brook dried up because of the drought, Elijah moved to Zarephath in Sidon, where God directed him to the home of a widow who would care for him. The widow was quite poor. When Elijah asked her for water and something to eat, she told him that she had only enough provisions of meal and oil to make one wheat cake to provide a final meal for herself and her only son before they both died of starvation. Elijah assured her that the source of both the oil and the meal would never be exhausted if she complied with his request, and so she fed him too (1 Kings 17:7–16). We recognize at once what will be a popular theme in the meaning of miracles in the biblical story. Moses provided food that did not cease so long as there was need by sending manna in the wilderness. Now Elijah would also expand the food supply to meet new critical needs, including his own.

In time the only son of this widow became ill and died. Elijah raised him from the dead, back into the life of this world (I Kings 17:17–24). This is the first time a raising-of-the-dead story appears in the Bible. Elijah next challenged, defeated and killed four hundred priests of the fertility god Baal, who was championed by King Ahab and his foreign-born wife, Queen Jezebel. Elijah accomplished this by calling down fire from heaven to burn up the sacrifice to Israel's God, Yahweh, that he had prepared. The priests of Baal had been unable to receive a similar response to their prayer to Baal to send fire. This further alienated Elijah from the king and queen (I Kings 18:20–40).

Once again Elijah went into hiding and felt quite alone. God comforted him, however, with a vision of others who were still faithful and directed Elijah to look for God not in the earthquake, wind or fire, but in a "still small voice." John Greenleaf Whittier used that passage in a poem that became the popular hymn "Dear Lord and Father of Mankind."* Then Elijah was instructed to plan for the future anointing of a new king (Jehu) to rule over Israel, a new king (Hazael) to reign over the Syrians and a new prophet, Elisha, to succeed him (I Kings 19).

The story of Elijah's departure from this world is told in II Kings 2 in a very dramatic way. It was on the way to this departure moment that another miracle occurred, linking Elijah once again with Moses and Joshua. As Elijah journeyed with Elisha into the wilderness for his final rendezvous with God, the two of them came upon the River Jordan. They could not get across, so Elijah took off his mantle and swept it across the Jordan, and immediately the waters parted and he walked across on "dry land" (II Kings 2:8). The primary supernatural act that distinguished first Moses at the Red Sea and then Joshua at the Jordan River was now retold about Elijah.

As for Elijah's dramatic departure from this world, mentioned

---

* From the poem "The Brewing of Soma," by John Greenleaf Whittier; adapted as a hymn by W. Garrett Horder in 1884.

above, we will examine that in chapter 25. Because the account
of the ascension of Jesus borrowed most of the details from the
story of Elijah's ascension, we will look at the two stories together
when we consider Jesus' ascension.

Moses, Joshua and now Elijah are said to have power over nature. Moses and Elijah have the power to expand the food supply.
Moses, Joshua and Elijah have the power to split a body of water
so they can navigate across it on dry land. Elijah adds to this collection of biblical stories the raising from the dead of the only son
of a widow. A pattern is clearly developing.

With Elijah's ascension, the story now shifts to Elisha in a primary way. He picks up Elijah's mantle, left in the wilderness, and
begins his journey back to his own country. Almost immediately
he comes to the Jordan River and cannot get across. Remember-
ing that he now wears the mantle of Elijah, he assumes that he
must, therefore, possess the power of Elijah. Taking that mantle,
he sweeps it across the waters of the Jordan River, and once
more those waters part and he crosses the riverbed on dry land
(II Kings 2: 13–14). Elisha is now the fourth biblical character to
perform this feat.

Then we read the details that accompany the career of Elisha.
He begins to sound familiar in other ways besides parting the
waters. Elisha, like his predecessors, is also capable of expanding
the food supply. A widow's bottle of olive oil becomes endless, no
matter much is used (II Kings 4:1–7).

Elisha also raises someone from the dead (II Kings 4:18–37).
He restores a child in stages, initially from a distance by having
his servant rush ahead with Elisha's staff and laying this staff
on the face of the boy. When Elisha arrives, he restores the child
to life and presents him to his mother. So Elisha was able, like
Moses and Joshua, to control nature and, like Elijah, to raise a
person from the dead.

Elisha adds one other category to the biblical development of miracles. He is the first to do a healing miracle (II Kings 5). The recipient is a foreigner whose name is Naaman. He is identified as a Syrian, a military captain and a person of great power. His disease is leprosy, a dreaded, incurable and fatal disease in biblical times. He becomes aware of the powers attributed to Elisha from a Hebrew maid, who was captured in battle and who now serves his wife. The king of Syria sends a message to the king of Israel, who in time contacts Elisha. Naaman then comes to Elisha bearing gifts and asking to be cured. Elisha directs him to bathe in the Jordan River. Naaman is incensed at the idea, noting that they have far greater rivers in Syria. Finally, however, with nothing to lose, he agrees to do as Elisha has prescribed. As he bathes in the Jordan, his leprosy is healed and he becomes "clean." He returns to Elisha in gratitude, offering abundant gifts that Elisha declines.

When the time comes for Elisha to depart this world, the details seem eerily reminiscent of the death of Elijah. When Elijah was taken up into heaven by a fiery chariot drawn by fiery horses, Elisha saw this miraculous event and cried out: "My father, my father! The chariots of Israel and its horsemen!" Then the text says: "He saw him no more" (II Kings 2:12). When Elisha is about to die the text reads: "Now when Elisha had fallen sick with the illness of which he was to die, Joash, king of Israel, went down to him and wept before him crying, 'My father, my father! The chariots of Israel and its horsemen!'" (II Kings 13:14). Then Elisha died. Surely the biblical writers intended for their readers to see the deaths of Elijah and Elisha in a similar fashion.

So now we have examined the second series of miracle stories in the Hebrew Bible. Let's summarize:

First there were Moses and Joshua, both of whom performed nature miracles. Both split bodies of water. Moses expanded the food supply.

Elijah and Elisha were featured in the second wave of biblical miracles. Both did nature miracles. Both split bodies of water so they could walk across on dry land. Both expanded the food supply. Both carried the miraculous theme to new levels.

Elijah became the first biblical character about whom the claim was made that he raised someone from the dead. The person raised was the only son of a widow. Elisha matched that Elijah miracle, but the person he raised was a child, and he did it in stages beginning from a distance. Elisha took it one step further with the first recorded healing miracle, curing Naaman, a foreigner, of leprosy.

That is the extent of the first two episodes of miraculous deeds that the Bible recounts. Keep them in mind. Remember some of the details. Miracles now once more go into an eclipse in the Bible and are heard about no more in any systematic way until we come to Jesus and the New Testament. When we look next at miracles associated with Jesus, we find many similarities. Jesus and his immediate disciples both do miracles. Their miraculous deeds fall into three categories: nature miracles, raising-of-the-dead miracles and healing miracles. The pattern we observed earlier becomes even stronger. The three series of biblical heroes who are associated with miracles show many similarities.

Perhaps when we look deeply enough, we will see that they were never intended to be supernatural stories of divine power operating through a human life. Perhaps we have been defending an idea that even the biblical authors never intended. If so, the insights of people such as Isaac Newton who challenged the possibility of miraculous actions of a heavenly power intervening in human affairs may have been—and may now be—destroying something the biblical writers themselves did not believe. Perhaps reformation might carry us back to original meanings!

18

The Miracles of Jesus

The third cycle of miracle stories that we find in the Bible is located first in the four gospels, with a spill-over in the book of Acts. It is hard to count the exact number of presumably miraculous events that are related in these sources because some of them are general claims and many of them are different versions of what was presumably the same event.

We are aware that both Matthew and Luke had access to Mark and that both incorporated Mark into their gospels. Not surprisingly, then, some miracles are recounted with only slight differences in all three of those gospels. It is sometimes even more complicated than that, however, for we find the story of Jesus miraculously feeding the multitude with a limited number of loaves and fishes upon six different occasions—twice in Mark and in Matthew, where the size of the crowd, the location and the number of both loaves and gathered fragments vary, and then once each in Luke and John. On only one occasion is there a miracle story that is told only in Matthew and Luke, without a version in Mark. That is the narrative of Jesus healing the servant of the centurion (Matt. 8:5–13, Luke 7:1–10). This unique combination may constitute evidence that Luke, in addition to Mark, had access to Matthew, a conclusion to which I am personally drawn.

When we come to the Fourth Gospel, miracles are presented in a quite different manner. In John they are never called "miracles," but are called "signs." John's gospel contains seven of these signs, all between chapter 2 and chapter 11, a part of the Fourth Gospel known as "The Book of Signs." The opening and the closing signs we find in chapter 2 and chapter 11 are dramatically different and appear nowhere else in the New Testament. The sign in chapter 2 is the story of Jesus changing water into wine at the wedding party in Cana of Galilee, and the sign found in chapter 11 is the account of Jesus raising the four-days dead and buried Lazarus. This is once again a story never mentioned in any other part of the New Testament. Between these two "bookend signs" John relates five episodes that at least sound familiar to readers of the earlier gospels, even if the details are sometimes quite different. They include the healing of the Gentile nobleman's son in Cana of Galilee (John 4:46–54), the healing of the man crippled for thirty-eight years at the pool of Beth-zatha (John 5:1–35), the feeding of the five thousand (John 6:1–14), the account of Jesus walking on the water (John 6:16–21) and the restoration of sight to the man born blind (John 9:1–41). This points to something besides a literal interpretation and may bring the original intention of this author to light. So while many people still wish to assert the historicity of the miracles connected with the life of Jesus of Nazareth, we are on guard not to accept that premise too quickly. John's signs certainly do not appear to have been literal acts of supernatural power performed at a particular time in history and in a specific space.* With our minds filled with questions we now begin the process of placing them under the spotlight of contemporary biblical scholarship.

First, we note the fact that miracles of any sort do not appear to have been connected to the life of Jesus until Mark's gospel

---

* I treated the signs in the Fourth Gospel more thoroughly in my book on John, *The Fourth Gospel: Tales of a Jewish Mystic*. See bibliography for details.

was written in the early years of the eighth decade, although the majority of the writings that would later be deemed canonical predated Mark. If there is no mention of a miracle being associated with Jesus for forty years after his death, can miracles really be viewed as literal accounts of historical happenings?

Paul never mentions a miracle being connected with Jesus in the entire body of his authentic epistles. An argument from silence is never a strong one, but it is a striking fact that when Paul wrote, miracles were so little identified with the life of Jesus that not even one single hint of a supernatural occurrence is alluded to in the Pauline corpus.

The next observation that comes crashing into our awareness is that Jesus was said to have performed miracles in the same three categories that we found in first the Moses/Joshua cycle and then the Elijah/Elisha cycle: nature miracles, raising-of-the-dead miracles and healing miracles.

There were many miracles in which Jesus, like those heroes of the Hebrew past, demonstrated power over nature. He could still the storm (Mark 4:35–41, Matt. 8:23–27, Luke 8:22–25). He could walk on water (Mark 6:45–52, Matt. 14:22–33). He could expand a limited amount of food to feed a host of people (Mark 6:30–44, Matt. 14:13–21, Luke 9:10–17). Nature was itself thought of as at the service of Jesus. Time after time the gospel texts remind us of the claims of miraculous power that were made in the Hebrew scriptures for the heroes of the past.

Jesus was also pictured as capable of raising people from the dead and restoring them to their interrupted lives in a very physical manner, as both Elijah and Elisha were said to have done. There are five gospel episodes in which Jesus was said to have raised someone from death back into life. Three of these narratives, however, are different versions of the same account, but sufficiently similar to convince us that in each it is the same person who was raised. That person was the dying daughter of Jairus, a synagogue ruler (Mark 5:21–43, Matt. 9:18–26, Luke 8:40–56). A careful reading of the details of this miraculous event will reveal, however, some striking similarities to the story of Elisha raising a child from the dead (II Kings 4:18–37). The most striking difference is that in II Kings the child was a boy whereas in the synoptic gospels* the child was a girl, but the similarities are otherwise clear.

The second person raised from the dead in the gospels occurs only in Luke (7:11–15). It is the account of Jesus raising from the dead the only son of a widow. It too, however, bears a striking similarity to the narrative in I Kings in which Elijah raised from the dead the only son of a widow (I Kings 17:17–24).

The final raising-of-the-dead narrative is the most popular of those stories in the gospels. It is the account of the raising of Lazarus, told in the Fourth Gospel (John 11:1–44). We look closely at this material to seek to determine its historicity.

First, there is the note about Lazarus being the brother of Mary and Martha. That is strange because Mary and Martha are written about in the synoptic tradition, where they are never identified as having a brother.

Second, John uses this story to locate all of his life-after-death teachings. One of the "I am" sayings is included here: "I am the resurrection and the life. He that believes in me, though he dies, yet shall he have life, and whoever lives and believes in me shall never die" (John 11:25–26). Since we know that none of these "I am" statements are historic—rather, they are metaphorical, equating Jesus with, for example, bread, a gate, a good shepherd, a true vine—this passage casts the whole Lazarus story into another realm.

---

* The three Synoptic Gospels are Mark, Matthew and Luke.

Then we look at the story itself. It has a strange feel about it. Jesus is notified of Lazarus' sickness and he deliberately postpones going to Bethany, where Lazarus is. When he finally does arrive, Lazarus is already dead and has been buried for four days. The crowd of mourners are still present. It was clearly a very public event.

Jesus, "greatly disturbed," walks with the crowd to the tomb of Lazarus and asks the people to remove the stone sealing the tomb. Martha objects: "Lord, by this time there will be an odor, for he has been dead four days." Jesus says to her that she will see "the glory of God." Then he cries, "Lazarus, come out," and the dead man arises and complies, still bound in his grave cloths. Jesus says: "Unbind him and let him go."

This Lazarus story appears only in John, which was written near the turn of the century, about 100 CE. In other words, for sixty-five to seventy years after this spectacular public event, no one wrote about it. The challenges to believing in this story as a literal narrative are considerable. So we search for clues.

There is a story, a parable in Luke, about a man named Lazarus, who begs at the gate of a rich man (Luke 16:19–31). In time both die. The rich man goes to a place of torment; Lazarus goes to a Jewish holy place identified as "the bosom of Abraham." There is in the parable a strange conversation among the rich man, the patriarch Abraham and Lazarus. The rich man asks Abraham to send Lazarus to bring water to his place of torment. Abraham replies that one cannot get to where the rich man is from where Lazarus is. Then the rich man says: "Well, send Lazarus to my brothers to warn them, lest they too come to this place of torment." Abraham responds: "They have Moses and the prophets. If they do not listen to Moses, neither will they be convinced if one returns from the dead."

It seems that Lazarus has been taken by John from the parable in Luke and turned into a figure of history to prove that the biblical message is accurate. In John's gospel the raising of Lazarus is a story that probes the point of Jesus' resurrection. That probing leads naturally into the story of the crucifixion. The Lazarus story is thus anything but literally true.

So we reach a conclusion of biblical scholarship: None of the raising-of-the-dead stories in the gospels appears to be treated by the gospel writers themselves as events that actually happened. Rather, an Elisha story and an Elijah story have been magnified and retold as events that happened in Jesus' life. Is this any different from having a splitting-of-the-waters story told about Moses, then Joshua, then Elijah and then Elisha? Is it any different from narratives about those Hebrew heroes expanding the food supply then being incorporated into accounts of Jesus feeding multitudes with loaves and fish? If this pattern becomes obvious to us, would it not also have been obvious to the original gospel writers, familiar as they were with Hebrew storytelling practices in which the presence of God was proclaimed in a successive, connected tradition of heroes? Have we been reading the miracle stories of the gospels as literal events of history in which the power of the supernatural invaded time and space, when they were intended only to communicate that the God of Moses was also the God of Joshua, Elijah and Elisha, and that this God had "in the last days" revealed the divine presence in Jesus of Nazareth? Each of these claims has a validity that we must engage.

We are not yet, however, at the end of our analysis of the miracles of the New Testament. There is one additional healing story connected to Jesus, to which we now turn.

We have thus far looked at nature miracles and raising-of-the-dead miracles and how they might have shaped the Jesus story. Now let's look at a New Testament healing story, one that parallels the Elisha story that involved the miraculous healing of the leprosy of a Syrian military leader named Naaman. Luke, who seems to borrow more from the Elijah/Elisha cycle than any other gospel writer, alone tells the story of Jesus healing ten lepers. One of them is a foreigner, a Samaritan (Luke 17:11–19). In both stories—the old and the new—the cleansing occurred by following a specific Jewish formula. Wash yourself in the Jordan River for Naaman; show yourselves to the priests in the cleansing of the ten. In both cases the foreigner returned to give thanks. It looks as if Luke borrowed the Naaman story from Elisha and reshaped and retold it about Jesus.

That may account for one of the healing stories in the gospels. There are, however, many more. They display Jesus' ability to give sight to the blind, hearing to the deaf, speech to those who are mute and movement to those with withered or paralyzed limbs. Many of these stories are wrapped around the memory of Jesus. Such stories make their first appearances in the gospel tradition at the very beginning of Mark, the earliest gospel, and they come in that first gospel immediately after the story of Jesus' baptism by John the Baptist. They include first a healing in the form of purging a demon from one who appears to be an epileptic person (Mark 1:21–28), then the healing of Peter's mother-in-law (Mark 1:29–31), followed by vast healings of undescribed maladies and demons (Mark 1:32–34). Next, there is a narrative in which an individual leper is cleansed (Mark 1:40–45), followed by the healing of a cripple let down on a sheet through an opening in the ceiling (Mark 2:1–12). Given both the prominent placement of these healing stories, and their quantity, they must be considered a major theme in Mark.

The same pattern, placing healing stories attributed to Jesus immediately after John the Baptist has affirmed Jesus' role as the messiah at the baptism, is used by both Matthew and Luke. It is a pattern that holds a clue to this third category of Jesus miracles—that is, healing miracles—in that it shows the relationship between Jesus as the worker of miracles and Jesus as the designated messiah. We will look more closely at this clue in the next chapter, as this section on miracles is brought to a conclusion.

19

Messiah Miracles— The Final Clue

When I wrote my book on the gospel of Matthew under the title *Biblical Literalism: A Gentile Heresy,* I noted the problem that Matthew and Luke had in dealing with the figure of John the Baptist. Both Matthew and Luke had expanded Mark into their longer and more provocative gospels, and in so doing they had to introduce John the Baptist earlier in their narratives. Mark had opened with John the Baptist and had related him to the Jewish observance of Rosh Hashanah. Rosh Hashanah, the Jewish New Year, was associated in a special way with Jewish messianic expectations.

In the sixth century BCE, following the Babylonian exile, Jewish messianic thinking had added to the Israelites' expectations a figure who would prepare the way for the messiah's coming, a figure that II Isaiah (as we call the unknown prophet who authored Isaiah 40–55) simply called the voice that "prepared the way." The voice of one crying in the wilderness, "Prepare ye the way of the Lord"—these were the exact words of this prophet (Isa. 40:3). These words entered deeply into the consciousness of Western Christianity when George Frideric Handel incorporated them

into his oratorio entitled *Messiah*. By the late fifth century BCE, in
the writings of an unknown and unnamed prophet whom we call
Malachi (a Hebrew word that simply means "my messenger"),
that theme is picked up anew. Malachi wrote: "Behold, I send my
messenger to prepare my way before me, and the Lord whom you
seek will suddenly come to his temple, the messenger of the covenant in whom you delight. Behold, he is coming, says the Lord
of hosts" (Mal. 3:1). One chapter later this prophet identified the
messenger as Elijah: "Behold, I will send you Elijah the prophet
before the great and terrible day of the Lord" (Mal. 4:5).

Mark applied those prophetic utterances and messianic expectations about Elijah to John the Baptist. He placed, for example,
II Isaiah's words about the voice crying in the wilderness to "prepare the way of the Lord" into the mouth of John the Baptist.
In Mark's mind John the Baptist was an Elijah-type forerunner
who prepared the way for the messiah. Because a major note of
the Rosh Hashanah observance in the synagogue was to pray
for the coming of the messiah, Mark chose to start his gospel at
Rosh Hashanah and to make the appearance of John the Baptist
and his baptism of Jesus the primary Jesus story told at Rosh
Hashanah.

Many people do not realize that the reason the gospel of Mark
is shorter than Matthew and Luke is that Mark related stories in
his gospel from Rosh Hashanah to Passover, or for just six and a
half months of the liturgical year of the synagogue. Matthew and
Luke, the two gospels that incorporated Mark into their narratives, sought to provide Jesus stories for the *entire* year and thus
also to cover the five and a half months between Passover in the
early spring and Rosh Hashanah in the early fall. This, however,
created for both of these later gospel writers a major problem.
They could not wait five and half months to introduce John the
Baptist and the baptism of Jesus, which inaugurated Jesus' public

ministry as the expected messiah; they had to use the baptism story much earlier in their gospel narratives. When they arrived at the Rosh Hashanah observance they could not retell the baptism story, which they had already used. So what did they do? They reintroduced John the Baptist into their texts at exactly the Rosh Hashanah moment by using the technique of a flashback in which John reappears, not in person, but in the voice of messengers sent from John. The story is essentially the same in both gospels and, in my opinion, constitutes another hint that Luke had Matthew to draw on as well as Mark.

When Rosh Hashanah rolls around, both Matthew (11:2–6) and Luke (7:18–35) tell the story of John from prison sending messengers to Jesus asking: "Are you the messiah?" Jesus never answers the question. Rather, he tells these messengers to listen and to look. His exact words are: "Go and tell John what you hear and see."

Then Jesus quotes from Isaiah 35, a passage regularly associated with Rosh Hashanah. In that chapter, Isaiah painted a portrait of the signs that would mark the arrival of the kingdom of God. First, he said, water would flow in the desert, causing even the crocuses to bloom in that sandy space. There the primary sign of the messianic inauguration of the reign of God was that human wholeness would replace human brokenness. The words are quite specific: "Then the eyes of the blind shall be opened and the ears of the deaf will be unstopped. The lame will leap like a deer and the tongue of the mute sing!" (Isa. 35:5–6).

In both Matthew and Luke, Jesus quotes this text in his response to the question from John's messengers. What those messengers were to tell John of the things they saw and heard was that "the blind see and the lame walk, the lepers are cleansed and the deaf hear, the dead are raised up and the poor have the gospel preached to them" (Matt. 11:5, Luke 7:22). It was Isaiah's list somewhat expanded. Matthew and Luke were issuing the claim that the messiah whom the Baptist had baptized at the beginning of his public ministry, Jesus, was the life around which the signs of the kingdom that the messiah would bring were seen. Think about that for just a minute. Does it not suggest that in order for Jesus to be proclaimed the messiah who was to come, the signs of the in-breaking kingdom had to be manifested in him? That was why the various healing miracles had to be wrapped around his life. These miracle stories were interpretive symbols, not biblical happenings. Later Christians, unaware of the healings' symbolic meaning in Jewish messianic thought, turned them into supernatural miracle stories.

We do not have to twist our brains into first-century pretzels in an effort to believe the unbelievable. We can read the miracle stories as the symbols they originally were and still read the gospels in a post-Matthew, post-Luke, and indeed post-Newtonian world. The gospels do not require that we suspend our intelligence and try to accept the premise of supernatural intervention as the only way to read or to learn from the Jesus story in the twenty-first century.

After centuries of laboring to understand stories that made no sense to us, we now discover that the problem was that we did not know how to read those stories. With this insight, our ability to chart a new reformation has passed another huge obstacle!

Now we know why miracles were not attached to the life of Jesus until the eighth decade. The miracles were interpretive signs. The writers of the miracle accounts saw Jesus as the messiah from whom miracles were expected. That understanding makes sense and it solves the biggest problem in contemporary Christianity. Isaiah predicted it. The gospel writers included it. We do not have to believe it. Jesus springs free.

PART VIII

Thesis 6: Atonement Theology

Atonement theology, especially in its most bizarre "substitution-ary" form, presents us with a God who is barbaric, a Jesus who is a victim and it turns human beings into little more than guilt-filled creatures. The phrase "Jesus died for my sins" is not just dangerous, it is absurd. Atonement theology is a concept we must escape.

Renouncing "Jesus Died for My Sins"

We double back in the examination of this thesis to things we have discussed before. I want to examine the traditional Christian way of talking about salvation. We call it "atonement theology." To accomplish this task we must of necessity go back, momentarily, to our earlier discussion of "original sin." Like love and marriage and even Jack and Jill, original sin and atonement theology go together; and because they do, the future of Christianity demands that we discuss both, even if it involves some repetition. I turn first to examine just how deeply atonement theology has distorted the Christian message.

Few people today use the word "atonement" in common conversation. When they do, normally the word simply bypasses most people's understanding. Familiarity breeds not only contempt, it seems, but also amnesia. Even when one points to the fact that the word "atone" was created by linking the words "at" and "one" together, and that what they then mean refers to the experience of being "at one" with God, still the essence of this word remains elusive.

For many people there appears to be a deep human yearning for

oneness with that which we call God or even what we call meaning, but little seems clear about that yearning. If we were to take
the time to explore the depths of human restlessness, the meaning
of human loneliness, the human desire (perhaps the human need)
to belong, then perhaps we could force the word "atonement" to
become once again a translatable concept. Even then, however, we
still might not connect those ideas with religion in general or with
the Jesus story in particular. Nonetheless, let me begin our discussion of atonement on this level of human experience and only then
seek to relate it to the Jesus story. The result just might be salutary.
At the very least I hope it will reveal a new dimension to the Jesus
story.

There is indeed a discernible and radical loneliness that appears to be part of every human life. Perhaps it is born in that
pre-conscious moment of our birth. Prior to the onset of labor,
each one of us was "at one" with our mother. The temperature
of the mother's body was perfect for the yet-to-be-born infant,
whether the mother was hot or cold. Prior to the birth, the fetus
was fed through the umbilical cord before it even experienced
hunger. The fetus had no awareness of the limits placed on life in
the womb, since he or she had never known anything else. Then
this apparently perfect womb-limited world was disturbed when,
as the Bible says, "in the fullness of time" the infant was propelled involuntarily into a much larger world. In that process the
infant experienced radical separation from that to which it had
been previously attached. In this broader world the typical infant
thus endures for the first time such things as hunger, thirst, soiled
diapers, temperature variations and a variety of other things never
experienced before. All of these things serve to create a sense of
separation and thus of loneliness in the human psyche, a loneliness that I suspect none of us ever fully escapes.

We overcome this separation only in relative ways. We attach our little mouth to our mother's breast. We lean against the warmth of her body while being rocked or cradled in her arms. As life expands, new dimensions of belonging are brought into contact with our innate loneliness. We learn first that we are part of a family that normally includes a father, siblings, grandparents and aunts and uncles, who in addition to our mother move in and out of the family constellation. Each person normally has a place at the family table, a bed, clothes, shoes that are his or hers alone. A sense of being in a unit of society is thus quickly built into the human experience for most of us. It is, however, never total and that sense of loneliness is never quite extinguished, creating our constant human yearning to be "at one." Friends enter our lives from time to time in powerful ways. Sometimes these friends are called "best friends" and are described as "inseparable," but such childhood attachments seldom last for a lifetime. People move, grow and change. For most people the "best friends" of childhood become finally little more than a happy memory.

There is also in the human experience an amazing ecstasy associated with what we call "falling in love." Falling in love is as if one had discovered the other half of one's self in one's mate and, in that union, feels strangely and wonderfully whole and complete, often for the first time. I do not wish to minimize or denigrate these feelings. Being in love is a powerful emotional experience for those of us privileged to know it. When one is in love, the grass appears to be greener, the sky bluer, the air fresher; life is almost always universally sweet. The ability to sustain such an "in love" relationship for a lifetime is rare enough to draw notice and admiration. While falling in love is real, it is never eternal. Life is mortal and lovers lose their loved ones. When abandoned by death or choice, lovers may be inconsolable in their grief. Yes, we adjust, life moves on, but empty spaces once filled by the love of another are so deep in our psyche that when we lose a partner or soul mate, we experience that loss as a wound to our psyche that remains forever.

wonderful

All of this is to say that there is in the heart of life an almost universal yearning for oneness, for at-one-ment, that never quite goes away. Much of what we call "the experience of God" is fashioned to meet us at this point of our human vulnerability. It was St. Augustine, writing in *Confessions,* who gave these words to that experience: "Thou, O God, hast made us for thyself alone and our hearts are restless until they find their rest in thee."* That is perhaps what atonement means at its deepest, experiential, religious level. As such it is a legitimate part of our humanity.

Inspired by a literalized understanding of the mythical fall into sin, however, Christianity took this valid human experience and transformed it into a doctrine. "Original sin" was the way the church articulated this problem. "Salvation" was the church's stated resolution of this problem. In the process of working out the details of original sin and salvation—that is, of the doctrine of atonement—the church turned God into a righteous judge who required satisfaction and was quite incapable of offering forgiveness. Jesus became someone whom God required to suffer in order to satisfy some presumed divine need. Every offense had to be punished, and human beings were loaded with life-destroying guilt. Atonement theology, as spoken about today in Christian circles, thus represents the deepest distortion of what Christianity means that I can imagine.

I begin this exploration with a statement that will offend some, amuse others and shatter a few, but that still needs to be said if we seek to move away from the almost unbelievable into a modern Christianity: *Jesus did not die for your sins or mine!* This distortion of Christianity, atonement as traditionally conceived, must

---

* See bibliography for details.

be lifted out of the unconscious realm of our faith story, challenged and expelled. It stands between us and any possibility of rethinking the meaning of Christianity. It is so deeply part of our religious jargon that precise, radical theological surgery may be required, for, like a malignancy, atonement theology has wrapped itself around vital Christian organs.

The way this idea has been explained in Christian history is straightforward. Let me state it briefly even at the price of being repetitious, but without the nuances that have been developed to ease our embarrassment. We human beings are all fallen people. Sin is the universal mark of our humanity. We were created in perfection, but we live in sinfulness. Our humanity is thus distorted, infected with a sickness that we cannot overcome. Our destiny is to live forever in the stance of a penitent, begging for mercy and hoping for a rescue that can only come from above. That is why in Christian liturgies we portray ourselves as groveling on our knees in the position of a slave, begging God for forgiveness. In the story of Jesus, so central to our faith, we describe just how it was that God effected our rescue. Salvation can come only at God's initiative, we said. That is why Jesus had to be clothed in divinity and portrayed as "God incarnate" (and ultimately even as the second person of the Trinity). If Jesus were not God, the rescue effort would not work, for human beings cannot save themselves from the effects of both original sin and "the fall." Salvation requires that Jesus be not just the agent of God, be not just of "similar" substance with God, but be of the "identical" substance of God. That was at least the conclusion drawn by the Council of Nicea in 325 CE, when a new creed was adopted to define orthodoxy.

How was this Jesus going to accomplish this task of saving the fallen? Here the doctrine of the atonement gets even stranger. God would force the divine Son to suffer the fate that all human beings deserved, but which no human being could possibly endure. Jesus had namely to absorb the punishment that God required in order for the justice of God to be totally satisfied. That is how the story of the crucifixion was told. Remember the scourging scene in producer and director Mel Gibson's 2004 motion picture *The Passion of the Christ*? No pain detail was left unexploited. Indeed the more grotesque the pain of Jesus' death was, the more secure, we were taught to believe, was our salvation. It was sadomasochism at its worst.

In our theological constructs, who was it requiring this suffering on the part of Jesus? The answer was clearly God! What kind of God would that be? A deity who had been wronged; a God to whom restitution had to be paid; a God who needed a human sacrifice and a blood offering before the restoration of the sinful could be achieved. So we were told that the "Father God" punishes the "divine Son" in order to achieve atonement with sinful human beings! Does this make sense to anyone? Did it ever make sense? Does this theology cause you or me to want to worship or even serve such a God? Does not this deity become the portrait of the ultimate child abuser? Paint it with beautiful colors as much as you will, perfume it with pious phrases, but nothing can rescue this understanding of God from the judgment of being evil.

Is this what atonement *really* means? Is this an essential aspect of Christianity? I think not. Thus any effort to reform Christianity must address this deep, internal theological sickness. Surely there must be another way to tell the Christ story. To that task we turn next.

Incomplete—Not Fallen

Everywhere one looks in the Christian religion, one discovers the pervasive sickness found in what we have called "atonement theology." In the church a fetish has even developed about the "cleansing power of the blood of Jesus" and its inherent ability to "wash away our sins." Protestants apparently want to bathe in the blood of Christ, because they sing hymns about fountains of blood in which they wish to be washed and they exhort the saving and cleansing power of Jesus' blood. Catholics appear to want to drink the blood of Christ to have its cleansing power operate from within. Perhaps Protestants are more obsessed with the external sins of the flesh and Catholics are more concerned about the sins of the inner self. No Christian, however, escapes this mentality.

The focus of each of the four gospels, one quickly notices, is on the fact of the crucifixion. From twenty-five to forty percent of the content of each gospel is dedicated to the last week of Jesus' life. The symbol of the cross in its various forms has become the universally recognized sign of Christianity itself. Hymns about the cross mark all forms of Christian worship. They appear in an almost infinite variety: "In the Cross of Christ I Glory," "Beneath the Cross of Jesus" and "Lift High the Cross,"* to name just a few. Crosses are also worn to signify our allegiance. Bishops wear elaborate pectoral crosses. Simple people wear simple crosses around their necks. The symbol is universally recognized.

The crucifix, focusing as it does on the specific and seemingly eternal suffering of Jesus, can be found hanging on the wall in the cell of almost every monk and priest in Christian history. It was the first thing each dedicated cleric saw upon awakening each morning and the last thing he saw before closing his eyes in sleep each night. When the grotesque nature of death by crucifixion got too unbearable, the suffering of Jesus was transformed into glory, but the cross still remained central. In the crucifix form called the Christus Rex, the cross became a throne from which Jesus reigned in glory, and the agony of his writhing body was transformed by the vestments of the great high priest. Every place we turn in Christian history, however, we see echoes of the Jesus who, as we say in the creeds, "came down from heaven" in order to be crucified "for our sins" on the cross of Calvary. We name our churches after the saving function of that Jesus who died for our sins: the Church of the Redeemer or the Church of our Savior. Salvation, understood as an atoning sacrifice and marked by great suffering and pain, has never been far from the heart of traditional Christianity.

Perhaps because we have heard these words and embraced these images for so long, their offensiveness has been largely removed. When the story of the cross is raised to consciousness and examined critically, however, it is hard not to see in that story cruelty, suffering and even elements of both masochism and sadism. Bulletins during Lent in many churches look as if they might have been purchased in a local sadomasochism shop. They feature

---

* "In the Cross . . . ," John Bowring 1825; "Beneath the Cross . . . ," Elizabeth C. Clephane 1868; "Lift High the Cross," George William Kitchin 1887.

whips and nails, and if they elicit any emotion at all, it is guilt. In some of the popular hymns of that season this guilt is overt and inescapable: "Who was the guilty? Who brought this upon thee? Alas, my treason, Jesus, hath undone thee. 'Twas I, Lord Jesus, I it was denied thee: I crucified thee."* That is the theology that arises from the Christian mantra, repeated so often that its meaning is supposed to be self-evident: "Jesus died for my sins."

Think about what that means. God has required that Jesus suffer because of my sins! Can one imagine a more powerful guilt message? No wonder our liturgies are filled with pleas for God to have mercy. Will that God who "spared not his own son" be more kindly disposed toward us than he was toward Jesus? Is that not why we have been taught throughout the centuries that the proper posture before God in worship is the position of a supplicant, a slave before a master who has the ultimate power of life and death over us? Yes, we've been taught that, but is kneeling as we beg for mercy truly the proper stance of a child of God before his or her deity? An abused child might beg for mercy as he or she stands before an abusive parent. A convicted felon might fall on his or her knees and beg for mercy before a "hanging judge," but is that ever a proper stance to mark the relationship of a child of God standing before the Source of his or her life, love or being? Have you ever known *any* human life to be helped by being told over and over again just how evil, wretched, vile and hopeless he or she is?

How did the Christian gospel ever get so distorted that it became the primary source of self-deprecation and guilt? How did the idea of the God of Abraham, Moses and Jesus devolve into this? Why has religion become primarily about behavior control? Is life embraced, made whole or saved by the threat of the punishment of

---

* "Ah, Holy Jesus," Johann Heerman 1630, trans. Robert Bridges 1897.

hell or even by the promise of the rewards of heaven? If our goal in life and in religion is to escape punishment or to gain reward, have we not failed to escape our own survival-driven self-centeredness? Is this what the Jesus of the Fourth Gospel had in mind when he defined his purpose as that of bringing "abundant life" to all (John 10:10)? Will abundant life ever be the result of a life in which guilt and fear are the primary motivators of behavior? Though the answer is certainly no, the only way to escape this theology, it seems, is to give up Christianity and walk away from the church forever. Many today are opting for that alternative.

How did such a destructive theology emerge in Christianity? It was born, I believe, out of Gentile ignorance of things Jewish. It emerged because the words and forms of Jewish worship continued to be used in Christian churches long after Jews were no longer part of that worshipping community and Gentile Christians totally misunderstood and misappropriated those Jewish words and forms.

So much of the language of Judaism is still found in Christian worship, but we Christians neither recognize nor understand it. We say, "Christ our Passover is sacrificed for us," without any awareness that we are identifying Jesus with the paschal lamb, whose blood was said to have kept the Angel of Death from killing the firstborn sons in Jewish households on the night of the exodus (Exod. 12). We sing the Agnus Dei, "O Lamb of God, who taketh away the sins of the world," without being aware that those words were taken almost verbatim from the Jewish day known as Yom Kippur, the Day of Atonement. On that Jewish holy day, a lamb was once slaughtered and its blood was smeared on the Mercy Seat, which was thought to be the throne of God, located in the temple in the Holy of Holies. People were then taught to think of themselves as coming into oneness with God because they were able to come "through the blood of the lamb."

In Jewish worship, however, the lamb was a symbol, not of a sacrifice that an angry God required, but of the human yearning to achieve the fullness of our human potential. The lamb, chosen carefully for the sacrifice, represented our longing to be all that God created us to be. That was why the lamb had to be physically perfect, with no scratches, broken bones or bruises. Since the lamb lived without the confusion and mistakes of human freedom, it also came to represent moral perfection. Thus the lamb of Yom Kippur was a symbol of our recognition that we had not become all that God wanted us to be. Human life, compromised as it was, did not share in God's perfection. So Jewish worshippers, on this one great day of penitence each year, acted out liturgically a means by which they could participate in God's oneness. They came to God under the symbol of the physically and morally perfect lamb.

Gentiles took that symbol and read into it the ancient animal sacrificial practices that once had even included human sacrifice. Under this limited and distorted understanding, God became the angry judge who had been offended by sinful people, for which this judge, in an act of divine wrath, deemed us worthy to be punished. The punishment we deserved, however, was greater than we could ever absorb. The wrath of God, it was said, nonetheless had to be served, since this God pursued justice with little thought of forgiveness. This God required the proverbial "pound of flesh." So, in order to satisfy the demands of this God, Jesus was made to take our place, enduring the wrath of this punishing deity in our stead. That is what happened, we have been told, on the cross. Jesus took my punishment from the hand of God for me. Jesus "died for my sins."

Does that make any of us feel better? Of course not! It destroys the goodness of God. It turns God into a monster, it turns Jesus into a masochistic victim and it turns you and me into grieving buckets of trembling, guilt-filled jelly. This was not originally, is not now and can never be the meaning of Christianity. Atonement theology must be abandoned if there is to be a Christian future. The repudiation of atonement theology is an essential step before Christianity can ever appeal to the emerging generation.

We now know that the entire theological superstructure of Christianity is built on a false premise. We are not fallen sinners, indelibly infected with original sin. Rather, we are incomplete people yearning to be made whole. As was noted earlier, we live today on the other side of the work of Charles Darwin. We are evolving people, not fallen people. We do not need to be saved from a fall that never happened. We need to be loved and empowered so that we are enabled to become all that we are capable of being. Atonement theology will never get us to this new goal. Jesus, perceived of as "savior," "redeemer" or "rescuer," will never bring us wholeness. Jesus as the "life of God" calling us to live fully, the "love of God" freeing us to love wastefully and the "being of God" giving us the courage to be all that we can be, will.

If Christianity is to have a future, the paradigm must shift from being saved from our sins to being called into a new wholeness from our sense of incompleteness. There can be no "substitutionary atonement" in the Christianity of tomorrow. The call to a new reformation is real, necessary and acute.

PART IX

Thesis 7: Easter

The Easter event gave birth to the Christian movement and continues to transform it, but that does not mean that Easter was the physical resuscitation of Jesus' deceased body back into human history. The earliest biblical records state that "God raised him." Into what? we must ask. The reality of the experience of resurrection must be separated from its later mythological explanations.

The Resurrection

Without Easter, there would be no Christianity! Whatever it was that constituted the Easter experience, the obvious fact is that there was enormous power in that moment that cries out for explanation. That power changed lives; it redefined the way people thought about God; it created a new consciousness; and in time it even caused a new holy day to be born. Each of these changes points beyond itself to something that must be big enough to account for these possibilities. At the same time, this undeniable explosion of power does not lend itself to a particular explanation, and thus it forces us to acknowledge that whatever Easter was and is, we can approach it only inside the time and space vocabulary of human existence, for none of us can escape the limits of our humanity. So over the years, the church has offered a variety of these time- and space-bound explanations. They are contained in what we call the gospels. In time, however, we discovered that these biblical explanations—these narratives of the Jesus story—were filled with contradictions. As these explanations were literalized over the intervening centuries, they served to make believing in the resurrection increasingly difficult, even unthinkable.

Nicholas Kristof, a writer for the *New York Times*, is a repre-

sentative of the perspective that treats the resurrection with something other than literalism. He describes himself as one "whose
faith is in the Sermon on the Mount, who aspires to follow Jesus'
teachings, but is skeptical that he was born of a virgin, walked on
water, multiplied loaves and fishes or had a physical resurrection."

Kristof interviewed former President Jimmy Carter, who, as an
evangelical Christian, is thought to believe in all of these things.
He probed Jimmy Carter on the resurrection. Mr. Carter replied:
"My belief in the resurrection of Jesus comes from my Christian
faith, and not from any need for scientific proof. . . . I look on the
contradictions among the gospel writers as a sign of authenticity,
based on their different life experiences."*

Suppose Mr. Carter had had the advantage of the study of the
Bible in the way it is done in contemporary theological settings,
and had learned the things which we have learned in that environment. Would he still consider the gospels, read literally, to be
believable, or would he say that they are unbelievable?

In today's world, the scholarly and critical explorations of the
biblical narratives inevitably bring two facts quickly into our
awareness. First, while not one word of the New Testament was
written without a firm commitment to the reality of the Easter
experience, none of the Bible's sources represents eyewitness,
first-generation reporting. Second, there is hardly an Easter detail
proclaimed in one part of the New Testament that is not contradicted in another. Traditional Christians seek to hide from these
two truths in biblical ignorance. The secular generation dismisses
Christianity because it makes so little rational sense. A quick
glance at the Easter stories of the Bible will make this case.

To begin this journey into the resurrection we start with the

---

* Both Kristof's and Carter's words are from Nicholas Kristof, "President Carter, Am I
a Christian?" *New York Times,* Apr. 5, 2017, https://www.nytimes.com/2017/04/15/
opinion/sunday/president-carter-am-i-a-christian.html.

fact that Paul and the gospels disagree on both whether there was a tomb into which Jesus was laid and whether that tomb literally became empty. From that initial fact the other disagreements flow with regularity. All of the gospel sources agree that women went to that tomb on the first day of the week, but they disagree on who the women were and on what they found there. They disagree on whether these women actually saw the risen Christ. Mark says no, Matthew says yes, Luke says no and John says yes! They disagree on where the twelve disciples were when the risen Christ supposedly appeared to them for the first time. Mark implies that it would be in Galilee; Matthew states that it was in Galilee; Luke says that it was never in Galilee, but only in Jerusalem; and John says that it was in Jerusalem first and in Galilee much later. They disagree on whether the resurrection occurred "on the third day" or "after three days"; the two descriptions do not give us the same day. They disagree on who saw the raised Christ first. It was Peter, says Paul; the women at the tomb, says Matthew; Cleopas in Emmaus, says Luke; and Magdalene alone, says John.

One cannot harmonize the contradictory content of the Bible's Easter narratives no matter how hard one tries. These sources have been available for people to read since the end of the first century, which means that these facts have been available to the Christian church for over two thousand years! Very few people, however, have taken the time to read, to think about or even to notice the contradictions. Perhaps in a believing age such participation was considered unnecessary. The twenty-first century, however, is not a believing age, and so we are troubled by these things in a way that our ancestors in faith did not seem to be. If we are seeking to start a new reformation, we must raise and address all of these questions. In our look at this thesis regarding the resurrection of Jesus and the Easter story, I intend to do just that and, in the process, to offer a new way to understand and to appreciate this cornerstone of the Christian faith. What does the resurrection of Jesus mean?

The resurrection of Jesus needs to be treated very differently from the way the virgin birth was treated. We dismissed the virgin birth earlier as a mythological explanation of the origins of Jesus. There we documented first the fact that the virgin birth was a later-developing tradition that entered the Christian story for the first time in the ninth decade of the Christian era. The resurrection, however, was the experience that brought Christianity into being. In addition, only two of the five major writers of the New Testament even mention a miraculous birth, making it tangential, not central, to the Christian story, while there is no verse of the New Testament that does not assume the reality of the Easter experience. So the thrust of this discussion on the resurrection seems fraught with peril to many, sometimes even to me, for if Easter is finally revealed as nothing substantial, then Christianity collapses. Thus this seventh thesis, like none of the others, goes to the very heart of our faith tradition. We start our probe with our earliest Christian source.

Paul, the earliest New Testament author, as we have noted before, wrote his authentic epistles before any gospel had been created. He describes Easter in the briefest of ways. Jesus "was raised from the dead in accordance with the scriptures," he says (I Cor. 15:3–4). Note two things about this first written reference to the resurrection. First, the verb Paul uses is passive. Paul does not say that Jesus "rose," but rather that he "was raised." The Easter action did not come out of Jesus himself, then. Something outside of Jesus acted on Jesus to "raise" him. Jesus, Paul asserts, was raised by God.

"Into what?" then becomes our next question. Did God raise Jesus back into the physical life of our world, thus restoring him to the life he had possessed prior to the crucifixion? From everything that Paul says in other parts of the body of his work, the answer to each of these questions is an emphatic no. In Romans, Paul indicates that this Jesus, who was raised from the dead, is at "the right hand of God" (Rom. 8:34). Oh, we say, but that simply describes the Jesus who, after his resurrection, ascended into heaven and thus into his exalted position in the presence of God. The only problem with that quick and easy explanation is that the story of the ascension of Jesus does not enter the Christian tradition until Luke writes some twenty-five to thirty years after Paul's death. Paul cannot be referring to something about which no one had ever heard. For Paul the resurrection itself places Jesus "at the right hand of God," not back into human history. For most of us that is a new idea.

Paul reinforces his understanding when he states earlier in Romans that "the spirit of him who *raised* Jesus from the dead dwells in you . . . [and] will give life to your mortal bodies" (8:11). There is a connection in Paul's mind between the spirit that raised Jesus and the spirit that will raise us and bind us to God in a new way. In these words there is no hint that this action could or would raise either Jesus or us back as resuscitated bodies, able to continue our mortal journeys. No matter what we may have thought before, resurrection was never resuscitation.

Another hint as to Paul's meaning is also found in Romans. Here Paul says: "Christ, being raised from the dead, *will never die again. Death no longer has dominion over him*" (Rom. 6:9, emphasis added). If resurrection meant being restored to life in this world, then resuscitated people would presumably have to die again. That is, however, not what Paul says. For Paul, the Easter event was a matter of being raised to a new dimension of life that he does not, perhaps cannot, describe, but it is beyond the power of death ever to threaten or strike again.

In the epistle to the Philippians, which was probably Paul's last authentic letter, the great apostle speaks of Jesus as "emptying himself." Was Paul not asserting that because Jesus had reached this new dimension of life, God had "highly exalted him and bestowed on him the name that is above every name, so that at the name of Jesus every knee should bow" (Phil. 2:5–11)? Jesus in the resurrection had not returned to his previous earthly existence, but had entered into the oneness of God. This is clearly what Paul understood the Easter experience to be. A deceased body walking out of a tomb to take up anew the life before his crucifixion simply is not the meaning of Easter that motivated the first author in the New Testament. The one thing that is clear is that Easter did not, in the earliest years of the Christian story for which we have any written record, mean that Jesus was restored to the life of this world.

Most biblical scholars do not today believe that Paul is the author of the epistle we have named Ephesians.* That epistle appears to have been written as a cover letter that served to introduce a collection of Paul's authentic epistles, which had been gathered together by his followers, in order to send them to other churches. It was the first step in proclaiming them as "scripture." The church in Ephesus may have been the first recipient of this collection. In any event, this epistle appears to have been written by Paul's disciples, who wanted to spread abroad his teachings. It is not a stretch, then, to suggest that while not being from the hand of Paul, this epistle might nonetheless be Pauline in content. It also appears to be dated earlier than any of the gospels. Given that early dating—in other words, before Luke's ascension story—it is noteworthy that this epistle also refers to God as raising Jesus "from the dead" in order to allow him "to sit at God's right hand in the heavenly places" (Eph. 1:20).

---

* Arthur J. Dewey, Roy W. Hoover, Lane C. McGaughy and Daryl D. Schmidt, *The Authentic Letters of Paul.* See bibliography for details.

The epistle we call Colossians is in that same category—that is, it was written within a decade after Paul's death by those who were disciples of Paul and thus sympathizers with the point of view expressed in Paul's teaching. Scanning through that epistle we discover these words about Easter: "If you have been raised with Christ, seek those things which are above, where Christ is ✲ seated at the right hand of God" (Col. 3:1).

So the first step that those of us who wish to explore the meaning of resurrection must take is to recognize that the founding moment of the Christian story is not about either an empty tomb or the resuscitation of a deceased body. Its original proclamation asserted that in some manner God had raised Jesus into being part of who God is. Jesus was raised by God into God. Is that not quite different from what we have been taught to think over the centuries of Christian history? It is indeed, and it will force us to look at Easter in a brand-new way.

23

Paul's List of Resurrection Witnesses

We have explored first the Pauline corpus of writings in the New Testament in order to learn what Paul meant when he wrote that "God raised Jesus" to the "right hand of God." We have also examined briefly two of the pseudo-Pauline epistles that nonetheless predate the gospels. Here we discovered the concept for which Paul used the word "resurrection." It is quite a different concept from what this word has come to mean in Christian history.

Before we leave Paul, we have to take seriously a list he included in I Corinthians, which he wrote around the years 54–56 CE. Here Paul states that the Christ, who was raised into God at his death, not into a life of flesh and blood in this world, nonetheless "appeared" to the people on this list (I Cor. 15:3–8). To what kind of experience was Paul referring in this part of his work?

The first thing we note is that the Greek word that has been translated "appeared" was *ophthe* (ωφθη). It is the same word used by the Septuagint translators to refer to the God who "appeared" to Moses in the burning bush in Exodus (3:2). It is also the word from which we get our term "ophthalmology," the science or study of seeing. We are so used to reading the Bible literally that we need to pause and ask what kind of appearing or seeing this is. Was the appearance of God to Moses in the burning bush an objective seeing? If others had been present, would they have seen what Moses saw? If Moses had possessed a smartphone equipped with a camera, could he have photographed the God who appeared during this experience? Is there a difference between sight and insight, between sight and second sight? What did Paul mean when he posted his list of those to whom the raised Christ "appeared"? For clues we examine his list.

"He appeared first to Cephas," Paul says. In the mind of Paul, it was Cephas-Peter who was the first to see. Then Peter appears to have opened the eyes of the other members of the apostolic band so that they too could see. How did that happen? Our minds seek to engage that "seeing." The language Paul uses seems to me to speak of a different kind of seeing from simply having a scene become visible before our eyes. It speaks of a breakthrough in our thinking, leading to a new understanding; it speaks of putting together things that had never been put together before and thus, in that innovative combination, forming a new insight. Was the resurrection of Jesus something like this? Did the tragedy that embraced the life of Jesus and led to his crucifixion get reinterpreted or understood in such a new way that it opened doors to life never before imagined? Can evil be transformed and made good simply by positing a victorious ending to its consequences?

There is a powerful story in the book of Genesis (chapters 37–50) that suggests this possibility. The brothers of Joseph, angry at what they perceived as their father's favoritism toward Joseph, resolved to remove him from their lives. First, they placed him in a hole from which he could not escape. They intended to leave him there to his fate, which was surely death. Then they saw a caravan passing by and decided to profit from their evil by selling their brother as a slave to this traveling band of people, who were

Midianites in one version of the story, Ishmaelites in another. Twenty pieces of silver was the agreed-upon price. As Joseph was carried off in chains, presumably never to be seen by his brothers again, they planned a way to explain his loss to his and their father: They would say that he had been eaten by wild animals. This was indeed what they told their grief-stricken father, Jacob, when they presented him with Joseph's multicolored coat, the sign of his special status to his father, but now drenched in an animal's blood, which they themselves had applied.

In the course of history, however, sometimes overt evil is but the prelude to life-giving insight. Joseph, the slave, ultimately gained the respect of his owners, and the opportunities he received from them opened door after door to him until he rose to become a ruler in Egypt, second only to the pharaoh. In that capacity he oversaw the storage of grain to prepare for a famine that he was sure was coming. When it came, starvation became rampant throughout the region and even threatened the lives of Joseph's brothers.

Hearing that grain was available in Egypt, Joseph's brothers took their money and grain sacks and traveled to that land in the hope of buying sufficient food to survive the famine. They confronted Joseph in his position of authority, holding in his hands, as he did, the power of life and death over them. They did not recognize him, but the story says that he recognized them. He now had the authority to sell grain or not to sell grain and thus to give or to withhold life over those who once had sold him into slavery and who had meant to destroy him. Would he finally gain his revenge? Or would he absorb this rejecting act of pain and return it to his brothers as love? This was Joseph's choice. In this story love won out, and because it did, life was enhanced—Joseph's life and the lives of his brothers as well.

In another part of the Hebrew scriptures a portrait was

painted by that aforementioned unknown prophet whom we
call II Isaiah (Isa. 40–55). This portrait depicted one called "the
servant," sometimes "the suffering servant." "The servant" was
created, we now believe, to be a poetic symbol of the people of
Israel. II Isaiah drew this portrait when he returned from exile
in Babylon in the sixth century BCE, filled with the hope of re-
establishing his defeated nation, raising up their destroyed city
of Jerusalem and rebuilding their demolished temple in order to
reclaim their messianic calling to be the nation through which
the nations of the world would be blessed. When this prophet
arrived back at what he called his homeland, however, the dev-
astation that greeted him was all-encompassing. He sank into
depression as he came to believe that there was no future, no
resurrection for his defeated and now destroyed nation. How
long he remained in depression I do not know, but when he
emerged, he sketched a new vocation for Israel that was rooted,
not in victory, but in defeat; not in power, but in weakness. It
forms perhaps the holiest writing in the Hebrew scriptures. The
vocation of the Jewish people, he suggested, was not to win, not
to achieve power or even nationhood again, but rather to live in
such a way as to absorb willingly the world's hostility, to drain
from people their anger, accepting it and returning it to them
as love. "The servant," a symbol for that nation, was to be a
willing victim, one who would be "rejected, despised, a man of
sorrows and acquainted with grief" (Isa. 53:3). He was to make
the people whole by accepting their abuse, never returning it in
kind, but responding to it only with love. That ancient portrait,
drawn by this unknown prophet, became the one which the followers of Jesus saw lived out in him.

Was Peter the first to see this? Was he the one who saw in
Jesus a life driven not by survival, but by the love that enabled
him to give his life away? Did this vision enable him to see God

in a new way, not as the almighty one, the heavenly father or the judge of the world, but as the Source of Life, expanding the early Christians' understanding of what it means to live; as the Source of Love, freeing them to love beyond their boundaries and their fears without the expectation of gaining love in return; and as the Ground of Being, giving them the courage to be all that they could be and, in the process, freeing others to be all that they could be? Was this the vision of God that they saw in Jesus, who called people beyond the barriers of tribe, race, ethnicity and gender? When he was victimized by those to whom he only offered love, when he died forgiving, loving, freeing, is that when they saw that God was in him? Was resurrection the ability to see that Jesus had taken his humanity to a new dimension and had now stepped into the being of that which they called divine? Was it a step from self-consciousness into a universal consciousness, into an awareness of the oneness of all things?

Is that how Peter's eyes were opened? Is that the vision to which he then opened the disciples' eyes, and then the "five hundred brethren" at once? Was not the next step to open the eyes of James, the Lord's brother, and then the apostles—that is, those sent out to all the people of the world? Finally, is that the resurrection message that embraced the self-loathing Paul, who believed that "sin dwells in my members," causing me to "do the things I do not want to do and to fail to do the things that I want to do" (Rom. 7:23, 19)? Was the resurrection the power that transformed Paul from the one who said of himself, "O wretched man that I am, who will deliver me from this body of death?" to the Paul who, when his eyes were opened to the meaning of Jesus, could then say, "Nothing in all creation can separate me from the love of God which is in Christ Jesus, my Lord" (Rom. 7:24, Rom. 8:38–39)? Could this transforming experience be the essence of resurrection?

Resurrection, I now believe, was not a physical act. No formerly deceased body ever walked out of any tomb, leaving it empty to take up a previous life in the world. For Paul and for the other early Christians to whom Paul says Jesus "appeared," resurrection was, rather, a moment of new revelation that occurred when survival-driven humanity could transcend that limit and give itself away in love to others, including even to those who wish and do us evil. This was the experience in which a new "seeing" of both God and life was born. Was this experience great enough to have been called resurrection? I submit that it was. That experience suggested that God and human life can flow together. It persuaded "believers" that every limit on our humanity can be broken. *That* is what those early Christians meant when they said: "Jesus lives. We have seen the Lord!" That same resurrection experience must now change the way we understand God and even the way we understand worship. Resurrection, understood as Paul and the early Christians experienced it, is an ongoing and life-reordering process, not an event that happened once in history a long time ago.

"The Lord is risen. He is risen indeed." This ancient salute that greeted Easter day did not mean that Jesus had been raised back into the life of human limitations, but that he opened to us access into the meaning of God, as the power to free us to live, to love and to be. How badly have we misunderstood the message of Easter! How limited has been our vision of resurrection! The last enemy to be destroyed is death; and with its destruction, we learn that God is one and all of us are part of that oneness. It is a new insight.

24

The Gospels'
Understanding of Easter

aul was the first, perhaps he was also the most important, but he was not the only witness to the resurrection
of Jesus in the biblical narrative. To complete our story
and to validate anew a different concept of resurrection,
we turn briefly to the gospel narratives. Be warned in advance.
There will be surprises that await us even here.

Mark, the earliest gospel to be written, has no account of the
risen Christ appearing to anyone at any time within its pages.
This fact surprises many. It so bothered the early Christians that
they kept writing new endings to Mark's gospel to cover up this
rather glaring deficiency.* If, however, the denial of a physical
resuscitation of the body was not a deficiency in the Easter story,
but an insight, as I am convinced it was, then those later editors

---

* Biblical scholarship is quite certain that the earliest copies of Mark ended with verse
8 of chapter 16—that is, with the women, having heard the resurrection message,
fleeing in fear and saying nothing to anyone. Verses 9–20 of Mark 16, a passage that
appears in some texts, was clearly added to Mark by later writers, who sought to
harmonize this first gospel with those that were written later. There is no dispute that
these verses are a later addition to Mark. The only dispute is whether or not Mark
intended to end his gospel with verse 8 of chapter 16 or whether perhaps the last part
of Mark's scroll was torn off and lost. The great majority of New Testament scholars
now accept the fact that Mark ended his gospel exactly as we find it at 16:8.

were revealing only that they did not understand what the original resurrection story was all about. The process of the literaliza-
tion of the Easter experience had clearly already begun.

Mark, in his telling of the Easter story in chapter 16 (vv. 1–8),
portrays some women coming to the tomb of Jesus at dawn on the
first day of the week. They are consumed with their worldly fears.
We are told that the thing they were discussing on their journey
was how they would be able to remove the great stone that had
been placed at the mouth of Jesus' burial cave. Presumably, in their
minds, the stone had to be removed to let them in, and in the mind
of the gospel writer, to allow Jesus to come out. When they arrived,
to their relief they found the stone already removed. A young man
was there; he was dressed in a white robe. He was not an angel.
Perhaps he was a liturgical functionary. I have worn a white robe
on many occasions during my career without being mistaken for an
angel. Perhaps this narrative reflected a developed liturgy. The role
this young man played in the Easter drama was simply to make an
announcement: "You seek Jesus of Nazareth who was crucified.
He has risen [or has been raised], he is not here; see the place where
they laid him. Go tell his disciples and Peter that he is going before
you to Galilee; there you will see him as he told you." The women
flee in fear, Mark says, and they say nothing to anyone, "for they
were afraid."

That is all there is to Mark's original story of Easter. How
strange a narrative it would be, if resurrection meant the resuscitation of a deceased body. These words point clearly, however, to
the fact that this is not and was not what resurrection originally
meant. You will see the meaning of resurrection, the white-robed
messenger seems to say, when you return to your homes and go
about the business of your life. Resurrection, you see, was not
just something that happened to Jesus; it is also something that
happens to and in each of us. For us, as for Jesus, it is a subjective

understanding, not an objective event. We will see him, the promise of Mark's messenger seems to say, when our eyes are open to the meaning of God found in the midst of life, in the expression of love and in the courage to be. That is, we are resurrected when we learn that God is present when, in the words I use over and over, we live fully, love wastefully and become all that we are capable of being. Easter is an experience which thus functions in a number of ways. First, it opens our eyes. Second, it calls us to open the eyes of others and to enable those others to live, to love and to be. It is in the authenticity of our humanity that the boundary between life and death is transcended. The first gospel so very clearly does not say what most of us have always thought and been taught that it says.

About a decade after Mark, the second gospel, Matthew, was written. Matthew has Mark in front of him as he writes, and he borrows extensively from that earlier source. He makes some changes, however. Matthew magnifies the miraculous and closes all of the loopholes that he believes Mark has left open. So Mark's "young man dressed in a white robe" becomes, in Matthew, a supernatural angel in translucent clothing (Matt. 28:2–3). The message of this angel has become much more supernatural: "[Jesus] has risen from the grave. He will go before you to Galilee. There you will see him" (Matt. 28:7). Matthew's women are faithful, far more so than they were in Mark. They go at once to tell the disciples what they have seen and heard. They are rewarded for that faithfulness by Matthew with an appearance of the risen Christ (Matt. 28:8–10). This is the first narrative of a resurrected Jesus being seen by anyone in the entire Bible. It is the ninth decade.

Matthew then relates the details of what had been in Mark only the promise of a Galilean appearance to the disciples (Matt. 28:16–20). To the surprise of many fundamentalists, however, it is not a vision of a resuscitated body. Examine the text closely.

Matthew's disciples are physical; they are bound by the laws of nature. They have to climb the mountain. Jesus on the other hand is quite unbound; he comes out of the sky. He has been raised into the meaning of God, and since God was still thought of as living above the sky, Jesus must come from above.

Please note an important distinction in this narrative. Jesus is not a victim; he is a victor, glorified and already endowed with heavenly power. He speaks. His words would later be called the "Great Commission": Go into all the world, make disciples of all nations and lo, I am with you always. Was this a missionary charge to go convert the heathen? Not a chance! There was no institutional church at that time that felt the need to gain converts. The risen Christ was saying, rather, go beyond your boundaries, your fears, your lines of security; learn to give yourselves away and know that you are part of who I am. We cannot now be separated! It is a different message of Easter from the one about which we have previously been told.

Next Luke writes, about a decade later. By this time, literal minds have begun to do their work of falsifying the message. The messenger in Mark, who became an angel in Matthew, has now become two angels in Luke (Luke 24:4). The body of Christ has become unmistakably physical. Luke's resurrected Jesus eats, he drinks, he walks, he talks and he interprets scripture (Luke 24:36–49). Yet he also seems to be able to materialize out of thin air and later to dematerialize into thin air (Luke 24:13–35). The symbols are confusing. He becomes so physical that the disciples feel his flesh and bones to make sure he is not a ghost (Luke 24:39), but then they begin to wonder how he will ever escape the limits of this life. The conclusion begins to grow that if he has been bodily restored from death, back into the physical life of this world, then somehow he must also be able to be bodily removed from the earth, since his eternal destiny is to be with God. Those were the assumptions that made the story of a physical ascension necessary. We will examine the details of the ascension narrative in the next chapters.

Finally, to complete our sweep of the four gospels, we move on to John. The Fourth Gospel, as it is called, has four resurrection stories, framed in two pairs. The first pair begins with Magdalene's discovery of the empty tomb (John 20:1). She goes at once to report this to a couple of the disciples, who apparently are close by. Their concern is not with the possibility of resurrection, one assumes, but with the suspicion of grave robbery. Peter, we are told, together with the one called only "the disciple whom Jesus loved," ran to the tomb. Entering it, they found it quite empty; only the grave clothes remained. No body appears to anyone. Peter is perplexed, but we are told that the "beloved disciple" believes (John 20:2–10). Belief in the resurrection is thus born in the Fourth Gospel, not in the vision of a resurrected body, but in the realization that the boundaries of death have been broken. These two disciples then return to their place of hiding.

Magdalene lingers at the tomb weeping. Jesus then, we are told, appears to her alone (John 20:11–18). She does not recognize him, thinking him to be the gardener. He speaks her name. Her eyes open with new understanding. She sees. She rushes to embrace him. "Do not hold me," Jesus says. Do not cling to this body. That is not what resurrection is about. Based upon this experience, Magdalene tells the disciples: "I have seen the Lord." With that, John's first pair of resurrection stories is complete.

The scene then shifts to the other disciples. Two almost identical stories are now told, covering a period of eight days. In the first of these stories (John 20:19–23), Thomas is absent. In the second (John 20:24–29), Thomas is present. The disciples see Jesus at once, at his first appearance, but the absent Thomas does not see and remains apart from their faith. Jesus then appears again eight days later. This time Thomas is present and he too sees. In response he makes the ultimate confession of faith: You, Jesus, are "my Lord and my God." Jesus responds with what was surely the reason those two stories were included: "Thomas, have you believed because you have seen me? Blessed are those who have not seen and yet believe."

The Easter experience in the New Testament, contrary to what we have traditionally been taught over the years, is not about bodies walking out of graves. It is far more profound than that. It is about God being seen in human life. By "God" I do not mean a supernatural, invasive God, who violates the laws of nature in order to enter time and space. I mean a transcendent dimension of life into which all can enter, an experience in which life is expanded, love is unlimited and being is enhanced. I mean the God whose presence and power calls us all into our essential oneness, our universal consciousness, our interconnectedness. We are part of who and what God is. God is not a noun we are compelled to define; God is a verb that we are invited to live. There is a difference, and it is in that difference that resurrection is both experienced and entered. That, in the last analysis, is what resurrection is all about.

PART X

Thesis 8:
The Ascension

The biblical story of Jesus' ascension assumes a three-tiered universe, a concept that was dismissed some five hundred years ago. If Jesus' ascension was a literal event of history, it is beyond the capacity of our twenty-first-century minds to accept or to believe it. Does the ascension have any other meaning, or must we defend first-century astrophysics?

25

Elijah Magnified

The gospels of Mark and Matthew were composed while the Christian movement was still part of the synagogue. The gospel of Luke may well have been written after the fracture that caused the Christians to be expelled from the synagogue, but because Luke based his gospel largely on the gospel of Mark, his work still reflects the organizing form of the synagogue. All three of these gospels were originally created, we now recognize, to provide Jesus stories for the seasons and Sabbaths of the synagogue's liturgical year. That is why the story of the crucifixion was told against the backdrop of the Passover and why Matthew placed what came to be called the Sermon on the Mount against the synagogue's observance of Shavuot, or Weeks, the day set aside to celebrate God giving the Torah through Moses at Mt. Sinai. That is also why John the Baptist was associated so deeply with the synagogue's observance of Rosh Hashanah. That holiday, also called the Jewish New Year, was the time when people prayed for the messiah to come. John the Baptist, as we saw in chapter 19, was cast in the role of the new Elijah, who according to Jewish messianic thought had to prepare the way for the messiah's arrival. So John the Baptist entered the gospel tradition not as a person of history, but as a Rosh Hashanah literary figure. The stories of Jesus as a healer were, as we noted in the section on miracles, told first as part of the Jewish observance of Yom Kippur, the Day of Atonement, in which the goodness of health overcomes the evil of physical distress. Being made physically whole was a sign that the kingdom of God was breaking in and that the messiah was at hand. The pattern of following the synagogue's liturgical year served as the organizing principle of the three synoptic gospels, so we find in each of them appropriate Jesus stories for Sukkoth, Dedication and even the minor festivals of the Ninth of Ab and Purim. Once we begin to understand the pattern, a crack opens into the original meaning of the synoptic gospels and we can begin to see just how it was that so many of the stories in the Hebrew scriptures were simply lifted out of the ancient texts, magnified and wrapped around Jesus of Nazareth.

The literary connections between Moses and Jesus were especially strong in Matthew's gospel, and they become quite obvious once the principle has been established. Both Moses and Jesus were subjected to the attempt by a wicked king to destroy them in infancy. Both were said to have fed the multitudes in the wilderness. Both had Red Sea–splitting experiences, wandering-in-the-wilderness experiences, and trials or temptations in that wilderness. Both went up on a mountain to get a new understanding of God's law. I have examined these connections in detail in my last book entitled *Biblical Literalism: A Gentile Heresy.*[*]

Luke, a gospel written to a congregation of diaspora (or dispersed) Jews that was just beginning to attract Gentile proselytes into its midst, had a rather different agenda from that of Matthew. So Elijah, the father of the prophetic movement, served Luke much better than did Moses, as the figure through whom Jesus was to be interpreted. A close reading of Luke reveals this broader world into which Jesus, as the new Elijah, fitted so well.

---

[*] See bibliography for details.

In Matthew's genealogy, the lineage of Jesus went back only to Abraham, who was regarded as the father of the Jewish nation. Luke, writing for his more expansive, cosmopolitan audience, took his genealogy of Jesus all the way back to Adam, the father of all humankind. This way Gentiles as well as Jews could be included.

We also see in Luke's gospel a much deeper dependency on the Elijah/Elisha narratives than anywhere else in the New Testament. In the Hebrew scriptures we are told that Elijah raises from the dead the only son of a widow. In Luke's gospel, as we noted in the section on miracles, Jesus repeats that Elijah story by raising from the dead the only son of a widow in the village of Nain. Elisha, Elijah's successor, healed a foreigner, a Syrian named Naaman, of leprosy. Luke has Jesus heal a Samaritan (also a foreigner) of leprosy in a story which no other gospel writer relates. The similarities abound.

The most obvious Elijah story that Luke retells about Jesus, however, is the story of Elijah's ascension. Here the way Luke uses Elijah to interpret Jesus becomes quite clear. I turn now to the story of Elijah's ascension so that we can examine these connections. This story is told in II Kings 2.

At the end of Elijah's life, the text informs us, he took his single disciple, Elisha, and they journeyed together into the wilderness to have a rendezvous with God. On this journey they talked about Elijah's imminent departure and Elisha's succession to the role of the "prophet of Israel." When they reached their destination, they began what would prove to be their final conversation. Elisha opened it by making a request of his master. I paraphrase for emphasis.

"Master, if I am to be your successor, may I make a final request of you?" Elijah responded by saying: "What is it, my son? Speak on." So Elisha continued: "If I am to do the work you have asked me to do, I need to be endowed with a double portion of your spirit!" To this request, Elijah responded: "I do not know that I have the power to grant you that," he said, "but if you see me ascending into the sky, then you will know that your request has been granted by God."

At that moment, according to this magnificent Jewish story, a magical, fiery chariot, drawn by magical, fiery horses, appeared out of the sky and swooped down to the ground, coming to a halt at exactly the spot where Elijah and Elisha were talking. It was as if this were a regular stop on this heavenly chariot's bus route! Without so much as a fare-thee-well, Elijah stepped immediately into that chariot to begin his ascension into heaven, perhaps waving his hand in farewell.

Even the ancients, however, knew that some kind of propulsion was required to transcend the forces of gravity, about which they knew almost nothing, but which they accepted as a fact of life. So the text says that God created a whirlwind that came roaring behind the fiery chariot. Pulled by the magical horses, this chariot bearing Elijah was thus propelled into the sky and to heaven by a whirlwind.

Elisha, standing on the earth below, we are told, watched in wonder. He cried out: "My father! My father! The chariots and horsemen of Israel!" The most important detail in this story was that Elisha, seeing the ascension of his master, knew that his request had been granted: He would be endowed with a double portion of Elijah's powerful, unique and yet still human spirit. It was and is a lovely story. The people of the Middle East were second to none as storytellers.

Luke saw Jesus as the new Elijah, but one whom he believed had become far more filled with the presence of God than had been the first Elijah. So Luke magnified this story. The new Elijah did not need the help of a magical chariot drawn by fiery horses. He did not need the heaven-sent whirlwind. As one who was God-sent and God-filled, he would return to God on his own.

Jesus also did not, as Elijah did, have a double portion of his enormous, but still human spirit to bequeath to his disciples. Luke had him go one better: The new and greater Elijah was said by Luke to be in possession of God's Holy Spirit, which he could bequeath not just to a single disciple, but to *all* of his disciples, then and throughout the ages. Luke's Jesus was Elijah magnified in the hope that by endowing him with these expanded images, Luke could capture and communicate to his readers the essence of this Christ, who had made God's presence so near and so available.

So it was that Luke took the story of the ascension of Elijah and his gift to his single disciple of a double portion of his spirit and expanded it almost, but not quite, beyond recognition. The result was the story of the ascension of Jesus into heaven and the subsequent outpouring of the Holy Spirit at Pentecost, both of which are uniquely Lucan stories, repeated nowhere else in the New Testament.

When one sees who it was upon whom the Holy Spirit fell at Pentecost, one sees immediately the universal message of Luke's gospel. "Men from every nation under heaven," Luke said, were gathered there at Pentecost. They included "Parthians, Medes, Elamites, residents of Mesopotamia, Judea, Cappadocia, Pontus, Asia, Phrygia, Pamphylia, Egypt, Libya, visitors from Rome, Jews, proselytes, Cretans and Arabians" (Acts 2:1–13). Given the knowledge of geography available in the first century, this was a remarkably inclusive list, even if it did call human beings "men"!

Luke knew that his ascension story, along with his Pentecost account, was not literal history, but he also knew that the inclusive love of God was universal, so he told this story. Today we are invited to hear its meaning, and to escape its literal understanding. Gospel truth can never finally be contained in the vocabulary of our humanity.

     The ascension story is both powerful and real, but it is not, and was never intended to be, literally true.

PART XI

Thesis 9: Ethics

The ability to define and separate good from evil can no longer be achieved with appeals to ancient codes such as the Ten Commandments or even the Sermon on the Mount. Contemporary moral standards must be hammered out in the juxtaposition between life-affirming moral principles and external situations. No modern person has any choice but to be a situationist.

26

Finding the Basis for Ethics

Finding a basis for making ethical decisions in our contemporary world is a far more complicated process than most people seem to imagine. This is especially true for those who continue to insist that ultimate authority lies in some ancient code of laws, such as the Ten Commandments or even the Sermon on the Mount. In this section of our attempt to inaugurate a new reformation, we bring ethical decision-making into the full focus of our attention. Doing so, we face the fact that, whether we like it or not, the mythology that has grown up around all ancient codes of law must be dismantled and ethical relativity will have to be embraced. We begin with an illustration that I invite you only to imagine, not to copy. It is designed to illustrate the fact that an identical action might be regarded as good in one context and as insensitive, inappropriate and wrong in another.

On a Sunday afternoon in America's "great cathedrals" of worship, our sometimes-billion-dollar sport stadiums, thousands of fans gather during the football season, often braving extreme cold, in order to see a game in person. Simultaneously, millions of additional fans view the game around the world on television. In the clear vision of literally millions of people, therefore, a 240-pound linebacker will be seen regularly walking back and forth between the tackles and guards, who form the football line of scrimmage. These linemen are now in a three-point pose, ready to charge at the next snap of the football. The linebacker will exhort the linemen verbally, and not infrequently he will even swat their upturned derrieres to urge them forward. Most of the people who see this interchange will think it so normal that they might not even notice it, much less remember it. No one watching would regard it as inappropriate.

Suppose, however, that we change the context from a football stadium to a church sanctuary during a Sunday-morning service of worship. The worshippers have come forward to receive the bread and wine of the Eucharist. They are kneeling in a row at the altar rail. Now imagine an usher, or even an acolyte, following the example of the linebacker, walking up and down behind these kneeling people and swatting each of them on their behinds. Would people notice? You bet they would! Not only would they notice, but this behavior would be viewed as weird, hostile, offensive, abusive and inappropriate.

Yet if we were to isolate the specific act from the two contexts, a football game and a service of worship, we would have to conclude that the deed done was identical. This leads us to our first ethical principle. The judgment as to the goodness or badness of a particular human action depends, not just on the act itself, but on the context in which the act is carried out. Subjectivity in ethical judgments is thus inescapable.

Look next at those substances which our human society has defined as "drugs." One of these drugs, the one we call alcohol, is used in the form of a fine wine to give grace and elegance to a banquet table. It is thus viewed as good. Alcohol, however, can be and often is used in other forms to perpetuate the hopelessness of a lost soul living on the fringes of society. The alcohol is the same; the context in which the alcohol is used renders the judgment.

This principle can be viewed from still another perspective. We have in our society become dependent on rather sophisticated drugs manufactured by a vast pharmaceutical industry. In the hands of a trained physician these drugs are dispensed to ease pain and to facilitate healing. In that context the drugs are life-giving. Sometimes, however, those same drugs are used as a coping device by a desperate person. In that context they can be and often are life-destroying. Good and evil are not fixed categories; they never have been. No matter what the religious claims of the past have been, it is now impossible to build an ethical system on the basis of an unchanging or eternal standard. Claims that some rule both is unchanging and comes from a divine source are today little more than lingering religious illusions. Those who seek to lead us to new studies and insights must face this reality, deal with it, dismiss it and look elsewhere for guidance in determining just what it is that makes good "good" and evil "evil."

It is the common practice of religious people not only not to acknowledge these uncertainties, but also never, ever to face them. The term "relativity" in ethics is considered a dirty word in conservative religious circles. Relativity, nonetheless, confronts human beings at every turn and in every decision they make. One of the reasons that religious people do not want to admit relativity is that it forces adult decision-making on them. It is so much easier to remain childlike and to pretend that there is a set of eternal rules which one just has to learn and agree to apply. Human beings want to believe that they can define the terms "moral" and "immoral" in a definitive way. It is, however, the existential context of life that more often than not determines what is good and what is evil.

We begin our search by asking a couple of questions. From where does the human sense arise that some things are good and others are evil? How do we cope with the slippery ethical slope which tells us that all rules are human and all rules are subjective? This apparently bottomless pit of uncertainty drives us in search of some essential ethical standard of ultimacy which forms an essential norm that we hope, and sometimes pretend, will define good and evil objectively for all time. We assume that such a norm must exist. Frequently, once we think we have found this norm or standard, we elevate it to a status that is beyond questioning. We treat it with great respect. In the Western Judeo-Christian world that has been the fate of the Ten Commandments. Look at the importance our whole society has attached to that traditional standard.

In many Christian churches built in the eighteenth and nineteenth centuries, the Ten Commandments were displayed in a prominent place on an inside wall for worshippers to see. The most popular form for this display was a depiction of the commandments inscribed on a stone tablet, for stone tablets are not only biblical, but they also give the impression of indestructability. Not infrequently, these commandments would be on not one, but two stone tablets, the first one including those commandments that we in our Christian catechisms have called "our duty toward God." These are the commandments (1–4) that tell us that God is one, that no "graven image" can be made to compete with God and that God's name and God's day must be honored. The second tablet would include those commandments (5–10) that are thought to spell out "our duty toward our neighbor": Honor your parents, do not kill, do not commit adultery, do not steal, do not bear false witness and do not covet.

In the early days of my life attending church, I was treated to the opportunity of hearing the Ten Commandments recited in worship on a regular basis. It happened on the first Sunday of each month. The prayer book instructed the members of the congregation to respond to the recitation of each individual commandment with the words: "Lord, have mercy upon us and incline our hearts to keep this law." When the final commandment was recited, we were taught to say: "Lord, have mercy upon us and write all these thy laws in our hearts, we beseech thee." Great power and authority were attached to these holy words.

In Sunday school in my church when I was in the fifth grade, the entire year was devoted to a study of the Ten Commandments. My teacher, a man named Herbert Darrow, whom I recall as a "godly man," led us meticulously through the sacred ten until we had completed our work on commandment number six: "Thou shalt not kill." Then to our surprise he went directly to the eighth commandment: "Thou shalt not steal." Being a perceptive student and literally having no idea what "adultery" meant, I raised my hand and when recognized said: "Mr. Darrow, you skipped commandment number seven. What does adultery mean?" His response was indelible. Flustered and upset at being asked, he responded: "You will learn about that when you get older!" Unfortunately, that is the only thing I remember from that entire Sunday school year.

A decline in the cultural power attributed to the Ten Commandments began to set in in the twentieth century. My church changed its liturgical directions to make the reading of the Ten Commandments voluntary, not mandatory. The result was that the Ten Commandments quickly fell into liturgical disuse. Why did my church take this action? Perhaps it was the fact that both the new scientific discourse and the period of history we refer to as the Enlightenment had served to erode our confidence in the supernatural deity, whose will these commandments were thought to express. Perhaps we discovered too many exceptions to the rules, which served to destroy the objectivity of this ancient moral code, or at least to weaken its authority permanently. Whatever the cause, a very real demise was felt, and that demise in the authority of the Ten Commandments was accompanied by a heightened sense of anxiety. To many conservative Christians, rampant immorality appeared to be the only real alternative to the cultural move away from this code of antiquity.

A judge in Alabama, Roy S. Moore, decided in 2001 that, in the service of his fundamentalist faith, he would install in his courtroom a two-ton statue on which the Ten Commandments were inscribed. Since he believed that these ten laws had been dictated by God, in his mind he was doing nothing other than defending God's truth. He was, however, charged with violating the constitutional amendment that guarantees the separation of church and state. His supporters rallied to his side. His critics were called "godless," "immoral" and "modernistic." Moore suggested that his enemies were those who were eager to remove God and God's words from America's courts of justice. The law prevailed, however, and Judge Moore's statue was removed.[*]

Most people do not know that there is a wide sectarian disagreement over the order and even the way the commandments are numbered. Judge Moore's Ten Commandments were not "objective" at all, as he claimed. On his statue he had followed the order of the Protestant version of these commandments.[†] I happened to be in Montgomery, Alabama, during the time of this controversy, and so I went with my wife to see Judge Moore's statue before it was removed. On the back were the words "copy-

---

[*] In the fall of 2017 Judge Moore won the Republican nomination for the U.S. senate from Alabama. Though we thought him largely discredited, he has returned to a place of prominence.

[†] Many people are not aware that the commandments are numbered differently by different faith communities. Roman Catholics and Lutherans combine the first two commandments, "You shall have no other gods" and "You shall make no graven images," into a single first commandment. Then they split the tenth commandment regarding coveting into two parts. Both ways, they come out to ten!

right 2001 Judge Roy S. Moore." Surely by this time, the Ten Commandments were in the public domain!

Are these commandments eternal? Are they unchallengeable? I do not think so. I will move next to trace the difference between religious rhetoric and religious practice in regard to the Ten Commandments. They are not the same.

27

How the Ten Commandments Have Changed Through History

One of the ways the demise of yesterday's religious power can be determined is to notice that things once held to be ultimately sacred now appear in jokes that not only cause people to laugh, but also cause them to be aware of the loss of those sacred symbols. Such jokes, therefore, produce nervous laughter and simultaneous fear. When James Watt, the secretary of the interior in the cabinet of President Ronald Reagan, told a racial joke, he was summarily fired. Yet the racist content of that joke had been commonplace in the social milieu of this nation twenty-five years earlier. Consciousness had grown over that quarter century. *One does not make fun of something so evil as racism* had become the new rule. This same sort of consciousness-raising experience is also observed when one discovers that one does and can laugh at what were once regarded as "the eternal laws of God." One politician came to the defense of the "inerrancy" of this code of laws by saying: "The Bible calls them the Ten Commandments, not the Ten Suggestions."

There was also a good news, bad news joke about the Ten Commandments that made the rounds. Moses, returning from Mt. Sinai, supposedly said to the people of Israel: "I have good news and bad news." "Give us the good news first," the people demanded. "Well," said Moses in obedience to their request, "I negotiated them down to ten!" "What is the bad news?" the people shouted in response. To which Moses responded, "Adultery is still in!"

Finally, there was a message on a church's lawn sign where people were given their "word for the day." This sign boldly advertised: "This week's special! Observe any seven of the Ten Commandments." Humor about the Ten Commandments clearly reveals a demise in the power once attributed to this code of ethics. Another indicator of the demise came for me with the realization that the *form* the commandments possess now has more importance than the *content*. Early in my career as a bishop, I went for my annual episcopal visitation to a congregation in Hudson County, New Jersey. On that Sunday we had about a hundred worshippers gathered to greet and welcome their bishop. When the time came for the sermon, I stepped out of the pulpit and walked into the nave, the body of the church. This was going to be an informal sermon.

When they were settled in their pews and adjusted to this new sermon position taken by their bishop, I began by asking: "How many of you believe that the Ten Commandments are still important?" Every hand in the church went up. No one actually in a church on Sunday morning wanted to be caught suggesting that this ancient code of conduct was not of great significance, authority and power. I took note of their unanimity. "That is good to see," I said, in effect congratulating them on their moral judgment.

Then I continued: "Since you all agree on their importance, who would now like to stand up and recite the Ten Commandments?" Every hand went down; there was not a volunteer among them. I enhanced the corporate guilt felt in that moment in a rather shameless way by saying: "You mean that you believe that the Ten Commandments are important, but none of you can tell me what they are?" I allowed that discomfort to be felt for just a moment before moving to dissipate it. "Well, let us see if all of us together can come up with ten," I suggested. There was an almost audible sense of relief. No one was now on the spot. "Who would like to begin by telling us what any one of the Ten Command-ments is?" Hands went up quickly. Prohibitions against "murder" and "adultery" were immediately mentioned; they are almost always recounted first. They were followed by another embar-rassing pause. Then a hand went up, but when I recognized this person, the commandment she referred to came out as a question: "Honor your father and mother?" Yes, I responded reassuringly; that is commandment number five. When her tentative offering was accepted, others were encouraged. Next the commandment to "observe the Sabbath" was offered. "Number four," I declared it to be, and continued to wait for more. Soon plenty of other commandments were mentioned, including: "Love the Lord your God with all your heart, mind and strength" and "Love your neighbor as yourself." I allowed that those two were very fine rules, but they had never been part of the official ten. Finally, we got "stealing," number eight; "false witness," number nine; and "coveting," number ten. No one could actually define coveting, but that was not required by this exercise. The fact was slowly and somewhat painfully being revealed that these hundred or so worshippers could not, even all together, name all Ten Command-ments, which they had universally proclaimed that they believed to be still very important.* I have little reason to think that this

---

* The missing one was number three: "You shall not take the name of the Lord your God in vain."

congregation would be much different from one in any other
church on any other Sunday morning.

This exercise revealed to me that if average churchgoers do
not know what the Ten Commandments are, then they can no
longer claim, with any sense of real conviction, that the commandments themselves are still important. For me it was a sure
sign of the erosion of any real objectivity still present in the field
of ethics. It also indicated to me very boldly that eternal rules
designed to govern human behavior will never again be written
in the permanence of stone, and that none of us who claim to
speak for the church can continue to pretend that these ancient
laws still provide the ethical basis on which anyone today lives.
The suggestion that moral absolutes could ever be codified for
all time violates our experience. The rules that must govern any
real debate on ethics are no longer obvious. Context always
modifies judgment. Life is never static. No rule, no ethical norm
is ever eternal. We all make our moral judgments based on the
situation in which we find ourselves, whether we can admit that
or not.

Who was it who proclaimed in the first place that the Ten
Commandments were the voice of God speaking? At this point,
we are driven to probe the mythology that has been built up
around that code. Mythology is always designed to prevent its
subject from being discussed, questioned or getting lost in relativity. Once we understand mythology's purpose, we can both ask
and access just how accurate this particular mythology is. "Not
very" is my conclusion, and I suspect it will be yours too, after we
engage in a bit of biblical study.

In many ways I must confess that I was unfair to my New Jersey congregation, because *no one* can name the Ten Commandments! This is a shocking statement to which most people react

with consternation. It does not jibe with what most all of us have been taught for so long. The fact is, however, that the Hebrew scriptures contain three versions of the Ten Commandments and they do not agree with each other. They cannot be rolled into a consistent ten! Tradition alone has dictated that the version found in Exodus 20 is the official version. A brief analysis of this Exodus list, however, will reveal that it is different from anything that Moses might have received.

How do we know? Because the commandment regarding the observance of the Sabbath in the Exodus 20 list was edited, we've learned through biblical scholarship, to bring it into conformity with the seven-day story of creation with which the Hebrew Bible opens. That Genesis chapter, we now know, was one of the last parts of the Hebrew scriptures to be composed. It was the product of the Jews living in the Babylonian captivity, which ended near the end of the sixth century BCE. Moses had been dead some six hundred years by that time. Furthermore, this was not the earliest version of the Ten Commandments, as we shall see.

So we have to assume, first, that an oral tradition carried the Ten Commandments from the time of Moses to the much later written form, which is in an earlier document of the Jewish people that we call the Elohist document. This strand of written history of the Jews probably appeared about 830 BCE. Second, we have to assume that a sixth-century-BCE writer, one of a group we today describe as "the priestly writers," then edited the commandments in such a way as to make the seven-day story of creation the standard version. Moses lived, according to most estimates, in the middle to last years of the thirteenth century BCE. Biblical scholarship thus challenges biblical mythology. We know this because the reason given for requiring the people to rest on the Sabbath was to emulate God who, on the seventh day of creation in that much later creation story, had rested from all of the divine labor and had enjoined that Sabbath day of rest on the people as a sign of their Jewishness (Exod. 20:11).

It is interesting to note that the version of the Ten Commandments found in Deuteronomy 5, which was written during the latter years of the seventh century BCE, also calls for the Sabbath to be observed, not on the basis of God resting on the seventh day (for that narrative had not yet been written), but on the fact that the Jews were to remember that they had once been slaves in Egypt and that even slaves, to say nothing of the cattle and other beasts of burden, deserved a day of rest (v. 15).

The third version of the Ten Commandments, but probably the oldest of the three lots, is found in Exodus 34. It is far more cultic and less ethical in its scope. The background to this narrative is that God was forced to rewrite the commandments because Moses had smashed the original tablets of stone on the ground in disgust when, on returning from Sinai, he found the people worshipping a golden calf. This version begins by defining God as "merciful and gracious, slow to anger and abounding in steadfast love and faithfulness." One is not to imagine, however, that these writers have made God soft or easy to manipulate. The text in Exodus 34 goes on to say that this God will not sit idly by when evil needs to be punished. On the contrary, God will visit "the iniquities of the fathers upon the children to the third and fourth generation." God then goes on to promise to drive out all the current occupants of the "Holy Land." Only then are the rules of the covenant stated: Israel is to have no other God, the Sabbath is to be observed and the sacrifices are to be done properly. The last commandment in this group of ten states: "You shall not boil a kid in its mother's milk." I must confess that I have never even been tempted to violate that commandment!

We can safely conclude that the Ten Commandments were never themselves meant to be an eternal code. They changed in history; they were edited. The ethical life has always been an adventure. The subject of ethical relativity is now open, and we will continue to pursue it until we reach new conclusions.

28

Meet Moses' Father-in-Law

We have thus far relativized the mythical claims made for the code by which the people of Israel claimed to live, by noting that even the Bible reveals confusion about the source of the Ten Commandments. These laws clearly emerged out of the common life of the people over a long period of time. They did not come down from on high, the revelation of the divine will. They grew over the centuries and were adapted to new circumstances as the Israelites' life changed and developed. That is why there are different versions of these commandments in the biblical text itself. The fact that the people themselves could not agree on the content of the code of law by which they claimed to live tells us that we are dealing with a human invention. Only once the code was widely accepted did mythology grow up around it.

Before pressing more deeply into the meaning of the Ten Commandments, I pause for a slight detour into that mythology. To understand this story, we go to the Exodus 20 version, which is closest to what people began to agree culturally constituted the "law of God." Even in this version, however, the biblical narrative makes it clear that these laws were designed to meet very real human needs. Not one in a thousand people will know this story, but it is in the Bible and has been available to us for hundreds of years. Because it didn't fit into the developed mythology around the Ten Commandments, we have tended to ignore it. If we seek to understand what the ultimate ethical demands are by which we can live, if we succeed in going beyond the response of earlier generations, then it is worthwhile to lift this story into our conscious minds. The details, presented in the chapters preceding the commandments themselves, are as follows (Exod. 18).

The Torah with its opening set of Ten Commandments arose, according to the Bible, from the suggestion of Moses' father-in-law, a man named Jethro, who was called in the Exodus story "a priest of Midian." This man, viewed by the people of Israel as a kind of elder statesman, on one occasion observed Moses acting as the judge, resolving all of the disputes that arose among the people of Israel. As their acknowledged leader, Moses was thought to be the only one who knew the will of God well enough to be capable of judging his people and adjudicating their conflicts. Only Moses was believed to have talked with God face to face on the top of Mt. Sinai, so only Moses could be trusted to interpret the law accurately in human disputes.

So Jethro, convinced that Moses could not long continue to be the sole judge of Israel, asked Moses to set up a tiered legal system of judges. For every ten members of the nation, he suggested, one man should be appointed judge to settle disputes that arose from within this group of ten. Any problems unable to be solved at the level of ten would then be appealed to the next level—to the judge who served as the decision-maker over a group of a hundred. If the person appointed judge over a hundred could not solve the problem, it would be appealed to the judge who was set up over a group of a thousand. Under this system of tiered decision-making, only those cases which could not be settled at the level of a thousand would come to the attention of Moses. Judging the disputes of the people would no longer be an overwhelming task falling on the shoulders of one man, but rather a manageable task resting on an appellate system.

This system's weakness lay in its lack of objectivity. By what standard would the judges on each level make their decisions? The will of God needed to be objectively applied, lest subjectivity destroy confidence in both the law and the judge. Moses saw the wisdom in Jethro's suggestion, and so the stage was set for this system to be put in place and for the law of God to be dictated to Moses in objective words that all could follow. Powerful symbols were then employed around the handing down of these "divine" rules. Those symbols included darkness, clouds, earthquakes and fire (Exod. 19). Mystery abounded, and the people were in a state of high expectation as they gathered at the foot of what came to be called God's holy mountain. They were prohibited, on pain of death, from coming too close to the mountain. Only Moses and Aaron the high priest, who was Moses' brother, could actually enter into the presence of God. Those who had been chosen as the judges over the people, however, could come partway up the mountain, but only after undergoing elaborate acts of ritualistic cleansing, which set them apart from the rest of the people. While they were not allowed into the literal presence of God, they could come close enough to be validated in their roles as judges.

So with the people aligned in tiers on that mountain according to their authority, with Moses and Aaron alone in God's presence, God spoke and the Torah was formed. The Ten Commandments were the first part of the Torah and gave voice to the universal principles. Then came the rest of the Torah, designed, as it was, to cover every individual breach that might occur among the people: how to act, how to worship, what was clean and what was unclean, all were covered. The law flowed from God, first to Moses and Aaron, then to the priests and judges and finally to the people. God's will for God's people was thus objectified and written down. Now those who judged the people had to judge them not by their own whims or with their own authority, but by the written law of God. Objectivity banished relativity, for "the law" was dictated by God and written down for all to see and to read. This provided the people with security, a single standard and at least the illusion of objectivity. The anxiety created by subjectivity was thus minimized.

The power of both truth and the will of God were now contained in written words, objective codes and articulated laws. That was always the way the laws were legitimized in the ancient world. Revelation as the source of truth was and is always mythological. Codes of law, thus attributed to God's revelation, were erected to minimize the anxiety of relativity. The fact is, however, that no code has God as its source and no code can or will endure forever. Knowledge changes; experiences expand; interaction with others challenges the version of truth by which a person or a community lives. How does one balance individual rights against the corporate welfare of the people? How does one define the stranger or even the enemy within one's gates that the law requires you to love? How does one determine justice when two virtues are in conflict? Remember the story of King Solomon, who was asked to determine who the real mother of a disputed child was? His solution was to draw his sword and threaten to divide the child into two parts, purportedly so that each mother would get equal justice (I Kings 3:16–28). That is sometimes the nature of life. Did not both Robert E. Lee and Ulysses S. Grant pray to the same God for victory?

How much relativity or ethical situationism can the average human life manage? The answer is not very much. The urge to have an objective standard of right and wrong, operating in every situation, is a response to authority, not to freedom. The ability to weigh the options presented in a particular set of circumstances requires a level of maturity that most people do not have and cannot embrace. As the world grows more complex, however, that is what is and will be required of us.

If God, defined theistically, is no longer a possibility for modern men and women to embrace, so is every claim that there are objective laws that express the will of this theistic deity. That being so, where do we go to determine what is right and good, what is wrong and evil? It can never be an objective code revealed by a theistic deity from any of the symbolic mountaintops where God is perceived to be speaking directly to you and me. The days of claiming to know the ultimate will of the theistic deity on any subject are over.

What then is left as an ethical norm for our times? Are we to be victimized by a code based on might as the ultimate arbiter of right? Is the "golden rule" to be reduced to the cynical, often quoted "Those who have the gold, rule?" Was Nikita Khrushchev, the former leader of what was then called the Soviet Union, correct when he said that God is always on the side of those who have the biggest army and the most powerful weapons? Or is there another standard that we must seek to discover? St. Augustine is quoted, perhaps apocryphally, as having said that ethical behavior is to be determined by this single assertion: "We are to love God and do whatever we please"—in other words, we cannot go wrong if love of God is at the heart of every decision we make and every action we take. Will that work? Not unless we define very carefully what it means to love God, but perhaps in this statement, we can find a new starting point for ethical conversations. At least we must try.

If God is love, as we constantly assert, then how does one live out this love? If God's call to us is to live abundantly, then how do we know what abundant life is? If God is the Ground of Being, then what does it mean to enhance the being of another? Perhaps this spiritual wrestling is what St. Paul meant when he exhorted us to work out our salvation with fear and trembling (Phil. 2:12). He added that it is "God who is working within us."

God is not a being, external to the world, prepared to invade life from on high to establish the divine will on earth. That claim, so familiar in religious circles, is nothing but an expression of the yearning present in the childhood of our humanity to explain the inexplicable. As we saw in earlier chapters, recent centuries of scientific research and discovery have refuted that theistic deity. God is, rather, a process into which we live. *Life*, *love* and *being* are the operative words. What actions expand life? What actions increase love? What actions enhance being? That is the arena in which good must ultimately be separated from evil. Our ethical answers will never be found within a code of yesterday. They will always be found in the struggle to live fully, to love beyond the boundaries of our security, in the affirmation found at the depth of our being. Do we then dismiss the great codes of the past? No, but we also do not endow them with the status of ultimate and unchanging laws. We do, however, ascribe to them the wisdom of the ages, and we give to our ancestors, who codified those laws, the courtesy of our attention.

We next will turn to look at the Ten Commandments from this perspective. They will look quite different.

29

The Questionable Relevance of the Ten Commandments Today

We have thus far exploded the myth found in the idea that the Ten Commandments or any other ancient code of law was ever dictated by God. A corollary of this insight is that our laws always arise out of the common experience of the people. We have examined the biblical data, which suggest that the Ten Commandments did not have a single source, but came in three versions (Exod. 34, Exod. 20 and Deut. 5) born out of different times and circumstances. Next we found evidence that this code has been dramatically edited at various points in history, destroying forever the idea that those laws were either eternal or unchanging. If the commandments have changed in the past, they are surely subject to change in the future. Thus relativity replaces certainty. The claim that we have ever possessed objectivity through the divine revelation of the laws of God becomes hopelessly compromised by every standard we apply. All of these ethical conclusions are startling to those who like to pretend that right and wrong are objective categories and not subjective evaluations.

We begin now to explore these rules that we once held in such reverence and respect. To our dismay, we will discover that there is not a single commandment of the ten that is not itself both time-bound and time-warped. There are none among the ten that cannot be set aside under the stress of human circumstances. Before we seek to find a way to define both good and evil in a post-religious world, we need to spend just a little more time on why the old rules do not work and why we must all become situational ethicists. We begin by doubling back on the content of the commandments themselves.

The first commandment, saying that God is one and that we are to have no other gods, returns us to the nature of the divine. If the moral code is said to be the word or the revelation of God, then who or what is God? Earlier in the book, we noted that the traditional, theistic way of thinking about God as a being, living externally to this world and equipped with supernatural power, is no longer a viable option for belief among modern men and women. This God has been slain by the explosion of knowledge. We traced that explosion earlier. Once we discovered the size of the universe, we understood immediately that we had thereby destroyed God's dwelling place above the sky, rendering this God forever after homeless. Next, when we discovered the laws by which the universe operated, breathtakingly precise as they are, we destroyed most of the things we once suggested that God did. There was no longer any room for either miracle or magic, to say nothing of divine intervention into the realm of the human. In that process, we rendered the theistic God unemployed. God no longer, for example, was thought to control the weather or sickness, using them as a means of divine punishment. With that insight theism began its relentless retreat out of life.

No theistic God was involved directly in either enterprise any longer. So then what does it mean to proclaim the reality of this theistic God in the Ten Commandments? The words of the first commandment fall quickly into irrelevance.

Next, what does it mean to be told not to make any "graven images"? Who among us in the twenty-first century is tempted to violate this ancient prohibition? The closest modern parallel that I can think of is the fact that some people today still place a statue of the Virgin Mary or perhaps of St. Francis of Assisi in their yard or garden. While the people who do this might still be superstitious enough to attribute "good luck" to these statues, seldom do these graven images become objects of worship to modern people. If I were to list the ten great moral laws of the universe, a prohibition against making graven images would certainly not be among them.

Then we come to the commandment about not taking the name of the Lord in vain. What could that possibly mean today? First, I need to state that this commandment never had anything to do with profanity. Perhaps you say, "God damn it!" when you accidentally break a valuable vase on a marble countertop, or "Jesus Christ!" when you hit your thumb with a hammer. This language may not be in good taste—it may even be blasphemous, as it assumes that we have the right to tell God who or what to damn— but such words, let it be clearly stated, have nothing to do with the commandment about prohibiting us from taking the name of the Lord in vain. What then was that commandment about, and is it still relevant in our world today?

In the primitive culture of ancient Israel, there were no lawyers to write legal contracts and no courts to enforce the terms of a legal deal. So when a business transaction was agreed to between two negotiators, they would clasp hands and swear in the name of the Lord that they would be true to the bargain to which both had agreed. If later one or the other of them failed to abide by the agreed-upon terms of this deal, they were guilty of having "taken the name of the Lord in vain." That was this commandment's original meaning. Is such a law necessary or appropriate today?

The Sabbath, which we are commanded to keep holy by refraining from labor, was, in the Bible, the seventh day of the week—that is, Saturday. The Christian world (except for the Seventh Day Adventists) has, however, long since ceased to observe Saturday as a day for either rest or worship. By what authority, then, did we abandon Saturday for Sunday? There is no divine command in any authoritative source we know of to justify this shift, but culturally we simply did it. If the Ten Commandments can be ignored whenever we wish, then it is hard to suggest that they have any binding integrity or eternal status.

Honoring one's parents sounds like good advice, but it too is situational. Should parents who are abusive to their children continue to be honored by them? If the statistic is correct that up to forty percent of adult women in America experienced some kind of sexual molestation as children at the hands of a family member—sometimes a father or a grandfather—are those women still under some obligation to honor their parents?

How do we explain the history of war in the Western Christian world when that world still claims that the commandment "Thou shalt not kill" belongs in its most sacred code? How do we understand the history of anti-Semitism by which Christians justified the killing of Jews from the time of the church fathers to the Holocaust? How could the Vatican have launched the Crusades of the eleventh, twelfth and thirteenth centuries, which were designed to kill "infidels," our name for Muslims, and still proclaim that the commandment not to kill was revealed as the law of God? How were we Christians able to give lip service to the commandment not to kill during the Inquisition, in which heretics were regularly burned at the stake? How were we in the Bible Belt of the South able to resist by the filibusters of our senators the passing of an anti-lynching law? Does the commandment not to kill have any force?

Are there exceptions to the commandment prohibiting adultery? I was pastor to a woman once, a schoolteacher, who was unknowingly married to a homosexual male. Because her husband appeared to have no interest in her, she began to think that she must be either unattractive or unworthy of male attention. In time she had an affair which served to restore her sense of self-worth. Is adultery always wrong?

The commandment against stealing seems clear and constructive, but in Victor Hugo's great novel *Les Misérables,** Jean Valjean steals bread to keep his family alive. Was his stealing a sin, or was the sin found in the social system that ground some people into such poverty that stealing was a necessary survival technique? By what standard do we judge?

Is the truth what we must always tell? What if truth is rude: "I had a miserable time at your home this evening and your dinner was inedible." What if one truth violates another? What if the truth puts someone's life at risk? What if the truth is cruel and serves no redeeming value? Can the injunction against "bearing false witness" sometimes be less than positive—less than life-giving?

How about desire? Is it always bad? Does "keeping up with the Joneses" have no redeeming value, even when it drives a poor youngster to stay in school and make something of him- or herself? Where does admiring end and coveting begin? Where does necessity stop and greed take over?

It seems that *none* of these Ten Commandments can be in-

---

* See bibliography for details.

vested with ultimate, absolute authority. On what basis, then, do we determine that good is good and that evil is evil? If it is not on the basis of some absolute standard, then to what do we turn in search of ultimate answers? Does relative truth mean *no* truth? Does relativity in ethics mean *no* ethics? To those questions we will turn next.

30

Modern Ethics

As we have seen, both in previous chapters and in life, something considered good in one generation may be looked upon as evil in another. Knowledge changes in both form and value. That is what has happened to the Ten Commandments. We still, however, have to make decisions in a complex world. We still seek ethical guidance. Where are we to find it? I seek now only to illustrate these questions and find that fixed conclusions are increasingly not possible.

For most of my life, for example, I have contended that sex can be both good and holy only inside the relationship of ultimate commitment called marriage. This point of view has been echoed in the pronouncement of ecclesiastical institutions. If love and sex are separated, I contended, then people begin to use one another for their own gratification. When you "use" a person, you are making out of them a "thing" and thus you have dehumanized them. To dehumanize another is surely to do evil. I am still convinced that sex and love, to be moral, must in the majority of cases not be separated. A true story, however, removes this assertion's ultimate authority.

I met a young man once whose story showed me that "good" and "holy" are words that cannot escape being tempered by the external situation. This man was gay. He had been raised by parents who abhorred his homosexuality. They told him over and over again that his "desires" were dirty, distorted and evil. Without recognizing what they were doing, they created in him such self-hatred that ultimately their definition of him became his own definition of himself. He loathed his body and its biological yearnings. He grew up refusing to admit to anyone outside the family what he knew he was. He looked upon himself as an object of hatred, his own and that of others. He had his first sexual encounter as a late teenager in a bathhouse in San Francisco. He had no idea who his first lover was. He knew only that he was an older man; how much older he did not even want to guess. No words passed between the two people who shared this experience. Bathhouses are not places in which relationships are formed, but where sexual needs are gratified.

The young man was scared, but driven. Impersonal though that bathhouse sex act was, he told me later, it was the first time in his life that he had ever experienced the fact that his body had value, that it could give pleasure to another. At last he had been in the presence of someone who did not define him as grotesque, but rather as desirable and even enjoyable.

Religious moralists might well judge this encounter as a shallow experience in which love and sex were totally separated, but, contrary to that assessment, my young acquaintance found it to be life-affirming and life-expanding. I make no judgment. I simply ask the ethical question: Was this act good or evil? My earlier moralistic standards were challenged by that story; perhaps they were relativized. They were eventually replaced by a simpler standard: The expansion of life is good, while the diminution of life is evil.

That young man's story was only one of thousands that have been shared with me over the years. Experience has time after time tempered my moral judgments. My career in the ministry spanned the years between 1955 and today. An enormous revolution in sexual understanding occurred during those years. Marriage as the precondition of sex has faded. It was a rare wedding that I performed, especially in the latter half of my ministry, in which the couple was not already sexually active, and in many cases, even living together. Sex *only* inside marriage may have been the norm once, but it has become the rare exception today. How am I to understand this changing pattern? Is the bitter judgment of rampant immorality my only option? I decided to look at history.

Sex only inside marriage was the unquestioned value of the medieval Christian church. That standard, however, was designed to fit the circumstances of that day. No effective birth control existed then, so sexual activity ran the risk of pregnancy. In that day, girls entered puberty later than they do today (from fourteen to sixteen) and tended to get married one to two years after the onset of puberty. Life expectancy was short. During that brief period between puberty and marriage a rigid separation of the sexes was mandated by society. A chaperone system that governed at least the socially prominent female population was fixed and real. The chief enforcer of sexual separation was usually an unmarried member of the parental generation, perhaps a maiden aunt. These women of the upper classes were regarded as rigid paradigms of virtue. No great effort was made to guard the virginity of girls born into the families of peasants, however, nor was any effort made to rescue prostitutes. A double standard was clearly in place. Males were almost encouraged to act out their sexual prowess, as long as they did not compromise the "virginal purity" of the girls of the upper classes. "Boys will be boys" was in fact a statement of permission. Sexual abstinence prior to marriage for proper young ladies was the standard (if not always the reality) that fit this worldview. Then came the revolution.

Democratic patterns smoothed out the class system. Girls began to be welcomed into careers from which they had previously been barred. The need for females to receive higher education then grew, which in turn began to increase significantly the time span between puberty and marriage. Better diet and better health practices began to drive the age for the onset of puberty down. Coeducational schools became the norm, not the exception. The chaperone system all but disappeared. The automobile opened new doors of mobility and privacy. Suddenly we awakened to the realization that we had stretched the time between puberty and marriage from one or two years to ten to fifteen years. Is it reasonable to expect sexual activity to be repressed for so long a period of time? Can moral rules control biology? Is such an expectation natural, healthy, possible or even desirable? The risk of pregnancy was almost totally removed by safe, effective and legally available birth control methods. Suddenly no one was listening to the words out of the old code that basically said only: "Thou shalt not!" If a sexual practice becomes almost universal, does condemning it allow you into a dialogue with reality? Or does it simply reduce your voice to the fringes of society? Can a medieval standard live in a modern world in which all the cultural patterns that undergirded the medieval standard have disappeared?

Another sexual conundrum: Is faithfulness to one's partner in marriage an absolute or is it a relative value? Once again, I share a true story.

I once knew a young married couple, who though deeply in love faced a debilitating tragedy. The woman suffered a stroke at age thirty-five, which rendered her both paralyzed for life and sexually incompetent. Should that tragedy also serve to end the sexual life of her husband, who was thirty-six? He loved her and he cared for her for a long period of time with both sensitivity and compassion. As the years went by, however, he found himself increasingly resentful and even bitter. He never considered the possibility of separation or divorce. He honored the fact that their marriage vows had been to take each other "for better, for worse, . . . in sickness and in health, till death do us part." Despite his best efforts, however, his relationship with his wife became fragile. Neither had much ability to give to the other what that other needed.

Almost by accident—it certainly was not planned—this young husband met a widow who was more than fifteen years his senior. They enjoyed many of the same things, despite that age difference, and their friendship grew. Ultimately, it became a sexually active relationship. That relationship in turn brought a new dimension to both of their lives. In traditional religious circles, however, this relationship would be condemned as adultery. Yet even this man's paralyzed wife seemed to be a beneficiary. Her husband was less resentful, less bitter and thus a far more loving caregiver. It was certainly true that the traditional rule of marital faithfulness had been violated, but the real issue was whether one should look at this situation through moralistic eyes or life-affirming eyes. Was anyone hurt by this extramarital relationship? No one in the triangle of persons made demands on another that could not be met. If the fullness of life is the goal and intention of the traditional moral code, then when this value and that code are in conflict, should the fullness of life or the moral code be followed? Must not the rigidity of the law always be set aside in the service of the fullness of life?

Another moral debate hinges on the question of suicide. Is it ever right to take one's own life? No, has been the answer to that question emanating from the Christian church for centuries. Until very recently, one who completed the act of suicide was not given the privilege of an ecclesiastical funeral. Suicide represented human pridefulness of making a decision that rightfully belonged to God and was thus condemned as sinful. Today, however, physician-assisted suicide is legal in several nations of the world and in some parts of the United States. The debate on this issue rages in our courts, in our legislative assemblies and even in our churches. What has changed?

The primary change agent has been modern medicine. Disease after disease has either been defeated or tamed, the survival rate stretching beyond formerly conceived limits. Today life expectancy is twice what it was in the Middle Ages. There are, however, some unintended consequences to our medical brilliance. Where is the line between expanding life and just postponing death? When the quality of life is gone and all that remains is a breathing cadaver, is the inability to avail oneself of the release of death a virtue or has it become a vice? Is not the ultimate freedom to which life can aspire the freedom to decide when to bring one's life to a peaceful end? Do people who are medically determined to be in the final months of their lives have no right to decide how and when they will die? This debate could not have occurred one hundred years ago. When the circumstances of life change, however, must not the rules created to guide us through life also change? In the case of suicide, an ancient value has been changed by new knowledge.

We have only scratched the surface of the modern debate on ethics, but what we have established is that every rule is ultimately relativized. Does this then mean that we will inevitably sink into a sea of relativity in which there are no rules, no ultimate standards? I do not think so. The ultimate law of the universe is still, I am convinced, the law of love through which the fullness of life becomes possible. The inescapable question thus becomes: How will love be practiced in the circumstances of our very modern world? The burden of freedom, with its relentless call to maturity, is found in the juxtaposition between life-affirming principles and our existential situations. It is there that modern ethical principles are born.

PART XII

Thesis 10: Prayer

Prayer, understood as a request made to an external, theistic deity to act in human history, is little more than an hysterical attempt to turn the Holy into the service of the human. Most of our prayer definitions arise out of the past and are thus dependent on an understanding of God that no longer exists. The God who answers our prayers has ceased to be a believable God in our day. A new way to understand prayer cries out to be developed.

The Death of Prayer

When I have lectured across the United States and indeed around the world on the task of developing what I call "A New Christianity for a New World," almost inevitably the first question I receive from my audience after the lecture is about prayer. It usually takes this form: "If what you say is true, then how do I pray?" It appears that whenever God is defined in any other way than as a supernatural being who stands ready to come to our aid, then prayer, as most people have traditionally understood it, loses most of its meaning. Perhaps it is a fact that the way one understands God is not really tested or even engaged until we begin to pray.

My first book, written in 1971, was entitled *Honest Prayer.** After being long out of print, it was recently revised and republished by St. Johann Press in Haworth, New Jersey. This book revealed quite clearly my early wrestling with the inadequacy of theistic religion and thus with the activity called prayer. A Christianity without prayer is to most people almost inconceivable. Has prayer died, a casualty of our secular age? Or does prayer still have a place in the Christian future that might be energizing? If it does still have a

---

* See bibliography for details.

place, what is it and how are we to understand it? Addressing these questions will not be easy, but they are unavoidable.

There are many ways that I might address this subject, but in the context of this book, in which the theological issues that surround prayer have been addressed under other topics, I have decided that the proper way for me to enter this subject here is by telling stories. They are true stories which pose the proper questions, but leave you, my readers, free to draw your own conclusions. From these stories you are free to extrapolate that which will lead to a new definition of prayer, perhaps one that can live in whatever our Christian future will be. Each of these stories illumines the prayer experience and will, I hope, reveal a vocabulary that is capable of communicating that experience to our questioning minds.

Before beginning this task, let me first make what will be to some a surprising statement about prayer in the Bible. The New Testament uses the word "pray" as a verb only fifty-nine times. It uses the word "prayer" as a noun only thirty-four times, and not once in the Fourth Gospel. Perhaps that relative infrequency will raise concerns, challenge our preconceptions and begin to erode some of our presuppositions.

My first story involves the former primus of the Episcopal Church in Scotland and my close friend and colleague, Richard Holloway. A theological gadfly, a man of enormous courage and deep convictions, Richard brought a level of honesty into the theological discourse of the Anglican Communion that was both bold and refreshing. On one occasion he was giving a public lecture somewhere in the United Kingdom, and when he had completed his presentation, he began to take questions from his audience. The first one came from a woman who was probably in the eighth decade of her life. She was outwardly pious and appeared to be very traditional, one who in all probability did not fit into Richard's typical audience. "Bishop," she said, "do you pray?" She asked this with some obvious anxiety; apparently some of the things that Bishop Holloway had said served in her mind to make this question seem appropriate.

The bishop responded, without a moment's hesitation, with a single word: "No!" He made no further comment, leaving that "no" to echo around the room for far longer than people were comfortable to have it linger. There was a shock quality to his answer that many of those present could not and did not easily process. Here was a high-ranking bishop, an international leader, clad in the symbols of his office—a clerical collar, a purple shirt and a pectoral cross around his neck—who had just stated publicly, "No, I do not pray." A bishop who did not pray seemed to many in that audience to be an oxymoron. Bishop Holloway had a flair for the dramatic, so he let the uncomfortable silence sit heavily upon his audience until overt anxiety had come quite close to engulfing everyone in that room.

Finally, breaking the silence, he said: "Madam, if I had answered your question with a 'yes,' you would have assumed that I accepted your definition of what it means to pray and your definition of God. That answer would thus have been both false and misleading, so I had to answer with a 'no.' Now, if we can discuss what we mean by the words 'God' and 'prayer' and get beyond the confusion between God and Santa Claus, which grows out of our childhood, then my answer might be very different." It was a teaching moment I have never forgotten. Is prayer something like a letter to Santa Claus? "Dear God, I have been a good boy or girl so I want you to do A, B, C and D for me." That is certainly the way that many people seem to understand prayer.

Most prayers assume that God is an external being, possessing supernatural powers. Prayer is thus often seen as the activity of last resort, when our own resources have failed us. "There are no atheists in foxholes," we are told. When danger approaches we cry out for God. We assume that this deity has the power to manipulate the forces of nature to bring about a desired result. Our prayers seem to assume that God might not "do good" or "be merciful" unless we ask God to do so. Our prayers also seem to assume that the mind of God can be changed, and with it the course of history. Do we really want to think that our prayers have that power? That is deep down not a comfortable, but a frightening conclusion.

If those are our primary prayer assumptions, then we can understand that the death of the theistic God causes nothing less than the death of that activity known as prayer, at least as prayer has been practised through the ages. The primus of Scotland could therefore in all honesty say to this woman's question, "No, madam, I do not pray." That did not mean, however, that this bishop had given up praying, so much as it signaled that he had come to a dramatically new and different understanding of what prayer is.

I cannot speak for or answer this question for Bishop Holloway, but I can answer it for myself. For me prayer remains a profound, life-giving experience, but I no longer understand it to be the petition of one in need to One who has the power to meet that need. Indeed, I regard that outdated concept of prayer to be like a delusional game of magic, a childhood concept out of which all of us need to grow. Perhaps the word "prayer" itself is where the problem lies. The Bible does appear to say that if we bring our concerns before God, God will address them, but is that what *prayer* is really all about?

A letter recently received through my website carried this request: "Please tell me how to pray. I have just been diagnosed with cancer and I need to know quickly." Did this person believe that prayer was the activity needed to cure her cancer? Does prayer in fact change the world of cause and effect? Yes, of course there are such things in the world of medicine as "spontaneous remissions," but if they are understood to be something brought on by divine intervention, then a host of other questions have to be faced. Why did this spontaneous remission occur in one person and not in another? If God has the power to intervene in history, why does God not do it with more frequency? If God has the power to cure sickness, to relieve pain, to help people escape danger or to bring a war and its consequent suffering to an end, then why does God not do this? If God has this intervening power in response to our prayers and does not use it, is God not malevolent? Not to use this power for good seems an absolute evil. If, on the other hand, God does not have the power to intervene in response to our prayers, then is God not impotent? That drives us to a tough conclusion, because a God revealed as either malevolent or impotent has very little remaining "shelf life." The "use before" date has long since passed.

Another true story will illustrate this same theme from a different angle. My youngest stepdaughter, Rachel, is quite adventuresome, as all our daughters tend to be. After working as a paramedic in both the South Bronx and Sarajevo, she decided she wanted to serve her country in a specific way, so she joined the United States Marine Corps. Given her ability and her athletic prowess, she quickly rose in the ranks of the Marine Corps, completing officer training school, pilot training and finally helicopter training to become the second American woman to pilot a Cobra, the Marine Corps' attack helicopter. She served three tours of duty in the second Iraq War, which included her participation in the battle of Fallujah, the bloodiest battle of that war. Those were days of high anxiety both for her mother and for me. People asked later: "Did you pray for your daughter while she was in Iraq?" The answer was: "Of course, we did!" How could we not pray for one we love, whom we knew to be in great danger? The real question was, however, how did we understand what we were doing when we prayed?

Did we, for example, believe that our prayers would keep our daughter safe? If her helicopter was hit by a ground-to-air-missile, destroying its ability to continue to be airborne, did we believe that our prayers would cause God to provide her with a safe landing? In biblical words, drawn from Matthew's story of Jesus' temptations, when he was told to cast himself off the pinnacle of the temple, did we believe that God had promised, Has not God given his angels charge of you—"lest you strike your foot against a stone" (Matt. 4:6)?

If we had believed that, then would we not also have been forced to conclude that all of those young men and women who died or who were injured in Iraq must have had no one praying for them? Did we assume that in the divine plan it was time for these people to die? Did we perhaps think that their lives were not worthy of continued existence because of their sinfulness? All of these alternatives have been offered in Christian history, designed as they are to soothe the human anxiety over the "shortness and uncertainties of human life," as liturgical language of old put it. What they reveal, however, is a monstrous God who would be unworthy of human worship.

We prayed for our daughter because that is what love does. We held her in our hearts before God as we do *all* those we love when they are in "trouble, sorrow, need, sickness or any other adversity," as the Book of Common Prayer advises, but that does not solve or illumine the question of prayer. It only poses the problem. We start our discussion of prayer here, but this only begins to scratch the surface of either the problem with prayer or the solution to this problem, so we must continue our probe ever deeper.

32

Prayer: An Act of Being or of Doing?

Prayer does not bring a theistic God rushing to our aid. It does not protect us from danger, sickness or death. Life confronts us with the truth of that reality time after time. What then is prayer? Is it anything more than pious smoke and mirrors? I think it is, but before I could see that, the paradigm by which I (and most Christians) understood prayer had to be turned upside down. That is what happened to me in an experience I shall now describe. This story does not define the nature of prayer, but for me it serves to illustrate its meaning. Prayer is not about the attempt to change reality; it is about approaching reality in a dramatically different way. The time of this story was around 1970. Its meaning, however, became for me not just memorable, but timeless.

I had been the rector of St. Paul's Church in Richmond, Virginia, for less than a year when I received a phone call in my office in the mid-morning. "Jack," the voice said, "this is Cornelia. I'm in the University Hospital in Charlottesville and I wonder if you could come to see me. It is fairly urgent. I would like to talk with you as soon as possible." I knew Cornelia fairly well. She was an active member in the diocese where I had previously served, working with me closely on a couple of vital projects. She lived in a small Appalachian town in southwestern Virginia. She was in her early forties, the wife of a "country" doctor and the mother of three children, who ranged in ages between nine and fourteen. About five years older than I, she was a lovely person in every way. Her home in Appalachia did not offer this well-educated woman many activities for intellectual engagement, so she met this need by becoming deeply involved in the life of the Diocese of Southwestern Virginia, which was centered in Roanoke as its "See City." Roanoke was Virginia's largest western city. It was in her pursuit of these goals that Cornelia and I met and developed a friendship.

I responded to her opening words on the telephone by saying: "What's wrong, Cornelia?"

"I would rather not talk about it on the phone," she said, "but if you could come, and soon, I would greatly appreciate it." Of course I could come and I did. Clearing my calendar for the next day, I left about noon for the hour and a quarter drive to Charlottesville. By the time I parked, made my way into the hospital, navigating the usual entry and directional procedures, and arrived at her room, it was about 2:00 P.M.

She greeted me with a smile. There was, however, an ominous mood in the air that did not lend itself to small talk. So I immediately pulled up a chair to the side of her bed and prepared to listen to her story. "Tell me what's going on," I said.

It was not easy either for her to speak or for me to listen. It started with a lingering cough, she said, followed by a lack of energy. Finally, following her husband's suggestion, she made an appointment to see her doctor, who lived and practiced in Charlottesville. He examined her in a routine manner and then ordered some diagnostic tests. When the results of these tests came back, alarm bells were set off. Additional, more sophisticated tests and X-rays were ordered. These confirmed a metastatic carcinoma, which almost always offers little hope. It is a kind of hidden malignancy that reveals no overt symptoms until it is already too late to treat it. Doctors then, as now, do not like to put time limits on life expectancy, for every disease and every patient is different. There was, however, an inexorable sense about this diagnosis, and she was already embracing the fact that in all probability she had a fairly short time to live, possibly six months or less. I reeled under the impact of what she was saying and tried to imagine how this relatively young woman, her husband and her children were coping with the news. Choking down my own emotions, I spoke softly to her and asked only one question, "Tell me what this does to you." That question opened the door to what was probably the most remarkable and meaningful conversation I have ever had with anyone in my entire life.

There is a radical honesty that engulfs both the person and all of his or her relationships when the conversation moves to the far side of a fatal diagnosis. All pretending ceases. It is as if every barrier were lowered, and people meet in a way that is rare indeed. I listened while she roamed over the terrain of her life. Her husband was the kind of doctor whose style of practice took him all over their part of Appalachia. He was a solo practitioner who was deeply involved in the lives of his patients. He thought nothing of going out at all hours of the night to deliver a baby, to set a broken bone, to attend to one having a heart attack or to treat a sick baby with a raging fever. This type of medical practice depended on his wife's presence in the home. She kept the children safe and got them off to school in the morning; she worked with them on homework in the afternoon. Though the children were increasingly independent, her death would necessitate radical changes in his life. It would either end his style of medical practice or require a paid round-the-clock caretaker for the children. Cornelia was at that moment embracing this reality.

Then she turned to the subject of her children and told me about the pain of wondering how they would cope without a mother. They not only needed her, but they depended on her for their stability. She was also dealing with the massive sense of loss that now seemed inevitable. She would never see any of her children graduate from high school or university. She would never know who each of her children would marry or how their lives and careers would develop. She would never know or see any of her potential grandchildren. The emotional landscape on which she was walking in this conversation was incredibly painful. She neither ignored nor repressed any of her feelings.

Next she turned to other relationships of both family and friends and described to me what she thought her death would mean to each of them. What happens when a relationship of love and friendship is suddenly removed? Life shrinks for the remaining ones. The pain of loss would create a vacuum in the lives of all those who were close to her, those who once encircled her with love. Who, she wondered, would fill the places she had once occupied? How would each family member and friend adjust? It is always harder for some to adjust to loss than others. Would there be some of those whom she loved the most, who would not be able to adjust at all? Would there be some who might never quite recover?

For almost three hours, we walked over the peaks and valleys of her life. I tried to feel her hurt and pain as best as I could. I sought to enter into those feelings. When one shares life that reaches this depth, a profound bond is created that I cannot adequately describe. Those three hours would forever remain indelible in my life. The time had flown by, it seemed, and looking at my watch I noted that it was 5:00 P.M. I had already violated one of the primary rules of pastoral ministry. One does not spend three hours at a patient's hospital bedside. I was emotionally drained and I suspected that Cornelia was also. So I began to draw the conversation to a close and prepared to take my leave.

At this time, I also found myself shifting gears away from my role as her friend and into my professional role as a priest. "Cornelia," I said as I stood to leave, "may I offer a prayer for you and with you?" She did not object. If I had some need to pray, she could deal with that. Perhaps she felt that she owed me this religious favor, since I had spent an inordinate amount of time with her. Whatever she thought, she acquiesced. Taking her hand in mine, I strung together a series of religious clichés that I had used many times before. I knew how to do that. These words clearly met some of my needs, but they added little, if anything, to the meaning or the depth of the visit. Then, promising to see her again, I departed and made my way back to Richmond feeling strangely ill at ease.

It was a slightly longer trip returning because of the traffic, so I had more time to think. On that journey home I compared the significance of our conversation, during which I had entered so deeply into her fear and anxiety, participating in a connection that made it at one and the same time both profoundly painful and profoundly real, with the shallowness of my "prayer," which was so mundane and so perfunctory. Which part of that visit was the "prayer," I asked myself. Was it the conversation that opened both of us to the shared experience of our common humanity, or was it those pious words that I addressed to a theistic deity, whose help I desperately needed? I felt that the conversation we shared had expanded and enhanced both of our lives. I sensed that the activity that I had called "prayer" had contracted us both and had forced us back into the stance of wearing our defensive shields and our security blankets. Clearly the conversation in which we had engaged each other and a painful reality on that day was holy time. The conclusion seemed so obvious: The conversation was in fact the real "prayer," while the thing I had called "prayer" was little more than a pious triviality. It was in the conversation that the meaning of God was shared between two people; it was in the conversation that the boundaries we humans erect to keep ourselves safe from the threat of another were transgressed. I vowed that day never again to engage in the activity that I had previously called "prayer" until I could pray with the same depth of honesty that I had shared with Cornelia at her bedside.

That day proved to be a turning point in my life and in my pilgrimage into learning to pray in a non-theistic world. To be able to live the meaning of prayer, rather than just to "pray," became the goal of my lifetime and indeed the goal of my priesthood. Prayer is the sharing of being, the sharing of life and the sharing of love. That hospital experience became a starting place for me in regard to the meaning of prayer. Prayer understood this new way became profoundly real for me, while the form that prayer had traditionally taken began to shift dramatically. From that day to this, prayer has been far more about "being" than it has been about "doing." This was for me a radical but necessary shift, which gave me a new starting place to enter a great and even transformative adventure into the depths of my faith. Experience always trumps explanation.

33

Driving Prayer Toward a New Understanding

Before prayer can be made real, our understanding of God, coupled with our understanding of how the world works, must be newly defined. Before prayer can have meaning, it must be built on an honest sharing of life. Before prayer can be discussed in the age in which we live, it must be drained of its presumed manipulative magic. It must find expression in the reality of who we are, not in the details of what we do. These were the insights that my fourth story, the one I am about to share, gave to me as I walked through what was probably the darkest period of my life, the years 1981–1988. The learning curve was steep; the depth of despair was real. I invite you now to enter that time period with me and to walk through that experience as I did. This narrative is true, personal and painful. I have spoken verbally of it before. I have not written about it. Doing so even now makes me feel quite vulnerable.

Around Christmas of 1981, my first wife, Joan Lydia Ketner Spong, was diagnosed with advanced breast cancer. She had never been fond of doctors and so had postponed seeing one until her fear of the symptoms, which she suspected were becoming critical, outweighed her dread of medicine. She had discovered a lump in her breast much earlier and decided to tell no one about it. It grew slowly, causing her to assume, perhaps to hope, that it had to be benign. It remained her secret. That December, as the holidays came into focus, however, the tumor erupted externally and became a draining sore. When that occurred, her secret was exposed. I was alarmed and got her as quickly as I could to a doctor. After an examination and later a biopsy, we heard the verdict. She had a stage four malignancy. Immediate surgery was required and massive chemotherapy would follow. Even after all that no guarantees were offered. In fact, we were told that about two years of life might be all that we could reasonably expect. We sank into the shock of that diagnosis.

At that time I was an active and fairly high-profile public figure as the bishop of Newark. We had been engaged in great controversies over the full acceptance in both church and society of gay, lesbian, transgender and bisexual persons. I was clearly identified in this fight and my name was widely recognized from press and television coverage. People in public life learn quickly that they really do not, perhaps cannot, have a private life. Within minutes, or so it felt, the news of both my wife's diagnosis and her prognosis spread until it seemed to me as if the whole world knew. From that day on, I never visited a congregation in my diocese for confirmation that prayers were not offered publicly for my wife and for me. Prayer groups all over New Jersey informed us that they were praying for us; some were Episcopal prayer groups, some were Roman Catholic and some were ecumenical. The one thing they all appeared to have in common was that they knew of the presumed two-year boundary that my wife and I were facing. I did not resent this invasion of our privacy. On the contrary, I was appreciative of their efforts, as was Joan. Their actions felt supportive and loving. In their own way, the people were telling us that they really cared for us and that, in whatever way they could, they wanted to be helpful. They were willing in this way to stand with us, to share in our pain and in our struggle. One never rejects love that is so freely offered, even when the form in which it comes might not be one's particular style. So Joan and I were carried by this wave of love from those who reached out to us in what was clearly our time of need.

The months passed and then the years began to mount. When we passed the two-year prediction date and things were still going positively, I noticed that these prayer groups began to take credit for my wife's longevity. In their letters to me, it almost sounded as if they believed that they had engaged the powers of evil in some profound contest that pitted them on God's side, holding back God's enemies. Their prayers, they suggested, were pushing back the advance of this demonic sickness. They were winning the battle and they felt good about their success. Once again, my response was not to debate the theological implications of their understanding of prayer, but simply to appreciate the level of caring that they were offering. It was, at least in its intention, sustaining. I could not help wondering, however, in the darkness of each night, about the implications of their understanding of prayer.

"Suppose," I thought to myself during a particularly sleepless time, "that a member of Newark's sanitation department had a wife with cancer." At that time, Newark, New Jersey, was either at or very near the top of the list of America's poorest-per-capita cities. I tried to envision just who it was who might occupy the bottom tier of Newark's socio-economic status system. My mind settled, whether rightly or wrongly, on the garbage collector working for Newark's sanitation department. So I focused on him.

In this long, dark meditation, I wondered how many prayer groups would have added the sanitation worker's wife to their prayer lists. I wondered how much public notice her illness would have achieved. If this couple went to church, perhaps their congregation might have been aware of their struggle, but would services have been interrupted with passionate petitions for healing? Would the gates of heaven have been stormed by massive numbers of prayer groups? Would God, therefore, I then wondered, have allowed this man's wife to die more quickly than my wife? Since it was my high public profile and my social prominence alone which caused more prayers to be uttered for my wife than for his, would those prayers be a factor in the course of my wife's sickness? Does prayer affect healing or encourage longevity? Does God operate on the basis of human status?

If I believed that prayer worked in this way, I concluded, I would immediately become an atheist! I could not possibly believe in such a deity. This capricious God would be demonic, it seemed to me. The cumulative power of many people praying existed in the case of my wife only because I was a fairly well known public figure. Is status a factor in what is presumed to be the healing power of God? When John Paul II lingered on his deathbed for so long, the whole world joined in prayer for him. Was that a factor in his long, lingering death? When a hurricane barrels down on a population center like New Orleans, the cries of millions are lifted heavenward in prayer. Can the cumulative power of many prayers actually change the direction of a storm? Is that what prayer does? If so, then prayer is a tool to be used by the mighty, the powerful and the well-known. If that is true, then God clearly cares more for the rich and famous than God does for the poor, the forgotten and the unknown. Such a conclusion is theologically violent, absurd and even hate-filled. Whatever prayer means, it cannot be that.

My wife lived for six and a half years from her diagnosis in December of 1981 to her death in August of 1988. In retrospect, I treasure that extension of time, but I did not fully understand then the gift that I was being given. Life is like that.

So I put these four stories with their varied and distinctive insights together. Then I seek to draw conclusions about what prayer means in the twenty-first century. Prayer is not and cannot be a petition from the weak to the all-powerful One to do for us what we cannot do for ourselves. Prayer does not bend God's will to a new conclusion. Prayer does not bring a cure where there is no possibility of a cure. Prayer does not create miracles to which we can testify publicly.

The beliefs that these conclusions refute are, in fact, delusions fostered by yesterday's world that we are now being called on to abandon. They are beliefs that arose out of the childhood of our humanity. Today a new question emerges, which we must face with honesty. Is prayer only the human act of last resort? Does praying reflect anything more than the fact that all else has failed? Why do we say so frequently to people, "You will be in my prayers," when we never stop to pray? Is it not our impotence in the face of life's pain that draws us to pretend that we actually possess the power to make a difference, creating nothing more than a comfortable fantasy in which we can hide?

Is prayer, as we have traditionally defined it, a holy activity, or is prayer the preparation for a time of engaging in a holy activity? Increasingly, I am moving to the latter conclusion. It is life that is holy. It is love that is life-giving. Having the courage to be all that I can be is the place where God and life come together for me. If that is so, are not living, loving and being the essence of prayer and the meaning of worship? When Paul enjoined us to "pray without ceasing" (I Thess. 5:17), did he mean to engage in the activity of praying unceasingly? Or did he mean that we are to see all of life as a prayer, calling the world to enter that place where life, love and being reveal the meaning of God? Is Christianity not coming to the place where my "I" meets another's "Thou," and in that moment God is present?

I pray daily. My way of doing that is to bring into my mind those I love, to cradle them in my awareness of the holiness in which my life seems to be lived. Do I expect miracles to occur, lives to be changed or wholeness suddenly to replace brokenness? No, but I do expect to be made more whole, to be set free to share my life more deeply with others, to be enabled to love beyond my boundaries and to watch the barriers that divide me from those I once avoided lowered. Prayer to me is the practice of the presence of God, the act of embracing transcendence and the discipline of sharing with another the gifts of living, loving and being. Can that understanding of prayer, so free of miracle and magic, make any real difference in our world? I believe it can, it does and it will. Beyond that conclusion I do not know what to say. Perhaps I have said all I need to say.

PART XIII

Thesis 11:
Life After Death

Can modern men and women continue to talk about eternal life
with any degree of intellectual integrity? Can Christianity survive
without it?

34

Life After Death—
Still Believable?

I have no use for life after death as a tool or method of behavior control. In many religious people that appears to be its only purpose. I do not believe that parents can effectively raise their children on the basis of promising them a reward for "good" behavior and punishment for "bad" behavior. Given that this style of childrearing has been all but universally dismissed by experts in child development, why have Christian people not banished the same mentality from the life of the Christian church? Heaven and hell are, quite frankly, badly dated, unbelievable concepts, which need to be dismissed at once from our minds and from the liturgical life of the church. Only the most irrelevant of our ecclesiastical thinkers appear not to see this; they alone cling to these archaic ideas.

Obvious changes in the meaning we attach to various words in our secular society make this shift very clear. Look at what has happened to the word "heaven." Since Gene Autry in the late 1920s sang, "You're the only star in my blue heaven," it has become little more than a synonym for the sky. When the word "heaven" is turned into the adjective "heavenly," it is used to describe everything from a new dress to good sex! Understanding this, Anglican theologian Don Cupitt could and did write a book entitled *Above Us Only Sky*.*

The word "hell" has fared no better. It has become a mild oath with little meaning. One can say in the summer, "It's as hot as hell today," and one can say in the winter, "It's as cold as hell today," and mean the same thing! The word "hell" no longer has any content.

We can trace the meaning of these concepts back to the early and medieval church, which constructed the realms that in ecclesiastical minds made up the afterlife. Those structures were constantly being adapted to meet human need. There was nothing unchanging or eternal about them. The major concern in the church with regard to life after death was not its reality, but the need that the leaders of the church felt to control human behavior on this earth. Originally, there were only two areas in the geography of life after death. By far the most graphic area was hell, in which sinners were eternally punished and fires burned forever. Then brimstone was added to heighten the fear and to motivate virtue. To this realm called "hell" were assigned not just the wicked, but also the non-believers, the heretics, the infidels and the unbaptized.

The other realm, called "heaven," was constructed as a place of bliss and reward; it was created and reserved for the virtuous, the saved, those who acknowledged "Jesus Christ as savior" and who were thus baptized. Please note that by adding the baptized and the "true believers," the church thus added "belief control" to "behavior control." One could not think outside the box of orthodoxy, the church was asserting, if one wanted to be "saved." This bicameral system of heaven and hell, however, did not fit reality. The experiences of life challenged it. Virtuous and godly

---

* See bibliography for details.

lives, we all know, had existed long before the time of Jesus, so
people in that earlier period of history could not possibly have
believed in Jesus or have been baptized, which was the established
standard for the "saved." In the early church this uneasy ecclesiastical discussion centered on great thinkers of the past like Plato
and Aristotle, who were indeed being read in that day to shape
the theology of the established church quite intentionally. That
shaping began once Christianity had received official recognition and had moved toward becoming the dominant religion of
the Western world. Could Plato and Aristotle be assigned to hell
appropriately and still be quoted regularly in the development of
creedal theology by the church fathers? It was an intolerable situation, and so church leaders set about to remedy this anomaly.
The fact that our image of life after death was changing even in
its early years is a clear indicator that the truth of this subject as
it was proclaimed by our church was not the product of divine
revelation, but of human adaptation. ~~who?~~ *Catholicism*

The church addressed this crisis by adding a third realm to the
structures of the afterlife, supplementing the original two desti-
nations of heaven and hell. This third place was called "limbo,"
and it was developed in the medieval church to be the eternal
destination of "noble pagans." Limbo was not a place of suffering, but it was also not a place where the beatific vision could ever
be achieved. Limbo served primarily to accommodate the human
conscience that could no longer assign to hell those noble pagans
who would have had no chance to encounter Jesus. In the twentieth century, Mahatma Gandhi, a deeply admired man of peace,
became a better illustration than Plato or Aristotle of why limbo
was so essential to our rational consciousness. It protected the
"justice" of God.

The moral outrage of assigning unbaptized babies to hell created another crisis in our belief in the afterlife. If heaven was

only for baptized Christians, what would become of unbaptized babies? In that era of widespread infant mortality, the stated conviction that their fate was hell was intolerable. Questions arose from many sorts of circumstances. What about stillborn infants? What about a miscarriage or even an aborted fetus? What kind of God would punish innocent infants for either the accident of their birth or the negligence of their parents? This debate raged for centuries in all parts of the Christian church.* Finally, in the fullness of time, a fourth structure was added to the geography of the afterlife. It was called "limbo for unbaptized children." Now the leaders of the Christian church could say that an unbaptized child would not be eternally punished, but would find his or her eternal dwelling place, in a place without punishment. In this new realm, there were no blazing fires for these "innocent ones," once again saving our sense of God's fairness and mercy.† This neutral outcome had the effect of saving Christian authority: A version of eternal life could now be had without either punishment or reward, but with fairness!

The next debate about the reality of the afterlife arose when people began to see "degrees of evil" in those who came to the moment of judgment. Right and wrong became selective categories. Were not some lives more overtly evil than others? Could Genghis Khan and Adolf Hitler be put in the same category as those who sinned by eating meat on Friday, cursed from time to time, violated their marriage vows or perhaps even got a divorce? The pressure arising from the sense of graduated evil found expression when yet another new room was added to the geography of the afterlife. This new room was started in the early Middle Ages and was called "purgatory."

---

* The debate continued into the twentieth century, and even within Protestantism, as Sinclair Lewis's 1927 novel *Elmer Gantry* reveals.

† The Vatican abandoned Limbo for children in the twentieth century.

Purgatory was an enormous step in a new direction for the Christian church. With the advent of purgatory the punishment of hell, but not the bliss of heaven, became time-related. Even those who had been the most evil of the world were no longer doomed to suffer through all eternity, but only to serve a longer sentence in purgatory. Those whose sins were either moderate or merely expressions of carelessness would spend less time in purgatory. In the last analysis, however, everyone, good and evil alike, would finally gain the promise of heaven. Purgatory was thus the first step taken by the church in the process of moving toward the healing hope of universalism.

The result of all of these changes was, however, that the after-life began to look like a house built by a committee! New rooms were being added to take care of every newly perceived human need. Those new rooms made it clear that the afterlife was a human construction, reflecting adaptations in the ever-changing human understanding of God. Despite the humble origins of these images, their power in the task of controlling human behavior was immense. Next these concepts entered into our literature and framed our consciousness. One thinks of such works as Dante's *Divine Comedy,* Chaucer's *Canterbury Tales,* John Milton's *Paradise Lost* and *Paradise Regained* and John Bunyan's *Pilgrim's Progress.*[*] Christianity was clearly now in the behavior control business! The feeling was that if these powerful controls were ever relativized, moral anarchy would be inevitable.

Is behavior control really the purpose of the Christian faith? One of the slogans of the American Humanist Association is "Good without a God." Does anyone really believe that goodness is dependent on a belief in God? The other side of the equation is even less ambiguous: Christian history surely reveals that the

---

[*] Dante Alighieri 1320; Geoffrey Chaucer 1386; John Milton 1667 and 1671; John Bunyan 1678.

Christians of the world can be and have been prodigiously evil even with a God. To separate reward and punishment, good and evil from any connection with life after death becomes, therefore, a necessary first step that must be accomplished before we can begin to examine anew the possibility of life after death. Heaven and hell, as aspects of the old reward-and-punishment behavior control system, will surely have to be discarded. For many people that theme has been such a dominant part of the meaning of the afterlife that once it is dismissed there appears to be nothing left.

So, then, does the possibility of life after death disappear when heaven and hell, reward and punishment disappear? Is that what life and death are ultimately about? I do not think so. To face this anomaly is, however, a necessary and essential first step. We take it and we move a step deeper into the subject.

35

A New Perspective
on Eternity

The hope for life after death is the almost universal fantasy of self-conscious people. Having known life in an individualized way, which is what self-consciousness provides, we find it difficult to think that this precious gift either originates or terminates in nothingness. So human beings have created mythological images to communicate their hopes and even their fantasies. Great debates throughout history have raged, for example, around the exact moment when God attaches an eternal soul to a developing human fetus. The modern controversy over abortion still reflects that debate. The Bible even suggests that God knew us before God formed us in the womb (Jer. 1:5).

Now, though, with our greater scientific understanding, everything about our birth and even our identity appears to be random, accidental and finite. The result of this evolution in thought is that the old images regarding eternal life have simply vanished from our awareness. My birth was made possible when a random sperm from my father, one of literally millions, connected with an egg from my mother, which she happened to produce at that time, a process she repeated about once every twenty-eight days. That chance collision determined my gender, my height, my hair color, my eye color, the range of my intelligence, the size of my feet and many other things. I am not a product of divine planning; I am rather a product of absolute randomness.

There is a biological clock that begins to tick the moment every individual zygote is formed between sperm and egg cell. All living things, whether human, plant, or animal, are finite. All living things have a beginning and will have an ending. Is there, then, any reasonable possibility that the finite can enter into the eternal, that the mortal can achieve immortality or that our dreams of life after death can be real? The odds seem very long, but I am determined to explore them in my quest to spell out a believable conviction.

The one thing of which we are certain, even as we begin this quest, is that the literalized post-death images of our religious past cannot be resurrected. There is no hell, no heaven, no limbo, no purgatory, no lake of fire, no milk and no honey. Those concepts no longer mark our lives. I have no interest in debating them. I am willing to pursue this subject only if we can explore and break new ground in a radical way. So I continue my attempt to discuss life after death by roaming into a very different place, revisiting a topic addressed earlier.

We have already looked at the history of the universe, but it is now essential that we recall that now. Our vast universe appears to have been born about 13.8 billion years ago in a massive explosion known as the Big Bang. We can determine today, with remarkable precision—almost one hundred percent—the exact elements that came into being in that explosion. In its initial state the universe consisted of lifeless physical matter and various chemical compounds. Hydrogen and helium seem to have been dominant at the beginning. This lifeless matter was hurled out into the emptiness of space, where it collided, interacted, linked by whom—from what?,

up and separated from other elements as galaxies were formed and stars were created. This lifeless universe of extreme temperatures seems to have expanded as matter was hurled further and further away. Inflation it was called. The universe existed in this lifeless form for about ten billion years. Wow!

Somewhere around 3.8 billion years ago, on this tiny planet revolving around a midsize star, in the galaxy we now call the Milky Way, life somehow emerged? It was a new thing, but we have to say that the possibility of life must always have been present or it could not have emerged. There is no evidence, however, to support the idea of a divine intervention to start life in this heretofore lifeless universe. Whether in the vastness of space there were other places where life developed is still unknown, but it seems probable.

That first life-form was very primitive, a microscopically small single cell, but it had the ability to reproduce itself. I suspect that even at that stage of development, life was survival-oriented. These single cells, as they proliferated, began the task of pumping oxygen into the atmosphere. (Oxygen is a product of living things.) Hundreds of millions of years passed with no other changes of significance. Then something new happened: Single cells began to form into clusters of cells. With these clusters, complexity was born and cell specialization became possible. One cell was no longer required to handle all the demands of a "living organism." With that step established and continuing to develop, hundreds of millions of years again passed.

Next this thing called life seemed to split into two distinct categories. One we now call animate life and the other, inanimate life. At first, this distinction was so slight as not to be noticeable, but as eons passed the differences became quite apparent. Yet animate and inanimate life-forms were and are deeply interdependent; one cannot live without the other.

Once again after the passing of hundreds of millions of years, from inside the animate side of life, primitive expressions of consciousness began to develop. At first these were little more than an antenna designed to relate the living thing to its environment, but that dimension of consciousness was destined to grow. We are today keenly aware of different levels of consciousness in the animate world. Is a clam aware of being conscious? If we really thought so, would we put a live clam into boiling water to make a chowder? We would not do that to our dogs or cats. There is a too deeply recognized kinship present there.

Higher forms of animate life began to develop systems of communication and to form social units called packs, herds or schools, but each unit was always organized around the survival needs of the species. Yes, there are examples in nature where one member of a pack is sacrificed for the life of the others. Heroic as it might appear, it is still regarded as instinctual, not chosen behavior. There was competition for supremacy among the various species of living things as each sought to occupy the top of the food chain. From about 180 million years ago to about 65 million years ago, reptiles, in the form of the dinosaurs, ruled the world and occupied that top position. They had limited brain capacity, but massive size and no natural enemies. Then some kind of catastrophe of nature annihilated the dinosaurs and scrambled the other life-forms on this planet.

With the end of reptile dominance the door was opened for the rise of the mammals to occur. As they gained prominence, a struggle for supremacy among the various mammals took place. The superior brain of the primates finally won out. The victory of hominids occurred about six million years ago. Then finally, sometime within the last quarter million years, came self-consciousness.

With that momentous development a self was born that was not just a part of nature, but a new center of consciousness. This creature had a mind that could transcend time's boundaries. This creature could remember and relive the past and dream about and even plan for the future. This creature knew that life had a beginning and an ending and that he or she would die. So this creature experienced the trauma of finitude, which drove him or her into the quest for meaning; no longer willing to see life as nothing more than repeating the biological cycle of being born, growing to maturity, breeding and dying, this creature *invented* meaning. The mind of this creature soared beyond all the boundaries of life and in some ways seemed to share in the timelessness of eternity.

These creatures, as they evolved and multiplied, could study and embrace the size of the universe and feel the smallness of being part of something so vast. They could learn about the connections that bind living things together. The discovery of DNA (deoxyribonucleic acid), which was first comprehended and named by James Watson and Francis Crick in 1953, helped these self-conscious creatures to embrace the oneness of life and to see their kinship with all other living things. Some of these *Homo sapiens,* as they were called, then began to probe the inner secrets of life and found such things as the "inner self" and became aware of what came to be called "the collective unconscious," which appears to bind us into being more than just finite. Assumed limits began to fade. We learned about non-verbal communication, and a new sense of both oneness and meaning.

Does the evolutionary process stop with human life as we now know it? No; indeed, we are aware of lives in our own history that seem to have been able to transcend generally recognized human barriers. We call such people mystics, prophets, even expressions of the divine. Perhaps what created these great religious leaders of history was that they were able to point beyond self-consciousness to a kind of universal consciousness.

All these things raise the possibility, perhaps even the probability, that we are somehow attached to and share in an eternity that we cannot ultimately identify. Is this just another delusion, or are we human beings moving to the edge of a new evolutionary breakthrough in which we acknowledge that our religious systems began as mythological attempts to understand that which we had no words to describe? For example, are we human beings so deeply connected that we can pass on vibrations of life and healing love to another? Is that what the activity we once called prayer was seeking to understand? Are we related to that which is timeless and eternal? Is that what our ancient views of life after death were trying to tell us? Is life the unfolding of the mystery that we once called God? Does eternal life find new content in these places?

Some years ago I did a full treatment of life after death in a book called *Eternal Life: A New Vision—Beyond Religion, Beyond Theism, Beyond Heaven and Hell.*[*] I weighed the odds of eternal life, newly defined. My conclusion was that I do believe in it. I find that it makes sense. We are up against an infinite system that we can experience only as finite. I see the edge of life break open, not in the picture of death being intercepted by life, but in the picture of life itself. All of those apocryphal stories about waking up restored to life after dying turn out to be wish fulfillment. Even the resurrection of Jesus, so long an object of faith, turns out to be not the resuscitation of the deceased body. This is not what resurrection means. It means being called into a new being, and it happens *within life*. It is found in grasping a new concept of life that lifts us beyond this mortal coil.

There is much that spells out this dimension of life. For example, there is the gift of survival. We all are bound by this urge, but very few creatures know it. The first actual change in our

---

* See bibliography for details.

evolutionary history at the dawn of time, according to Professor Stephen Nowicki of the Biology Department at Duke University, was the ability of some cells to separate and yet still be connected *in order to have a better chance of surviving*. The regular routine of fight-flight that is also present is, in Professor Nowicki's view, an elaborately prepared for, adrenaline-caused rush to leave the liver and to go throughout the body—raising blood pressure, enabling the body to be successful under stress.* No part of this is known until we pass the consciousness test. Then we fight to survive. We human beings battle between being and non-being. When the day comes for us to die, that inevitable death goes against our whole life plan.

The out-of-body experiences sometimes reported by individuals near death are another possible indicator of a transcendent dimension of life. I do not know how they work, but I cannot help but wonder: Is there something within ourselves that can escape the end of life? Is there a division between body and soul that can give us some hope?

Still another indicator lies in connections between certain people that link them in an almost mystical way. How many people have awakened at night thinking about someone dear to them, for example, and then the next morning have learned that the person they had had on their mind the night before had been in an auto accident or had had a heart attack? They often conclude, perhaps rightly, that somehow "the message got through." Similarly, what is the meaning of hypnosis? Can one person control another person with the power of the mind alone—and if so, how? The hypnotist and the subject do not even have to be close to each other for the process to work.

The list of indicators goes on. What is "the collective uncon-

---

* From lectures on the subject by Professor Stephen Nowicki of Duke University. See bibliography for details.

scious"? Are we linked with people who lived before us or after us? Is life still a mystery?

What do we make of people who seem to have a peculiar spiritual insight? Can men and women, shamans, holy people, make contact with others?

When this book was nearing completion I listened to some lectures by Cornell University Professor Steven Strogatz on the Theory of Chaos.* The lectures expressed that ultra-modern concept of disorder. It was proposed that chaos was the next boundary that we must cross. I was fascinated. There is so much left that we do not understand. How is it possible for human life to be composed of millions of physical properties, but always to create a sense of consciousness that can fall in love? It was amazing.

I do not think we know enough about life to rule such things out. I know I do not.

I cannot draw pictures, evaluate data or even share facts. I can only say that at the edges of life, on the boundaries of expanded self-consciousness, the concepts of transcendent reality, infinite love and eternal life still make sense to me. I am not deluded. I believe that I have touched the eternal and that I share in what that means. Reward and punishment are dismissed. Expanded life, life beyond finitude, is embraced. I am convinced that it is real. I will live as if that is so and be prepared for the next adventure that self-consciousness brings my way. The only place I can hold this conviction and prepare for what comes next is in a community of seekers. That is what I ultimately believe the church must be.

So to that church with all its imperfections I cling, for that provides me with the place to touch and enter "the eternal."

---

* See bibliography for details.

Part XIV

Thesis 12: Universalism

We are called by this new faith into radical connectedness. Judgment is not a human responsibility. Discrimination against any human being on the basis of that which is a "given" is always evil and does not serve the Christian goal of offering "abundant life" to all. Any structure in either the secular world or the institutional church that diminishes the humanity of any child of God on any external basis of race, gender or sexual orientation must be exposed publicly and vigorously. There can be no reason in the church of tomorrow for excusing or even forgiving discriminatory practices. "Sacred tradition" must never again provide a cover to justify discriminatory evil. The call to universalism must be the message of Christianity.

36

The Marks of Tomorrow's Christianity

Christianity is called to be a community of self-conscious people who have transcended all of the boundaries that divide one human being from another. It is also called to be a community of people committed to a journey into the future going beyond even "the cloud of unknowing," as a fourteenth-century mystic termed it. Christianity is charged with the task of creating a place in which all can hear about and contemplate the meaning of life and thus be introduced to that which is ultimately real. Such a community of believers will of necessity give up any role in judgment, sacrifice all claims to possess the truth in any concrete form and refrain from ever again hiding documented evil under the guise of "sacred tradition." Christianity must be a place in which human oneness is practiced and where human engagement with that which is eternal can be probed. This is finally what Christianity must come to mean.

Christianity did not come into being with a Bible that contained "the Word of God." It was not born with creeds fully formed that its constituents had to believe. It did not place God upon a throne to dispense justice, nor did it place worshippers on their knees in the stance of beggars. It did not possess political power, seek to maintain behavior standards or define good and evil for all to follow. All these things were added later.

If this institution is to live into the future, it must recover its original meaning and identity. It must shed those aspects of its past that are divisive, condemning and authoritarian. It must abandon creeds and tribal oneness in favor of universal inclusiveness; it must use its formulas to include, never to ban. In short, to live into the future, the Christian church must become a universal community.

The challenges are great: Can Christian theology once again be enabled to interact with contemporary knowledge? Can Christian liturgies be made to reflect reality rather than nostalgia? Can Christianity affirm human oneness while still embracing its radical diversity? Can this faith create a new institutional form that fosters a truth-seeking, universal community?

These are the questions which this book has tried to raise, and to some extent address. I now bring this work to a conclusion with the hope that a resounding yes will be heard from a newly enlightened faith tradition. Hints of this kind of purpose have always been present in Christianity. We do not have to create them out of nothing. Perhaps, as G. K. Chesterton has said: "Christianity has not been tried and found wanting; it has been found difficult and not tried."*

When Matthew brought his gospel to a conclusion, he placed words to this effect into the mouth of the risen Jesus: "Go into all the world and make disciples of all nations" (28:19). We have met these words before and we tend to hear these words as an institutional charge calling the church's members to "convert the heathen." When Matthew wrote, however, the Christian move-

---

* G. K. Chesterton, *What's Wrong with the World,* Dover Publications, 2007; first published 1900.

ment was still part of Judaism. There *was* no institutional church seeking to grow. So these words must have meant something quite different to its first readers. Indeed they did!

Matthew was, I believe, sounding the call to a universal humanity. "Go make disciples of all nations" meant, to Matthew, "Go beyond the boundaries of your religion, your security system and your fears." It meant, "Go to those whom your religious tradition has defined as unclean, uncircumcised, unsaved, unbaptized and unbelieving; those denounced as infidels, heretics, agnostics or atheists." It meant, "Go beyond the barriers you have erected in your biologically driven search for survival."

What then are you to do? Matthew's Jesus was quite clear, but only if we know how to translate the meaning of those early words: "You are to proclaim the gospel." To Matthew, that did not mean that we are to provide our converts with a set of formulaic Christian answers. It meant rather that we are to make all persons aware that they are included within the infinite love of God. When Matthew's words, which we have called "the Great Commission," were first attributed to Jesus, it was not a call to missionize the world, but rather a call to build a world in which human oneness can flourish. It was a call to universalism.

This essential aspect of the Jesus message was not struck in Matthew's final chapter alone. We have noted earlier that when the gospel of Luke described Pentecost, the event in which the Holy Spirit fell upon the disciples of Jesus (Acts 1:1–13), the author made sure that it was understood as a universal happening.

When Paul tried to describe to the Galatians what was involved in his call to "put on Christ," he said that it meant that human divisions must disappear. In Christ there is no longer "Jew nor Greek," "slave nor free," "male nor female." All are "one in Christ Jesus" (Gal. 3:26–29). That is what Jesus meant, and that is what the original Christ experience was, before the Bible came to be called the "Word of God," before we became scripture's defenders and before the creeds became the "essence of our faith." It was also before any form of liturgy became the "only way to worship."

From its very inception, Christianity has kept this sense of human oneness, but it has been buried under many layers of ecclesiastical power expressions. The original vision of Christ was not captured within the church's power needs, but within such universal hymns as "In Christ There Is No East or West, in Him No South or North," or more modern hymns to universalism such as "All Are Welcome" or "For Everyone a Place at the Table."* The Christian invitation to the world has always been: "Come unto me, all ye that travail and are heavy laden, and I will give you rest" (Matt. 11:28). It was never meant to have a limit, to be only for "some of ye"! Were these words attributed to Jesus intended to be a call for us to "rest from human labor"? I do not think so. The passage was a call to rest from the eternal human struggle to become. It was an invitation for all to dwell in the joy of capital-B "Being." Christianity has never been about believing correctly. It was never meant to provide the basis upon which believers would separate heresy from truth. It was always a call to practise the task of living, loving and being. In the words of the new baptism liturgy of the Episcopal Church, we are "to seek Christ in every person loving our neighbors as ourselves."

When charting a new reformation, however, we must engage in the task of going even deeper into this vision of universalism. It has to do not only with erasing human division, but also with relativizing our most cherished beliefs. Creeds can no longer bind Jesus. Doctrines such as the Incarnation and the Trinity can never again pretend that they have defined either God or Jesus. Can a

---

* "In Christ . . . ," John Oxenham, 1852–1941; "All Are Welcome," Marty Haugen 1994; "A Place at the Table," Shirley Murray 1998.

church set these things aside without cutting all ties to what is called "historical Christianity"? I think we can and I think we must. The Christianity of the future cannot live inside the doctrines of the past. Doctrines are always a description or definition of our God experience, they are never a definition of God. For example, I can say that I am a Trinitarian because that term describes my experience of God. The Father element of the Trinity means the experience of God as an external Other that is beyond anything that I can imagine. The Spirit means the experience of God as an internal reality that is deep within me and inseparable from my humanity. The Son means the experience of God made manifest in a particular life. The Trinity is not a description of my God, then, but of my God experience. It does not mean that God *is* a Trinity. That would be an idolatrous claim. My experience of God and God are not the same. God is not beyond my ability to experience, but the nature of God is beyond my ability to describe.

The same thing is true about the fundamental doctrine of Christianity known as Incarnation, as I have previously mentioned. That doctrine makes Jesus not unlike the comic strip character Clark Kent, who turned out to be Superman in disguise. We must move beyond this now-irrelevant dualistic pattern to discover the Holy in the heart of the human. A doctrine called Incarnation will never get us there.

I find this unity between the divine and the human powerfully expressed in the parable of the judgment, a parable told only in Matthew's gospel (Matt. 25:31–46), which was discussed in chapter 7. No one asked those being judged whether or not they had recited the creeds, attended worship regularly or even lived moral lives! Judgment in this parable was both simple and universal: Did you discern and respond to the presence of the Holy in the life of the "least of these" your brothers and sisters? It is one more example of the theme of universalism present in the heart of Christianity.

When I contemplate the meaning of Jesus, I come back again and again to his image as the ultimate boundary-breaker, in whom what it means to be human is constantly being expanded. The meaning of the incarnation to me is that the life of God is always met in the human. Christianity is not about religion; it is about life. God is not an external being; God is "Being itself," manifested in all that is. So we look anew at the biblical portrait of Jesus and see it in terms of *being*, not *doing*. In the New Testament, who is it that comes to Jesus? It is the Samaritans, the Gentiles, the lepers, the adulterers, the thieves, the broken, the warped, the damaged; and each finds in him the love and acceptance of God. That is what Christianity has always been and that is what the Christianity of tomorrow must reflect.

The language that refers to Jesus as the "Son of God," I am now convinced, has nothing to do with some literalized version of mythology, but has everything to do with the fact that God was experienced as the Source of Life in the life of Jesus, as the Source of Love in the love of Jesus and as the Ground of Being in the being of Jesus. So in Jesus the human and the divine flow together, for they are one. The dualism of the past simply fades away. The doorway into the divine is to become deeply and fully human!

The church of the future will not dismantle and dispatch the gospel narratives, but will recognize them for what they are, a first-century attempt to explain the Christ experience. We will not jettison the creeds, but will recognize them as fourth-century love songs, sung to those people's understanding of God. We can thus join in singing these ancestral songs. We do not literalize their words, nor do we bend the church of tomorrow to the liturgical patterns of antiquity. We will allow the Christ experience to create new forms through which ultimate truth might be allowed to flow in our time.

All of this is to say that the Christianity of tomorrow will set aside the literal formulas of our Christian past, but Christians will not ever set aside the power of the experience that expressed itself in scripture, creed, theology and liturgy. We honor each, but we literalize none!

The Christianity of the future must also be willing and able to dialogue with the other great religious systems of the world without defining any of them as lacking or deficient. Our task is not to judge, but to accept them as they are, to call them to live fully, love wastefully and be all that they can be in the infinite variety of our humanity. We see the Christian life as a journey into the mystery of God, into a new humanity, into the ability to give ourselves away to others as the mark of the presence of Christ in us. The reformation we chart is scary, but it is noble, compelling and freeing. Even more, however, it gives the Christian story a chance to live in a new time in history. I pray it will. I pray it can. I believe it must.

PART XV

Epilogue

37

My Mantra:
This I Do Believe

Prior to his death in 2009, Forrest Church was the senior minister of the famous All Souls Unitarian-Universalist Church in New York City. He was also the son of a former Democratic senator from Idaho who sought the nomination of his party for the presidency of the United States in 1976. Forrest Church had an amazing gift with words. For example, the title of one of his books was *God and Other Famous Liberals*. I always wished I could have thought of that title before he did!

He also once said: "God is not God's name. God is our name for that which is greater than all and yet present in each."[*] I had that definition in mind when I began to draw together my thoughts into one coherent statement that would sum up the content of these twelve theses. I needed to be clear about what it is that I do believe, about why I insist on identifying myself without apology as a Christian and about why I think that a radical theological reformation is essential to a Christian future.

---

[*] Forrest Church, "Born Again Unitarian-Universalism" (talk delivered at the UUA General Assembly, Boston, MA, June 29, 2003), http://www.allsoulsnyc2.org/publications/sermons/fcsermons/bornagainuuism.html. *lookup*

I call this statement "My Mantra." It is not designed to be an incipient form of a new Christian creed which might be imposed on tomorrow's Christianity. The days for believing that anyone can ever reduce the experience of the Holy to a set of propositions that can be recited and believed are over. I do not want to go back to that world of traditional religion. I live rather in time and space, where there is not, nor ever can there be, something that might be called a "timeless creed" or a set of beliefs that might endure forever. So my mantra is intended to be only a statement of where I am today, the place at which I have arrived in my journey at this moment. I want to state positively something about the conclusion that I presently hold and to bear witness to why I continue to see in the Christian story something that compels me into discipleship. I long ago walked beyond a literal interpretation of the Bible, but I do not therefore feel a need to abandon the Bible or to suggest that this book no longer has great worth for me. Instead, I journey deeply into the Bible's content, moving far beyond the literal surface, and discover there both meaning and insights to which I continue to feel a deep allegiance.

I long ago moved beyond what I call creedal theology, which as we saw was developed in the fourth century, but I have not moved beyond the hope that I can place the insights of Christianity into a coherent form, at least for my generation. I long ago moved away from the worship patterns of the thirteenth century, which portray God as a parent figure who needs to be flattered or a judge before whom I am compelled to grovel on my knees in penitence while I beg this God to "have mercy." I have not moved, however, beyond that sense of the reality and that holiness of what I call the "infinite Other."

Human language is woefully inadequate when one seeks to speak of that which cannot be embraced inside the human boundaries that mark the edges of the world of existence. I must, however, continue to use human words since I have no other way to communicate thought. So I do, but with the caveat that words might point to but cannot ever capture or hold that truth of which I seek to speak. With that warning clearly stated, I bring these chapters to a close by sharing my mantra, my current statement of belief.

I cannot tell you who God is or what God is. No one can do that. That is not within the capability of any human mind. All I can do is tell you how I believe I have experienced God. God and my experience of God are not the same. I also must face the fact that I may be delusional; I may be referring to something that does not exist except in my deluded mind. Many people have had delusional experiences in which God has been otherwise perceived. I do not believe that this is the case with me, but I must always be aware of that possibility. So under the rubric of full disclosure, I file this acknowledged possibility and continue to press on.

I believe I have experienced God as the Source of Life. Life was born as a single cell and, as such, began its journey in time until it arrived at its present stage, which includes the self-conscious complexity of human beings, producing for the first time, so far as we know, a creature who can define life, contemplate its beginnings, anticipate its termination and raise the question of its meaning. If God is the Source of Life, then the only way I can appropriately worship God is by living fully. In the process of embracing the fullness of life, I bear witness to the reality of the God who is the Source of Life.

I believe I have experienced God as the Source of Love. Love is the power that enhances life. It flows through the universe, finding expression in the care that nature in all its living forms gives to its young, but love reaches self-consciousness only in human beings. If God is the Source of Love, then the only way I can worship God is by loving "wastefully," a phrase that I like. By "wasteful" love I mean the kind of love that never stops to calculate whether the object of its love is worthy to be its recipient. It is love that never stops to calculate deserving. It is love that loves not because love has been earned. It is in the act of loving "wastefully" that I believe I make God visible.

Finally, I believe I experience God, in the words of my greatest theological mentor, Reformed German theologian Paul Tillich (1886–1965), as the Ground of Being. That is a difficult phrase to embrace. It was borrowed and refined by Tillich from the philosopher Plotinus, an early-third-century-CE Greek philosopher, who was himself not a Christian. If God is the Ground of Being, then the only way I can worship God is by having the courage to be all that I can be; and the more deeply I can be all that I can be, the more I can and do make God visible. So the reality of God to me is discovered in the experience which compels me to "live fully, to love wastefully and to have the courage to be all that I can be."

The mission into which this understanding of God drives me is not to build a religious institution or to help people become religious people. Indeed, if the truth were known, I am more repelled by those attracted to what people might call religion than I am drawn to them. No, the mission to which my mantra calls me is the task of building or transforming the world so that every person living will have a better opportunity to live fully, love wastefully and be all that each of them was created to be in the infinite variety of our humanity. There can be no outcast; there can be no one regarded as "unclean." There can be no prejudices which are allowed to operate in this vision of Christianity. The essence of Christianity, as I now understand it, is that everyone is to be accepted "just as I am, without one plea" and that everyone is called into the task of growing into all that each of us can be. The first stage of this process is what traditional Christianity once called "justification"; the second stage of this process is what traditional Christianity called "sanctification."

To this mantra I add one thing more. I am a Christian. I am a disciple of Jesus. Why? Because when I look at the life of Jesus, as that life has been refracted to me through both scripture and tradition, I see a person who was so fully alive that I perceive in him the infinite Source of Life. I see one who loves so totally, so wastefully, that I perceive in him the infinite Source of Love. I see one who was profoundly capable of being all that he could be, whether it was on Palm Sunday when he was hailed as a king—there is nothing so seductive as the sweet narcotic of human praise—or on Good Friday when he was being put to death, when even the threat of non-being did not alter his humanity. In both experiences, Jesus was and is what he was and is. He was not changed by flattery, nor was his being diminished by the imminence of his death. So I join with St. Paul in the affirmation of faith, "God was in Christ," bringing oneness out of diversity, wholeness out of brokenness and eternity out of time.

This is the God to whom I am drawn and worship. This is the Christ that points me toward the fullness of God. This is the faith I seek to share with the world. To embrace life, to increase love, to have the courage to be—these, for me, are the doorways through which I walk into the mystery of God. This God is real to me and Jesus is still my doorway into this reality. In this Jesus the future of Christianity becomes visible once again. I walk eagerly into this life-centered God experience. I welcome the Christianity to which this vision beckons me. I bear witness to the faith that leads me and the whole world to live fully, love wastefully and be all that we can be.

Shalom.

John Shelby Spong

Bibliography

Altizer, Thomas J. J. *The Gospel of Christian Atheism*. Philadelphia: Westminster Press, 1966.

———. *The New Gospel of Christian Atheism*. Aurora, CO: Davis Group, 2002.

Aquinas, Thomas. *Summa Theologica*. Vol. 55, *The Resurrection of the Lord*. New York and London: Blackfriars and McGraw-Hill, 1963.

Ardagh, Arjuna. *The Translucent Revolution*. Novato, CA: New World Press, 2005.

Arendt, Hannah. *The Human Condition*. Garden City, NY: Doubleday Anchor Books, 1959.

Armstrong, Karen. *A History of God*. New York: Ballantine Books, 1993.

———. *The Great Transformation: The Beginning of Our Religious Traditions*. New York: Knopf, 2006.

Augustine. *Confessions*. Edited by Temple Scott. New York: E.P. Dutton and Company, 1900.

Bacik, James J. *Apologetics and the Eclipse of Mystery: Mystagogy According to Karl Rahner*. Notre Dame and London: University of Notre Dame Press, 1980.

Bonhoeffer, Dietrich. *Letters and Papers from Prison*. Edited by Eberhard Bethge; translated by Reginald Fuller. New York: Macmillan, 1952.

Bowker, John. *God: A Brief History—The Human Search for Eternal Truth*. London: DK Publishing, 2002.

———, ed. *The Cambridge History of Religion*. Cambridge: Cambridge University Press, 2002.

Bowman, George W. *Dying, Grieving, Faith and Family: A Pastoral Care Approach*. New York and London: Haworth Pastoral Press, 1998.

Brown, Raymond. *The Gospel According to John*. 2 vols. Garden City, NY: Doubleday, 1966–1970.

Buber, Martin. *I and Thou.* Translated by Walter Kaufman. New York: Scribner, 1970.

Bultmann, Rudolf Karl. *The History of the Synoptic Tradition.* Translated by John Marsh. Oxford: Basil Blackwell, 1963.

Calvin, John. *The Institutes.* Edited by John J. McNeill; translated by Ford Lewis Battles. 2 vols. Library of Christian Classics. Philadelphia: Westminster Press, 1975.

Cerminara, Gina. *Many Mansions: The Edgar Cayce Story on Reincarnation.* New York: New American Library, 1999.

Chaucer, Geoffrey. *The Canterbury Tales.* Edited and translated by Nevill Coyhill. Penguin Classics, 2003.

Chopra, Deepak. *Jesus: A Story of Enlightenment.* San Francisco: HarperOne, 2008.

———. *Life After Death.* New York: Random House, 2006.

Cox, Harvey. *The Secular City.* New York: Macmillan, 1965.

Cullman, Oscar. *Christ and Time.* Translated by Floyd Filson. Philadelphia: Westminster Press, 1964.

Cupitt, Don. *Above Us Only Sky.* Santa Rosa, CA: Polebridge Press, 2008.

———. *The Great Questions of Life.* Santa Rosa, CA: Polebridge Press, 2005.

———. *The Sea of Faith.* London: BBC Publishing, 1984.

———. *Taking Leave of God.* London: SCM Press, 1980.

Dante, Alighieri. *The Divine Comedy.* Penguin Classics, 2006; originally published 1320.

Darwin, Charles R. *On the Origin of Species by Means of Natural Selection.* Philadelphia: University of Pennsylvania Press, 1959; originally published 1859.

———. *The Journal of the Beagle.* Edited by Paul H. Barrett and R. B. Freeman. London: William Pickering Press, 1986.

Davies, Paul. *God and the New Physics.* London: Dent 1984; New York: Simon and Schuster, 1992.

———. *The Mind of God.* New York: Simon and Schuster, 1992.

Dawkins, Richard. *The Selfish Gene.* New York and Oxford: Oxford University Press, 1976.

———. *The God Delusion.* London: Bantam Books, 2006.

Dewey, Arthur J., Roy W. Hoover, Lane C. McGaughy and Daryl D. Schmidt. *The Authentic Letters of Paul.* Santa Rosa, CA: Polebridge Press, 2010.

Dodd, Charles H. *The Interpretation of the Fourth Gospel*. Cambridge: Cambridge University Press, 1968.

Dollar, Jim. *The Evolution of the Idea of God*. Greensboro, NC: Outlands Press, 2006.

Einstein, Albert. *Relativity: The Special and the General Theory*. Translated by Robert W. Lawson. London: Methuen, 1920.

Elias, Norbert. *The Loneliness of Dying*. Translated by Edmond Jephcott. Oxford: Blackwell, 1985.

Epperly, Bruce G., and Lewis D. Solomon. *Finding Angels in Boulders: An Interfaith Discussion on Dying and Death*. St. Louis, MO: Chalice Press, 2004.

Erickson, Erik H. *Identity and the Life Cycle*. New York: Norton, 1980.

Farrer, Austin. *Saving Belief: A Discussion of Essentials*. London: Hodder and Stoughton, 1964.

Filippenko, Alex. *Understanding the Universe: An Introduction to Astronomy*. 96 Lectures recorded on DVDs from the University of California, Berkeley. Chantilly, VA: The Teaching Company, 1998.

FitzRoy, Robert. "An Essay by the Captain of the Beagle." Recorded in a taped reading of Darwin's *The Voyage of the Beagle*. Old Saybrook, CT: Tantor Media, 2006.

Frankl, Victor. *Man's Search for Meaning*. Boston: Beacon Press, 1959.

Freud, Sigmund. *The Future of an Illusion*. Translated by James Strachey. New York: Norton, 1975.

———. *Moses and Monotheism*. Translated by Katherine Jones. New York: Vantage Books, 1967.

———. *Totem and Taboo*. Translated by James Strachey. New York: Norton, 1956.

———. *Civilization and Its Discontents*. Translated by James Strachey. New York: Norton, 1962.

Friedman, Edwin H. *From Generation to Generation*. New York: Guildford Press, 1985.

Fromm, Eric. *The Art of Loving*. New York: Harper and Row, 1956.

———. *The Heart of Man: Its Genius for Good and Evil*. New York: Harper and Row, 1964.

Frost, Robert. "The Road Not Taken." *The Collected Poems of Robert Frost*. New York: Holt McDougal, 2002.

Funk, Robert, and Roy Hoover. *The Five Gospels: The Search for the Authentic Words of Jesus*. New York: Macmillan, 1992.

Geering, Lloyd. *Christianity Without God*. Santa Rosa, CA: Polebridge Press, 2002.

Goulder, Michael D. *Luke: A New Paradigm*. Sheffield, UK: Sheffield Academic Press, 1989.

Goulder, Michael D., and John Hick. *Why Believe in God?* London: SCM Press, 1983.

Grof, Stanislav. *Beyond the Brain: Birth, Death and Transcendence in Psychotherapy*. New York: State University of New York Press, 1984.

Groopman, Jerome. *The Anatomy of Hope: How People Prevail in the Face of Illness*. New York: Random House, 2004.

Hamilton, William. *Radical Theology and the Death of God*. Indianapolis: Bobbs-Merrill Press, 1966.

Harpur, Tom. *Life After Death*. Toronto: McClelland & Stewart, 1992.

Harris, Sam. *The End of Faith: Religion, Terror and the Future of Reason*. New York: Norton, 2004.

Hawking, Stephen. *A Brief History of Time: From the Big Bang to Black Holes*. Introduction by Carl Sagan. New York and London: Bantam Books, 1988.

Hedrick, Charles W., ed. *When Faith Meets Reason: Religious Scholars Reflect on Their Spiritual Journeys*. Santa Rosa, CA: Polebridge Press, 2007.

Hegel, G. W. Friedrich. *Early Theological Writings*. Translated by T. M. Knox. Chicago: University of Chicago Press, 1948.

———. *The Phenomenology of Spirit*. Translated by J. B. Baillie. New York: Macmillan, 1949.

Heidegger, Martin. *Being and Time: A Reading for Readers*. Translated by E. F. Kaelin. Tallahassee: Florida State University Press, 1987.

Hick, John. *Death and Eternal Life*. San Francisco: Harper and Row, 1976.

———. *The Fifth Dimension: An Exploration of the Spiritual Realm*. Oxford: One World Press, 1999.

———, and Michael Goulder. *Why Believe in God?* London: SCM Press, 1983.

Horgan, John. *The Undiscovered Mind: How the Brain Defies Replication, Medication and Explanation*. New York: Simon and Schuster, 1999.

Hugo, Victor. *Les Misérables*. Translated by Lee Fahnestock and Norman MacAfee. New York: Signet Classics, 2013.

Ireton, Sean. *An Ontological Study of Death: From Hegel to Heidegger.* Pittsburgh: Duquesne University Press, 2007.

James, William. *Pragmatism: A New Way for Some Old Ways of Thinking.* London: Longmans, Green, 1949.

Jaspers, Karl. *Nietzsche: An Introduction to the Understanding of His Philosophical Activity.* Translated by Charles F. Wallraff and Frederick J. Schultz. Tucson, AZ: University of Arizona Press, 1965.

Johnson, Steven. *Mind Wide Open: Your Brain and the Neuroscience of Everyday Life.* New York: Scribner, 2004.

Jonas, Hans. *The Gnostic Religion: A Message of the Alien God and the Beginnings of Christianity.* Boston: Beacon Press, 1958.

Kohn, Rachel. *Curious Obsessions in the History of Science and Spirituality.* Sydney: ABC Publishers, 2001.

Küng, Hans. *Eternal Life: Life After Death as a Medical, Philosophical and Theological Problem.* Translated by Edward Quinn. Garden City, NY: Doubleday, 1964.

Lewis, C. S. *A Grief Observed.* New York: Phoenix Press, 1961.

Lewis, H. D. *The Elusive Mind.* London: George Allen and Unwin, 1965–1968 (the Gifford Lectures).

Luther, Martin. *Luther's Works.* Vol. 28 on I Corinthians. Edited by Hilton C. Oswald. St. Louis: Concordia Press, 1923.

Madigan, Kevin J., and Jon D. Levenson. *Resurrection: The Power of God for Christians and Jews.* New Haven and London: Yale University Press, 2008.

Marx, Karl. *Das Kapital.* 3 vols. Edited by Frederick Engels; translated by Ernest Untermann. Chicago: Charles Kerr, 1906–1910.

Millay, Edna St. Vincent. *Conversation at Midnight.* New York and London: Harper and Brothers, 1937.

Miller, J. Kenneth. *The Secret Life of the Soul.* Nashville, TN: Broadman and Hardan, 1997.

Milton, John, *Paradise Lost.* Edited by Christopher Ricks. Signet Classics, 2001.

———. *Paradise Regained.* Edited by Christopher Ricks. Signet Classics, 2010.

Mitford, Jessica. *The American Way of Death.* New York: Simon and Schuster, 1963.

Moltmann, Jürgen. *The Crucified God.* London: SCM Press, 1973.

Moody, Raymond A., Jr. *Life After Life.* New York: Bantam Books, 1976.

Neuhauser, Robert G. *The Cosmic Deity: Where Scientists and Theologians Fear to Tread*. Lancaster, PA: Mill Creek Publishers, 2005.

Newton, Isaac. *The Principia*. Edited by Alexander Kayre and I. Bernard Cohen. Cambridge, MA: Harvard University Press, 1972.

Newton, Michael. *Journey of Souls: Case Studies of Life Between Lives*. Woodbury, MN: Llewellyn Publications, 1994.

Nietzsche, Friedrich. *Thus Spake Zarathustra*. Translated by Walter Kaufman. Princeton, NJ: Princeton University Press, 1974.

Nineham, D. E. *St. Mark*. London: Penguin Books, 1963.

Novak, David. *The Soul's Refinement*. Chicago: Non Fit Press, 1996.

Nowicki, Stephen. Biology as the Source of Life. Lectures produced by The Teaching Company, Chantilly, VA, 2002.

Ogden, Schubert. *The Reality of God and Other Essays*. San Francisco: Harper and Row, 1963.

Ogletree, Thomas W. *The Death of God Controversy*. Nashville, TN: Abingdon Press, 1966.

Pagels, Elaine. *Beyond Belief*. New York: Random House, 2004.

Pagels, Heinz R. *The Cosmic Code: Quantum Physics as the Language of Nature*. New York: Simon and Schuster, 1982.

Pannenberg, Wolfhart. *Jesus, God and Man*. Translated by Lewis Wilkins and Duane Priebe. London: SCM Press, 1968.

Pascal, Blaise. *Pensées*. Oxford World Classics, 2008.

Patterson, Stephen, *The Gospel of Thomas and Jesus*. Sonoma, CA: Polebridge Press, 1993.

Phillips, J. B. *Your God Is Too Small*. New York: Touchstone, 1997.

Pike, James A. *A Time for Christian Candor*. New York: Harper and Row, 1964.

———. *If This Be Heresy*. New York: Harper and Row, 1967.

Pittenger, Norman. *God in Process*. London: SCM Press, 1967.

Robinson, Daniel N. *Consciousness and Its Implications*. 12 lectures delivered at Oxford University. Chantilly, VA: The Teaching Company, 2003.

Robinson, John Arthur Thomas. *Honest to God*. London: SCM Press, 1963.

———. *In the End: God*. London: Collins, 1968.

———. *The Human Face of God*. Philadelphia: Fortress Press, 1974.

Ryken, Leland. *Bunyan's The Pilgrim's Progress*. Crossway Books, 2014.

Sartre, Jean Paul. *Being and Nothingness: An Essay on Philosophical Ontology*. Translated by Hazel E. Barnes. New York: Philosophical Library, 1956.

Schleiermacher, Friedrich. *The Christian Faith*. London: T. & T. Clark, 1908.

———. *The Experience of Jesus as Lord*. New York: Seabury Press, 1980.

Schulenberg, Michael. *Getting to the Promised Land Without Spending Forty Years in a Wilderness*. Pittsburgh: Dorrance, 2005.

Segal, Alan F. *Life After Death*. New York: Doubleday, 2004.

Smart, Ninian. *Philosophy and Religious Truth*. New York: Macmillan, 1964.

Smith-Tilly, Kelly. *At Life's End: A Portrait in Living and Dying—The Story of Dr. Maynard Adams*. Raleigh, NC: Privately published, 2003.

Smoley, Richard. *Conscious Love: Insights from Mystical Christianity*. San Francisco: Jossey-Bass, 2008.

Spong, John Shelby. *A New Christianity for a New World*. San Francisco: HarperCollins, 2002.

———. *Biblical Literalism: A Gentile Heresy*. San Francisco: HarperCollins, 2016.

———. *Born of a Woman*. San Francisco: HarperCollins, 1992.

———. *Christpower*. Arranged by Lucy Newton Boswell Negus. Richmond, VA: Thomas Hale, 1975; republished Haworth, NJ: St. Johann Press, 2007.

———. *Here I Stand: My Struggle for a Christianity of Integrity, Love and Equality*. San Francisco: HarperCollins, 2000.

———. *Honest Prayer*. New York: Seabury Press, 1973; republished Haworth, NJ: St. Johann Press, 2000.

———. *Rescuing the Bible from Fundamentalism*. San Francisco: HarperCollins, 1991.

———. *Resurrection: Myth or Reality?* San Francisco: HarperCollins, 2005.

———. *The Sins of Scripture*. San Francisco: HarperCollins, 2005.

———. *This Hebrew Lord: A Bishop's Search for the Authentic Jesus*. San Francisco: HarperCollins, 1974, 1985.

———. *Why Christianity Must Change or Die*. San Francisco: HarperCollins, 1998.

Spong, John Shelby, with Jack Daniel Spiro. *Dialogue in Search of Jewish-Christian Understanding.* New York: Seabury Press, 1975; republished Haworth, NJ: St. Johann Press, 1998.

Strauss, David Friedrich. *Leben Jesu, or The Life of Jesus Critically Examined.* London: SCM Press, 1973; originally published 1834.

Streeter, B. H. *Immortality: An Essay in Discovery.* New York: Macmillan, 1922.

———. *The Four Gospels: A Study of Origins.* London: Macmillan, 1930.

Strogatz, Steven. *Chaos.* Lectures produced by The Teaching Company, Chantilly, VA, 2008.

Tattersall, Ian. *Becoming Human: Evolution and Human Uniqueness.* New York: Harcourt Brace, 1998.

Taylor, Charles. *Hegel.* Cambridge: Cambridge University Press, 1975.

Temple, William. *Readings in St. John.* New York: Macmillan, 1945.

Thielicke, Helmut. *Death and Life.* Translated by Edward Schroeder. Philadelphia: Fortress Press, 1970.

Thompson, Francis. *The Complete Poetical Works of Francis Thompson.* New York: Modern Library, 1913.

Tillich, Paul. *Systematic Theology.* 3 vols. Chicago: University of Chicago Press, 1951–1963.

———. *The Courage to Be.* New Haven: Yale University Press, 1952.

———. *The Eternal Now.* New York: Scribner, 1963.

———. *The New Being.* New York: Scribner, 1953.

———. *The Shaking of the Foundations.* New York: Scribner, 1948.

Tippler, Frank J. *The Physics of Immortality.* Garden City, NY: Doubleday, 1994.

Tournier, Paul. *The Seasons of Life.* Translated by John S. Gilmore. Richmond, VA: John Knox Press, 1961.

Vahanian, Gabriel. *The Death of God: The Culture of Our Post-Christian Era.* New York: George Braziller, 1964.

Van Buren, Paul. *The Secular Meaning of the Gospel.* New York: Macmillan, 1963.

Von Hügel, Baron Friedrich. *Eternal Life: A Study of Its Implications and Application.* Edinburgh: T. & T. Clark, 1912.

Vosper, Gretta. *Amen.* Toronto: HarperCollins, 2011.

———. *With or Without God: Why the Way We Live Is More Important Than the Way We Believe*. Toronto: HarperCollins, 2008.

Wilber, Ken. *A Brief History of Everything*. Boston and London: Shambhala Press, 1996.

Wolfe, Thomas. *You Can't Go Home Again*. New York: Harper and Row, 1934.

Scripture Index

Subject Index